REPORTS AND RETURNS

AAT Intermediate NVQ/SVQ Level 3 in Accounting

British Library Cataloguing-in-Publication Data

A catalogue record for this book is available from the British Library.

Published by
Kaplan Publishing UK
Unit 2 The Business Centre
Molly Millars Lane
Wokingham
Berkshire
RG41 2QZ

ISBN: 978-1-84710-605-6

Printed and bound in Great Britain.

We are grateful to the Association of Accounting Technicians for permission to reproduce past assessment materials. The solutions have been prepared by Kaplan Publishing.

CONTENTS

STUDY TEXT

CONTENTS

WORKBOOK

PREFACE

STUDY TEXT

The study text is written in a practical and interactive style:

- key terms and definitions are clearly defined
- all topics are illustrated with practical examples with clearly worked solutions
- frequent practice activities throughout the chapters ensure that what you have learnt is regularly reinforced
- test your knowledge section at the end of each chapter helps you to check that you have really understood the topics covered.

WORKBOOK

The workbook comprises three main elements:

A question bank of key techniques to give additional practice and reinforce the work covered in each chapter. The questions are divided into their relevant chapters and you may either attempt these questions as you work through the study text, or leave some or all of these until you have completed the study text as a sort of final revision of what you have studied.

Practice simulations.

Mock simulations which closely reflect the type of simulation you may expect.

STANDARDS OF COMPETENCE

Unit commentary

This unit relates to the preparation of reports and returns from information obtained from all relevant sources. You are required to calculate ratios and performance indicators and present the information according to the appropriate conventions and definitions to either management or outside agencies, including the VAT Office. The unit is also concerned with your communication responsibilities which include obtaining authorisation before despatching reports, seeking guidance from the VAT Office and presenting reports and returns in the appropriate manner.

Elements contained within this unit are:

Element: 7.1

Prepare and present periodic performance reports

Element: 7.2

Prepare reports and returns for outside agencies

Element: 7.3

Prepare VAT returns

Knowledge and Understanding

To perform this unit effectively you will need to know and understand:

		Chapter
The business environment		
1	Main sources of relevant government statistics (Elements 7.1 & 7.2)	1
2	Relevant performance and quality measures (Element 7.1)	5
3	Main types of outside organisations requiring reports and returns: regulatory; grant awarding; information collecting; trade associations (Element 7.2)	6
4	Basic law and practice relating to all issues covered in the range statement and referred to in the performance criteria. Specific issues include: the classification of types of supply; registration requirements; the form of VAT invoices; tax points (Element 7.3)	8, 9
5	Sources of information on VAT: Customs and Excise Guide (Element 7.3)	8
6	The process and systems required to complete and submit VAT returns in accordance with current legislation (Element 7.3)	8
7	Special schemes: annual accounting; cash accounting; bad debt relief (Element 7.3)	8, 10
Accounting methods		
8	Use of standard units of inputs and outputs (Elements 7.1 & 7.3)	5
9	Time series analysis (Element 7.1)	4
10	Use of index numbers (Element 7.1)	4
11	Main types of performance indicators: productivity; cost per unit; resource utilisation; profitability (Elements 7.1 & 7.2)	5
12	Ratios: gross profit margin; net profit margin; return on capital employed (Elements 7.1 & 7.2)	5, 6
13	Tabulation of accounting and other quantitative information using spreadsheets (Elements 7.1 & 7.2)	3, 7
14	Methods of presenting information: written reports; diagrammatic; tabular (Elements 7.1 & 7.2)	2, 3
The organisation		
15	How the accounting systems of an organisation are affected by its organisational structure, its administrative systems and procedures and the nature of its business transactions (Elements 7.1, 7.2 & 7.3)	1
16	The purpose and structure of reporting systems within the organisation (Element 7.1)	1
17	Background understanding that a variety of outside agencies may require reports and returns from organisations and that these requirements must be built into administrative and accounting systems and procedures (Elements 7.2 & 7.3)	1, 6
18	Background understanding that recording and accounting practices may vary between organisations and different parts of organisations (Elements 7.1, 7.2 & 7.3)	Throughout
19	The basis of the relationship between the organisation and the VAT Office (Element 7.3)	8, 10

Element 7.1 Prepare and present periodic performance reports

	Chapter in this text book
Performance criteria	
In order to perform this element successfully you need to:	
A Consolidate information derived from different units of the organisation into the appropriate form	5
B Reconcile information derived from different information systems within the organisation	5
C Compare results over time using an appropriate method that allows for changing price levels	4
D Account for transactions between separate units of the organisation in accordance with the organisation's procedures	5
E Calculate ratios and performance indicators in accordance with the organisation's procedures	5
F Prepare reports in the appropriate form and present them to management within the required timescales	2,3

Range statement

Performance in this element relates to the following contexts:

Information

- Costs
- Revenue

Ratios

- Gross profit margin
- Net profit margin
- Return on capital employed

Performance indicators

- Productivity
- Cost per unit
- Resource utilisation
- Profitability

Methods of presenting information:

- Written report containing diagrams
- Tables

Element 7.2 prepare reports and returns for outside agencies

Performance criteria

In order to perform this element successfully you need to:

A	Identify, collate and present relevant information in accordance with the conventions and definitions used by outside agencies	6
B	Ensure calculations of ratios and performance indicators are accurate	5,6
C	Obtain authorisation for the despatch of completed reports and returns from the appropriate person	6
D	Present reports and returns in accordance with outside agencies' requirements and deadlines	6

Range statement

Performance in this element relates to the following contexts:

Raios

- Gross profit margin
- Net profit margin
- Return on capital employed

Reports and returns

- Written report
- Return on standard form

Element 7.3 Prepare VAT returns

Performance criteria

In order to perform this element successfully you need to:

A	Complete and submit VAT returns correctly, using data from the appropriate recording systems, within the statutory time limits.	10
B	Correctly identify and calculate relevant inputs and outputs.	8,9
C	Ensure submissions are made in accordance with current legislation.	10
D	Ensure guidance is sought from the VAT Office when required, in a professional manner.	8,10

Range statement

Performance in this element relates to the following contexts:

Raios

- Computerised ledgers
- Manual control account
- Cash book

Inputs and outputs

- Standard supplies
- Exempt supplies
- Zero-rated supplies
- Imports
- Exports

INTERNAL AND EXTERNAL REPORTING

INTRODUCTION

Welcome to this introductory chapter of the Unit 7 Study text and Workbook. In this first chapter we shall be looking at the different types of business that exist and how these organisations can be structured. We shall also be looking at the different types of report that are prepared by businesses, for example, internal and external reports and the data and information that are required to prepare such reports. The contents of this chapter are designed to introduce you to the subject of preparing reports and returns and will form essential background information to the rest of the material covered in this study text.

KNOWLEDGE AND UNDERSTANDING

- Main sources of relevant government statistics (Elements 7.1, 7.2)
- How the accounting systems of an organisation are affected by its organisational structure, its administrative systems and procedures and the nature of its business transactions (Elements 7.1, 7.2, 7.3)
- The purpose and structure of reporting systems within the organisation (Element 7.1)
- Background understanding that a variety of outside agencies may require reports and returns from organisations and that these requirements must be built into administrative and accounting systems and procedures (Elements 7.2, 7.3)

CONTENTS

1 Internal information systems

1.1 Introduction

In assessments you may be required to prepare a report for internal management purposes or for some external agency.

A large amount of the data and information for preparation of reports will be **produced within the organisation itself**, from its accounting and administrative systems.

An organisation's size, type of business, objectives and structure will have an impact on its internal information systems.

1.2 Size of business

A small 'corner shop' type of business will have fairly **basic** reporting requirements. The management and ownership of such a business are likely to overlap and there will be little need for formal internal reports.

The main source of information concerning the business that will satisfy both internal and external requirements will generally be the **financial accounts**, probably supported by a cash flow statement. The accounting system may thus consist mainly of cash records and files of invoices and other source documents.

Larger businesses will have a more defined management structure and will often be organised into **separate operating units for reporting purposes** (by different products/services or geographical location, for example). It is likely to have a greater demand for reporting to external parties such as investors, tax and government authorities, regulatory bodies (e.g. the Stock Exchange) and trade associations. Thus its accounting and administrative systems need to be more sophisticated to cope with the range of both internal and external information needs; these systems are invariably computer-based.

1.3 Type of organisation – objectives

An organisation may be **private sector** or **public sector**, both of which have different objectives and reporting requirements.

DEFINITION

A **public sector** enterprise is owned and funded by central or local government – for example, hospitals, libraries, schools, etc.

They are generally run to provide services rather than to make a profit. Their information systems will thus be geared towards recording and reporting on expenditure levels and productivity/efficiency measures.

DEFINITION

A **private sector** business is owned and funded by individual investors.

It may be a sole trader, partnership or limited company and will generally be profit-seeking to give a return to its investors. **Charities** are a typical example of the exception to this. Reporting requirements will primarily focus upon **revenue, cost and profit information**, although secondary objectives – such as staff development, product innovation, increasing market share and environmental considerations – will also affect the design of information systems.

Externally, companies (particularly public limited companies), will be required to provide quite **extensive information** and the systems must also be able to cope with these demands.

1.4 Type of business

Businesses can generally be categorised into **retailers, manufacturers** and **service** organisations.

Manufacturers and retailers will deal with distinct products, for which detailed unit cost and revenue information will be required for internal control and decision-making.

Service organisations may keep records by client (accountants, solicitors), by department (hospitals, schools, etc) or by location/branch (estate agents, restaurants). Employee time will be an important feature of costing; pricing and efficiency reports and systems will need to incorporate timesheet and charge-out aspects.

1.5 The organisational structure

A profit-seeking manufacturing business is used here for illustration purposes, although the general principles can be applied to all types of business.

Such a business may be organised along the following lines:

(a) A **chief executive** and **main board** are appointed who have overall control of the business unit. They are responsible for achieving the stated objectives and report primarily to the shareholders.

(b) The chief executive/board may appoint certain **key managers** who take responsibility for the various management functions of:
   (i) finance
   (ii) marketing
   (iii) production
   (iv) personnel.

(c) These key managers may further **delegate responsibility** within their functional areas for certain activities.

1.6 Organisation chart

The organisational structure of a business is often illustrated in an organisation chart.

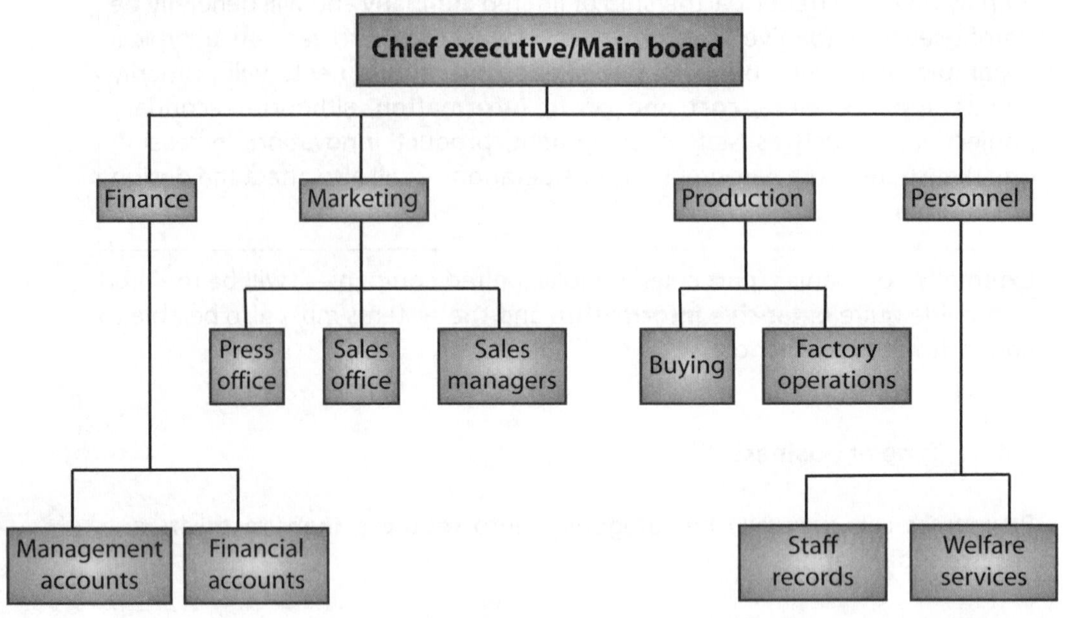

There is a sub-division of responsibilities between these areas, but in practical terms there is a considerable degree of **interdependence** between each functional area.

This type of organisational structure is based upon the functions within the business.

1.7 Other organisational structures

Other structures may be according to:

- **Products/services** – The initial tier below the chief executive/main board is split according to the individual or groups of products or services offered by the business. Each of these will then be progressively split by function and/or geographical location.
- **Geographical region** – The initial tier is split by region (within the UK: North, South, etc or worldwide: Europe, America, Far East, etc). Subsequent tiers may then be split by product, function, etc.

1.8 Effects of organisational structure on information systems

However an organisation is initially structured, all will have the common functional elements as illustrated by the above chart. These will deal with the **basic recording, processing and analysing of the business's transactions** and the production of financial and management accounts.

Organisations that are split at some level by **product/service or geographical region** will have additional requirements from their systems.

- **Product/service split.** The revenue earned and costs incurred by particular products/services need to be separately identified. This causes particular problems on the cost side, where items of expenditure must be allocated between products/services. Suitable coding systems can be used for direct expenses (labour, materials, etc) but there will also need to be a system for splitting shared overheads between products/services.
- **Geographical split.** Revenues and costs must again be split, this time between geographical regions using appropriate codes. Particular problems arise with overseas regions where different currencies, legal and reporting requirements can make consolidation and comparison of information difficult.

2 Internal reports – management information

2.1 Management activity

Internal reports will form an important means of providing management information. Information will be provided for various purposes and at various levels, but will generally be tied in with one or more of the commonly defined areas of management activity:

- forecasting
- planning
- organising
- co-ordinating
- decision-taking
- controlling.

All these tasks are directed at the **achievement of corporate objectives** that were mentioned earlier. It also follows that, if these tasks are to be carried out, managers must have some system for communication, either with the outside world or within the business.

Managers need information in order to manage.

2.2 Information purposes

The information associated with managerial activities can be analysed as being needed for three purposes, often identified with **senior (i.e. strategic), middle (i.e. tactical)** and **shop-floor (i.e. operational)** management levels:

(a) **Strategic level** – Information is needed on long-term plans and corporate objectives as well as strategies to improve the size of the organisation and ultimately the performance. Information will be drawn from both internal and external sources.

(b) **Tactical level** – Information is needed for short-term decision-making and may be concerned with yearly production plans, forecasts of cash and sales analyses. Such information is typically internally generated and of a financial nature.

(c) **Operational level** – Information is needed here for the day to day running of the business to ensure that the company's activities are carried out in an orderly and efficient manner. This will often be non-financial, relating to scheduling and other operational policies of the organisation.

2.3 Information levels

Most business organisations require information at various levels:

- **International** information, such as the state of commodity markets, relative strengths of currencies, and political affairs
- **National** information, such as government policies, trading conditions and the impact of new legislation
- **Corporate** information, such as business performance and financial results
- **Departmental** information, such as individual budgets for costs and actual expenditure compared therewith
- **Individual** information, such as sales made by individual salespersons and remuneration of individuals

2.4 Types of internal report to management

Management may require various types of reports for their various purposes:

- **Regular reports** – These are reports which relate to a cycle of activities (e.g. payroll processing and sales ledger processing).
- **Exception reports** – These are reports prepared to highlight some unusual occurrence and prompt the user to take corrective action (e.g. significant variances of costs from budget).
- **Analyses** – Analyses are items of data which are considered and commented on. Analysis may be done on a regular or on an ad hoc basis.
- **Forecasts** – Forecasts are merely the result of intelligent conjectures about the future based upon the past. Forecasting methods vary from naive methods to more advanced methods using mathematical models which attempt to simulate the degree of uncertainty that arises in business life.

2.5 Qualities of good information

What makes information of good quality?

- **Promptness** – The value of information declines with the length of time that the user has to wait for it. Information that is out of date is a waste of time, effort and money.
- **Brevity** – The information provided should concentrate on the essentials and ignore trivia. Too much information can blind the user to the truly important matters contained therein.
- **Accuracy** – Inaccurate information is of little use for strategic, tactical or operational purposes. The degree of accuracy of information will vary; the managing director may be concerned with the reporting of profit to the nearest thousand pounds. On the other hand the sales ledger supervisor will be concerned with a high degree of accuracy with regard to the balancing of the control account.
- **Discrimination** – Information should be tailored to the needs and level of understanding of the recipient. The degree of detail required by the credit controller to monitor the level of debt is different from the level of detail required by the chief executive.

- **Economy** – Information has no intrinsic value. Its value can only be gauged by the benefit that management obtain from its use. Information should not be produced wastefully. Only essential reports are produced which enable management to take effective action.
- **Capability for exception reporting** – The information system should be capable of highlighting the unusual so that appropriate action can be taken by the recipient.

▷ ACTIVITY 1

Employment information (AAT CA D93)

An organisation has started to collect monthly information regarding employment and labour costs from its various departments. At the moment it only records average rates of pay in each department. Suggest three other items of management information that you believe should be collected relating to employment. [Answer on p. 14]

3 External reports and returns

3.1 Introduction

The second element of Unit 7 is concerned with the **preparation of reports and returns for outside agencies**. The accounting and other information systems of a business organisation must take the requirements of such agencies into account, as far as is practicable.

The main types of external organisations requiring reports and returns have been identified as **follows:**

(a) regulatory organisations
(b) grant-awarding organisations
(c) information-collecting organisations
(d) other external reporting requirements.

We will be looking at these in detail later on in this study text.

3.2 Other external reporting requirements

As well as the requirements of the organisations discussed above, a business will need to cater for the information demands of external parties who have a particular interest in it. These will include **shareholders** (existing and potential), **customers and suppliers, banks, debenture-holders** and other lenders.

3.3 Problems of reporting for external agencies

Much of the information required for external reports and returns will be available from the normal accounting/administrative systems of the organisation (e.g. VAT, PAYE, NI information). However, some of the information required is

specialised (financial statistics, non-financial data) which may or may not be part of the organisation's own management accounting requirements.

Thus there may be a need to set up **special data collecting exercises or routines** (computerised or manual) to pick up the relevant data and sort it as required by the particular report or return.

▷ ACTIVITY 2

Agency return (AAT CA J93)

(a) Give an example of a periodic report which has to be made to an outside agency by any organisation.
(b) What is the main purpose of this return? [Answer on p. 14]

4 Sources of data for internal and external reports

4.1 Introduction

Most of the work involved in producing a report is in the initial stages of **collection and organisation of the required data and information.**

4.2 Data and information

The terms **data** and **information** are commonly used to mean the same thing, but it is important to distinguish between the two.

□ DEFINITION

Data is raw facts, numerical information and figures, unassembled and frequently unrelated to one another.

□ DEFINITION

Information is obtained by processing the data in some way. It can be defined as an organised collection of related pieces of data.

4.3 How data becomes information

Without some sort of analysis, **raw data can be rather unhelpful** since it is often impossible to see any trends in a mass of figures. In general data may be transformed into information in a number of ways:

- bringing related pieces of data together, i.e. **grouping** data
- **summarising** data
- performing basic calculations, i.e. **processing** data
- **tabulation** and diagrammatic techniques
- **statistical analysis**
- **financial analysis.**

Statistical information is needed to run any business organisation. For example, planning future sales targets requires analysis of past sales data and calculating employees' wages requires analysis of data from clock cards. Managers will use available information to obtain the best results consistent with the objectives of the organisation.The data from which the information is obtained may arise from **internal sources** and/or external sources.

4.4 Internal sources of data

Business organisations themselves produce **huge amounts of data.** For example:

(a) There are 25 employees in the export department.
(b) Last year's budget for the personnel department was £265,000.
(c) In December 20X2, 1,500 type LA31 engines were produced.
(d) Last month 358 expense claims were submitted.

These are all items of data internal to the organisation. Data produced within an organisation will obviously vary from organisation to organisation. For a 'typical' organisation, five major activities might be considered:

(1) **Production** – amount of stock available, quality of goods produced, productivity, frequency of machine breakdowns;
(2) **Marketing** – sales figures, expenditure on advertising and promotion, results from market research surveys, travelling expenditure by representatives;
(3) **Purchasing** – price of raw materials, consumption of stationery, occurrence of overdue deliveries;
(4) **Finance** – wage rates of employees, cash in hand, bad debt details, details of loans held;
(5) **Administration** – number of employees, costs of maintenance, number of mailings.

4.5 External sources of data

Organisations frequently need to make use of **data obtained outside the organisation itself.** For example:

- a **survey** may be commissioned to determine customer satisfaction with service arrangements in a large store
- data on the size and the characteristics of a **section of the population** may be useful to determine the number of potential customers for a product
- if a company is to compete successfully, it will need details of the **activities of its competitors.**

5 Primary and secondary data

5.1 Introduction

Data can be categorised into **primary** and **secondary data**

□ DEFINITION

Primary data is any data which is used solely for the purpose for which it was originally collected.

□ DEFINITION

Secondary data is data that has already been collected for some other purpose but can also be used for the purpose in hand.

An important distinction is made here since information collected for one purpose by a business and then, at a later date, used again for another purpose would **no longer be primary data.**

EXAMPLE

Decide which of the following are primary data and which are secondary data.

(a) Information from clock cards when used for making up wages.
(b) Data from a government publication on the toy industry used by a new toy shop to determine which items to stock.
(c) Expense claim forms submitted by sales representatives used to estimate the car mileage they have travelled.
(d) Results of an election opinion poll published in a newspaper.

Solution

(a) This is primary data, since the data is collected to make up the wages.
(b) This is secondary data; government statisticians collate data from various sources and the data is used in a variety of ways (see later in this chapter).
(c) This is secondary data since the expense claim data is collected for a different reason initially.
(d) This is primary data since the data was collected specifically for the purpose. If you said secondary data you were probably thinking that the results were being used to predict the result of the election; this is different from the reason why it was collected.

5.2 The problem of using secondary data

Primary data (if available) is preferable to secondary data since data collected for a specific purpose is likely to be **better** than data acquired for some other purpose. Some of the **problems with secondary data** are:

- **The data has been collected by someone else.** There is no control over how it was collected. If a survey was used, was a suitable questionnaire used? Was a large enough sample taken (was enough data collected)? Was it a reputable organisation that carried out the data collection?
- **Is the data up to date?** Data quickly becomes out of date, for example, people's consumer tastes change and prices may fluctuate wildly.

- **The data may be incomplete.** Certain groups of people are sometimes omitted from the published data. For example, do you know which groups are included in the unemployment figures?
- **What is the data?** Is it actual, seasonally adjusted, estimated or a projection?
- **The reason for collecting the data may be unknown.** Statistics published on motor cars may include or exclude three wheeled cars, vans and motor caravans. Readers need to know which categories are included in the data.

If secondary data is to be used, these questions need to be answered. Sometimes the answers will be published with the data itself or sometimes it may be possible to contact the people who collected the data. If not, users must be aware of the **limitations of making decisions based on information produced from secondary data.**

5.3 Sources of secondary data

Sources of secondary data are numerous and can be broadly categorised as of two forms – those produced by individual organisations and those produced by the government.

5.4 Data from individual organisations

Some examples of such data are:
Bank of England Quarterly Bulletin – reports on financial and economic matters.
Financial Times (daily) – share prices and information on business.
Company reports – information on performance and accounts of individual companies.
Labour Research – articles on industry, employment, political parties and trade unions.
South Yorkshire Statistics (annual) – a selection of statistics relevant to the area.

5.5 Government statistics

The **Office for National Statistics (ONS)** is a government agency which exists primarily to meet the needs of government. However, much of the information compiled is readily usable by business and other organisations. Since its creation in 1996 (from a number of other government agencies) the service to business has been extended and CD ROMs and books have been published which has encouraged businesses to make more use of government statistics.

The service works in the following way.

- Each government department prepares and publishes its own statistics via ONS outlets.
- If any series of data from these departments is of sufficient interest it is usually included in more general publications like the Monthly Digest of Statistics.

The ONS publishes an **extensive range of statistical digests.** To help find the publication most suitable to anyone's needs two useful guides are available:

- *Government Statistics* – a brief guide to sources, listing all the main publications and departmental contact points
- *Guide to Official Statistics* – a more comprehensive list.

Some of the more important digests are **general** and some more **specific.**

5.6 General digests

- *Monthly Digest of Statistics* – a collection of the main series of data from all government departments
- *Annual Abstract of Statistics* – similar to Monthly Digest but containing more series and over longer periods of time
- *Social Trends* – a collection of key social and demographic statistics, presented using charts and tables

5.7 Specific digests

- *Economic Trends* provides a background to trends in the UK economy.
- *British Business* contains statistics and commentary from the Department of Trade and Industry. The contents vary (weekly) but include statistics on capital expenditure, investment intentions, industrial production, company liquidity, acquisitions and insolvencies, regional development grants.
- *National Accounts* contains detailed estimates of national accounts, including consumer expenditure.
- *Overseas Trade Statistics of the UK* gives detailed statistics of exports and imports.
- *Employment Gazette* includes articles, tables and charts on manpower, employment, unemployment, earnings, labour costs and stoppages due to disputes.
- *New Earnings Survey* contains statistics relating to earnings from employment by industrial occupation and region.
- *Financial Statistics* contains key financial and monetary statistics for the UK.
- *Business Monitors* is a series of publications in which a wide variety of statistics are produced, examples of which are:
  (a) annual data relating to cinemas
  (b) monthly data on road vehicles and new registrations
  (c) quarterly data on insurance companies and private pension funds
  (d) annual analysis of the accounts of listed and unlisted companies
  (e) monthly list of price indices for current cost accounting.

If a business is to remain successful and competitive then it will need a wide variety of data about the environment within which it operates. Government statistics are a useful source of this data.

▷ ACTIVITY 3

Employment Gazette (AAT CA D94 – amended)

A manufacturing company has a copy of the Employment Gazette which contains statistics relating to:

(a) employment and unemployment
(b) earnings.

State to what practical purposes both (a) and (b) could be used by the company. [Answer on p. 14]

6 Test your knowledge

1. What would the information system of a small business, e.g. a sole trader typically comprise?

2. How will the information systems' primary requirements differ between public and private sector organisations?

3. What is an exception report?

4. Name at least four necessary qualities of information if it is to be useful to management.

5. How does raw data become information?

6. Give three potential problems with using secondary data.

7. Give three sources of secondary data and examples of the types of information they provide.

[Answers on p. 14]

7 Summary

In this initial chapter we have looked at the general reporting requirements and systems of organisations. We have seen that the particular reporting system of an organisation will depend upon the size, nature and organisational structure of the organisation.

We then looked at the need for internal management information and the fact that in order to manage a business successfully information must be provided on the strategic, tactical and operational level. When providing information for management, it is also important that this is useful information which means that it must be prompt, accurate and understandable.

Information may also need to be provided to external agencies in the form of reports or returns. Such information must be accurate and also may not be the normal information provided by the internal management information system.

It is important to distinguish between data and information. Data is unanalysed facts whereas information is data which has been analysed in some way. Another important distinction is between primary and secondary data, the former being of more direct use and the latter requiring care with its use.

Finally the information made available by the government was considered. This vast array of information can be useful to most organisations in assessing their position within the UK market.

Answers to chapter activities & 'test your knowledge' questions

ACTIVITY 1

Employment information

(i) Numbers employed.
(ii) Vacancies.
(iii) Hours worked, etc.

ACTIVITY 2

Agency return

(a) Return to trade associations, returns to government agencies, etc (e.g. VAT return).
(b) Compliance requirement, statistical trends and seasonal variations.

ACTIVITY 3

Employment Gazette

(a) Employment and unemployment details – where to locate a new factory.
(b) Earnings – how does the company compare with national averages?

Test your knowledge

1 Cash records (e.g. analysed cash book, bank statements, petty cash vouchers), sales and purchase invoice files, supplier catalogues, simple customer database.

2 Public sector organisations will require information on expenditure and productivity/ efficiency measures; private sector businesses' information requirements will focus upon revenue, cost and profit information.

3 An exception report is one that highlights unusual results to prompt the user to investigate and take corrective action where necessary.

4 Promptness/timeliness; brevity; accuracy; discrimination/relevance; economy.

5 Data may be processed into information by grouping, summarising, tabulation, diagrammatic representation, and statistical and/or financial analysis.

6 Lack of knowledge about its method of collection; not necessarily up to date; could be incomplete, e.g. not covering all parts of population; accuracy/nature (forecast/actual) of information unknown.

7 *Financial Times* – share prices, exchange rates, company news.

Social Trends – key social and demographic statistics, e.g. household disposable income, population trends, leisure activities.

Employment Gazette – manpower, employment, unemployment, labour costs.

(For others see main text.)

WRITING REPORTS

INTRODUCTION

Reports are one of the most effective means of business communication. In this chapter, we will be looking at the variety of different ways in which reports can be structured and how you need to go about writing a report. In most assessments you will be required to prepare a report of some sort and, in most cases, the report required will be fairly short and informal. However, in practice, you may be required to prepare longer, more formal reports and therefore all aspects of report writing will be covered in this chapter.

KNOWLEDGE AND UNDERSTANDING

- Methods of presenting information: written reports; diagrammatic; tabular (Elements 7.1, 7.2)

CONTENTS

PERFORMANCE CRITERIA

- Prepare reports in the appropriate form and present them to management within the required timescales (Element 7.1)

1 Reports as a means of effective business communication

1.1 Introduction

In most assessments you will be required to prepare a report of some sort. Normally these will be fairly short informal reports but in practice you may be required to prepare longer, more formal reports, therefore all aspects will be covered in this chapter.

A **report** could be defined as an orderly and objective **communication of factual information** which serves some business aim. Its purpose is to convey information to particular readers or to answer a question.

Report is a general term. A letter containing specific information could be classified as a report or a memo drawing someone's attention to certain details could be classified as a report.

Reports do not even have to be written; it does happen that people are requested to, or offer to, make **oral reports.**

1.2 Functions of a report

Reports have five different functions as follows:

- informing – gathering information
- analysing – analysing the information gathered
- evaluating – so the reader can make a decision based on the report
- recommending – recommendation of a future course of action
- describing – noting observations.

2 Structure of reports

2.1 Introduction

Reports can take **many forms** and can vary in length and status from:

(a) **simple reports** in memo, letter or short report form, to
(b) **fixed format reports,** such as accident reports, to
(c) reports on **internal matters within a company** which may be formal or informal, to
(d) **formal reports,** such as the findings of public enquiries.

2.2 Simple reports in memo, letter or short report form

Many written reports in industry are **simple reports** concerning day-to-day problems and these tend to be short and informal. As such, they have a short life and are intended for only a few readers who are familiar with the problem and its background. The reader will generally be interested in the findings of the report and any action it will lead to.

Of the conventional short forms of informal report, three in particular deserve special attention: **the short report,** the **letter report** and the **memorandum report.** These will vary widely in form and arrangement, depending on the purpose for which they have been written.

2.3 The short informal report

This is generally only a **two or three section report.** The main areas are:

(i) the name of the person requesting the report
(ii) the title
(iii) an introduction, which may also give the background
(iv) the procedure, information, findings and 'overview' of the problem
(v) the conclusion
(vi) the name and position within the company of the writer
(vii) the date.

The following example shows the basic structure but may be adapted to suit different requirements.

EXAMPLE

To: D Fagen

Date: 29 July 20X6

Accounts Department reaction to proposed hot drinks vending machine installation

Introduction

This report describes the reaction of staff in the Accounts department of the Kenilworth branch office of Teck Bros to a proposal to replace existing tea and coffee-making arrangements with a hot drinks vending machine. The report was prepared on the instructions of D. Fagen, Branch Manager and written by J. Ely, Office Junior, Accounts Department. Instructions to prepare the report were received on 24 July 20X6 and it was submitted on 29 July 20X6.

Procedure

It was decided to interview personally all 12 members of staff in the Accounts Department. All staff were notified in advance. Questions were devised, three to establish staff reactions and a fourth inviting comments. All staff were then interviewed and the results noted. (A copy is appended to this report.)

Findings

(a) In response to the question 'Would you be happy to see a vending machine installed?' EIGHT people said yes, THREE said no and ONE was uncertain.

(b) In response to the question 'Are you happy with the present arrangements?' THREE people said yes, EIGHT people said no and ONE appeared unconcerned.

(c) In response to the question 'Would you like to have a wider range of hot drinks available to you?' EIGHT people said yes, THREE people said no and ONE was uncertain.

(d) Amongst the comments made when staff were invited to comment on the proposal were 'Will fixed times for coffee and tea breaks disappear?' 'What about the tea ladies?' and 'I would prefer to obtain drinks at my own convenience'.

Conclusion

A clear majority of the staff (two-thirds) are in favour of this proposal.

J Ely
Office Junior
Accounts Department

2.4 The letter report

As the name implies this is a report written in **letter form.** It is used primarily to present information to or by someone outside the company. For example, an outside consultant may write his analysis and recommendations in the form of a letter, signing the letter as normal.

2.5 Memorandum reports

Memorandum reports are used primarily for routine reporting within an organisation, although some companies use them for external communicating. Because they are largely internal communications, they are often written on standardised inter-office memorandum stationery.

Following the company's identification or logo, if there is one, the words From, To and Subject appear at the top of the page. Sometimes the date is also part of the heading. Like letters, the memorandum may carry a signature or the writer may merely initial the heading.

The business supplies buyer of Datewise has asked one of his clerks to investigate the costs and supply of 108mm x 219mm white envelopes, with a view to finding a cheaper source.

EXAMPLE

Memorandum

To: Mr Hopkins

From: A Clerk **Date:** 4 January 20X7

Subject: Supply of envelopes

As requested I have investigated the local suppliers of the 108mm x 219mm white envelopes and compared the costs.

There are three main office suppliers to choose from: Paper Products, Office Treasures and Bestbuy.

Our current supplier, Bestbuy, has free delivery and offers us a 25% discount on orders over £100.

Paper Products offer boxes of 1,000 envelopes £3 cheaper than Bestbuy on orders of six or more boxes. They offer the same discount and have a free delivery once a fortnight in this area. Special deliveries carry a charge of £20.

Office Treasures are the same price as Paper Products but, as we would be new customers, they will not discuss discounts.

Paper Products would be most suitable for us as we always order more than six boxes and rarely need special delivery. I would recommend them for future supplies of envelopes.

2.6 Fixed format reports

Some reports, such as **accident reports** and **personnel appraisal reports,** will be a fixed length and style because the report is a fixed format.

EXAMPLE

Vehicle accident report

Branch & reference....................................Claim number...

Important – Reports in respect of accidents to motor and electric vehicles should be forwarded to the Distribution Director no later than 24 hours after the accident has occurred.

PLEASE COMPLETE IN BLOCK CAPITALS

Date of accident............ Hour.......am/pm Condition of road Wet or Dry
Driver's name..........................Age............................Licence No................................
Address...

State if person was injured...
Place where accident occurred..
Did you give any warning and how?..
What was the speed of your vehicle immediately before impact?.........

Company details	**Opposing vehicle or property (third party)**
Vehicle Reg No..	Description of opposing vehicle or property
Make..	....
Damage to vehicle.................................	Driver's name ....
Goods damaged, value as on ledger (attach a/c)..	Address... ....
Did police witness accident? Yes/No	Name & address of any injured third party
If so, officer's No. & Station	....
Name of witness (1)................................	Nature of injuries................................
Address	Which hospital?..................................
	Damage to third party property
Name of witness (2)...............................	....
Address	....
	Third party insurers.................................

ON A SEPARATE SHEET DESCRIBE HOW THE ACCIDENT OCCURRED

3 Structure of formal reports

3.1 Introduction

Formal reports (such as the findings of public enquiries) may be internal or external to the organisation, and are used for the more complex and important investigations commissioned by senior management.

In general, they will include the following:

(a) **introduction,** including terms of reference and background to the report
(b) **approach to the investigation**
(c) detailed **findings** (some of which may be presented as an Appendix)
(d) **conclusions** and **recommendations,** as appropriate.

The findings of **public enquiries** are presented in terms of a formal report. In terms of length and style, these are likely to be the longest and most formal of reports.

Structure is very important. The report will be used for reference so readers need to be able to find the information they need quickly and easily. Formal written reports usually contain the basic sections listed below, though there are often slight variations.

3.2 Title page

The title. This should give a good idea of what the report is about, without being too long. It should be easy to find in a filing system.

- The date of issue
- Circulation list (if appropriate)
- Name of author(s)
- Author's position and department
- Name and address of organisation

3.3 Summary or synopsis

The major **uses of summaries** are:

- to help readers decide whether to read the whole report
- to enable readers to see the key points
- to focus attention on the aim of the report.

Write the summary after the report is finished. As a rough guide, it should be about 10% of the length of the report and should only contain material included in the main report.

Include in the summary:

- a brief statement of the problem investigated
- a summary of the main points, concentrating on the conclusion
- an outline of any recommendations.

3.4 Table of contents

A list of **headings** and **sub-headings** and their page numbers. The contents page should provide an overview. The headings should be meaningful.

3.5 Introduction

Introduce and clearly state the main topic of the report. Give background factual information sufficient to 'set the scene', familiarise the reader with the context and prepare him for what is to follow. You may also be required to give terms of reference.

3.6 Main text

- A fuller statement of the problem.
- How it was investigated and what was discovered.
- Informative **headings** for each section and sub-section. A section may comprise one or more paragraphs, consisting of a main point, reasons and factual evidence.

3.7 Conclusion

(a) **Summarise** the key points made in the main body of the report and summarise findings, showing briefly but clearly how they are logically derived from the supporting evidence presented.
(b) **Evaluate the findings,** questioning whether they are a complete answer to the problem.
(c) **No new information** is to be included in the conclusions.

3.8 Recommendations

Recommendations, if required, can be included with the conclusions or treated separately.
(a) They should recommend a certain course of action in accordance with the conclusions reached.
(b) Any recommendations made should be prepared for in the main body, along with consideration of their viability.

3.9 Appendix

Appendices should be given informative headings and structured so that the reader can understand them. They should not include information which readers will need in order to follow the main text.

(a) Their use is to provide more detailed information which is of interest but either too technical or too peripheral for most readers of the report.
(b) This is also the place to provide documentation for facts presented in the report, e.g. letters, faxes, tables, etc.
(c) Computer programs might be presented in the appendix.

3.10 Acknowledgements

These can be at the beginning or at the end if it is felt appropriate to **thank people.**

3.11 References

The **references** must contain a list of books, articles, etc. which have been consulted, if the report has required it. When referring to information from these sources in the body of the report, they must be acknowledged by means of a referencing system.

References need the following details:

- **Books:** Author, Title, Publisher, Edition (unless 1st), Place of publication, Date, Chapter, and page number if relevant.
- **Journals:** Author, Title, Journal, Volume, Number, date and page number if relevant.

4 Writing a report

4.1 Overall structure

The structure of the report should reflect the function. The questions that need to be answered are:

- Is there a specific aim?
- Is it just a presentation of facts?
- Does it need a demonstration of analysis used?

All reports, whether short or long, formal or informal, need the basic structure of **beginning, middle and end.**

The **beginning** should determine:

- what the document is about
- the relevance for the reader.

The **middle** should contain:

- the main analysis
- the detailed argument supporting your conclusions, recommendations or proposed action.

The **end** should tell the reader:

- what will happen or what you want them to do
- conclusions and recommendations.

4.2 Checking the report

After writing the report, the next step is the checking and preparation of the work for distribution.

The steps to follow when checking your report are:

(a) Checking should not take place immediately after writing. If it is possible to come back to the report after a few days have lapsed, then checking is likely to be more effective.

(b) Edit the report yourself before asking a colleague to look at it. Look at it with the following structure in mind.

- **Material:**
  Does the report contain all that should be included?
  Has unnecessary padding been taken out?
- **Language** (see later section on effective business communication):
  Are the words well chosen, precise and appropriate?
  Is their meaning clear?
  Is the report easy to read and understand?
- **Design:**
  Is it well planned?
  Are the sections in the right order?
  Are the paragraphs in logical sequence?
  Is it attractively set out?

(c) Ask a **colleague to review it** and to identify:
- parts which are unclear.
- areas or points which you have missed.
- flaws in your argument.

(d) Arrange a **meeting** to discuss your colleague's comments.

4.3 Physical appearance

As far as **physical appearance** is concerned, first impressions are very important and the report's physical appearance should be designed to create the desired impression.

4.4 Page layout

Good layout impresses readers. Make sure there is plenty of space between the various parts of the report and leave a good margin.

The different sections of the report usually begin on a **new page**, though the sub-sections of the main body of the report will generally follow on from one another.

4.5 Headings

Headings are the titles of the various **divisions of the report.** Usually, it helps if you make generous use of headings and sub-headings. Headings break text into manageable sections and help by increasing the 'white space' around the blocks of type, especially when the type is single spaced. They also act as sign-posts, pointing out what is to be found in each section.

Formal headings such as PROBLEM or EXPERIMENTAL or DISCUSSION are not as useful as informative headings that genuinely focus attention on the essence of the following paragraphs.

The importance of headings (sometimes called **captions**) is emphasised by type and position. There are four major positions of headings.

(a) Highest of these four in order of rank is the **centred heading**. This is on a line by itself and is centred between the right and left margins.

(b) Next in order is the **marginal heading**. Beginning on the left margin, this is also on a line by itself.

(c) The **box heading** is the next in the ranking. It begins on the left margin and is surrounded by a box of space formed by indenting the first few lines of the text.

(d) The fourth is the **run-in heading**. This simply runs into the first line of the text it covers and is distinguished from the text only by underscoring or using a bolder font or italics.

These are illustrated below.

(a)

SUB-CONTRACTING THE CANTEEN SERVICE

(b)
The proposal

xxxxxxxxxxxxxxxxxxxxxxxxxxxxxxxxxxxxxxxxxxxxxxxxxxxxxxxxxxxxxxxxxxxxxxxxx
xxxxxxxxxxxxxxxxxxxxxxxxxxxxxxxxxxxxxxxxxxxxxxxxxxxxxxxxxxxxxxxxxxxxxxxxx
xxxxxxxxxxxxxxxxxxxxxxxxxxxxxxxxxxxxxxxxxxxxxxxxxxxxxxxxxxxxxxxxxxxxxxxxx
xxxxxxxxxxxxxxxxxxxxxxxxxxxxxxxxxxxxxx

(c)
Considerations xxxxxxxxxxxxxxxxxxxxxxxxxxxxxxxxxxxxxxxxxxxxxxxxxx
xxxxxxxxxxxxxxxxxxxxxxxxxxxxxxxxxxxxxxxxxxxxxxxxxx
xxxxxxxxxxxxxxxxxxxxxxxxxxxxxxxxxxxxxxxxxxxxxxxxxxxxxxxxxxxxxxxxxxxxxxxxx

(d)
Staffing requirements xxxxxxxxxxxxxxxxxxxxxxxxxxxxxxxxxxxxxxxxxxxxxxxxxx
xxxxxxxxxxxxxxxxxxxxxxxxxxxxxxxxxxxxxxxxxxxxxxxxxxxxxxxxxxxxxxxxxxxxxxxxx

A numbering system may also be used:

1

THE PROPOSAL

1.1
Introduction

Xxxxxxxxxxxxxxxxxxxxxxxxxxxxxxxxxxxxxxxxxxxxxxxxxxxxxxxxxxxxxxxxxxxxxxxx
xxxxxxxxxxxxxxxxxxxxxxxxxxxxxxxxxxxxxxxxxxxxxxxxxxxxxxxxxxxxxxxxxxxxxxxxx

1.2
Considerations xxxxxxxxxxxxxxxxxxxxxxxxxxxxxxxxxxxxxxxxxxxxxxxxxx
xxxxxxxxxxxxxxxxxxxxxxxxxxxxxxxxxxxxxxxxxxxxxxxxxx
xxxxxxxxxxxxxxxxxxxxxxxxxxxxxxxxxxxxxxxxxxxxxxxxxxxxxxxxxxxxxxxxxxxxxxxxx

1.2.1
Staffing requirements xxxxxxxxxxxxxxxxxxxxxxxxxxxxxxxxxxxxxxxxxxxx
xxxxxxxxxxxxxxxxxxxxxxxxxxxxxxxxxxxxxxxxxxxxxxxxxxxxxxxxxxxxxxxxxxx

4.6 The reader of the report

Whatever type of report you are preparing, it is vital to consider the **reader's interest** if you wish to convey your message. The audience you are trying to reach via the report will determine:

(1) the language you use
(2) the length of the report
(3) the style of the report.

4.7 The language you use

Ideally a report should communicate its messages as quickly, as easily and as precisely as language will permit.

To achieve a **more effective business writing style** there are a number of points to note.

4.8 Short words not long

Never use a long word where a short one will do.
Short words are easy to spell and understand and tend to communicate better than long words.

Can you think of short words for perception, initiate and utilise? It might be easier to use view, start or use instead of the longer words.

Readability studies show that a heavy proportion of long words tends to slow up the reading and makes understanding difficult. Thus, wise report writers will use long words with caution.

The following contrasting **sentences** show the effect of long words on writing clarity. Without question the simple versions communicate better.

A decision was predicated on the assumption that an abundance of monetary funds was forthcoming.	The decision was based on the belief that there would be more money.
They acceded to the proposition to terminate the business.	They agreed to end the business.
During the preceding year the company operated at a financial deficit.	Last year the company lost money.

▷ ACTIVITY 1

Finding the right word

In the following sentences, replace the words printed in italics with more-suitable words:

(a) One statesman thought the treaty *derogative* to his country's honour.
(b) The Frenchman regards the *observation* of the Sabbath from a different standpoint.
(c) The town officials did their best to make the buses popular and *payable*.
(d) Among the typists she raised such *dissent* that no pair of them remained on speaking terms.
(e) Your best plan is to treat him as *contemptibly* as you can.

(f) The body was so mangled that it could hardly be recognised as *humane.*
(g) It seemed that the patient ought to *decease.*
(h) The girl was *sick with nostalgia.*
(i) By these remarks do you mean to *infer* that I know something about your savings?
(j) I have photographed the children of that school now for thirty years without a *breakage.*
(k) The island is famous for its *luxurious* vegetation.
(l) The murderer was seen in the very *action* of firing his gun.
(m) After the *invention* of chloroform surgical operations had a higher rate of success. [Answer on p. 35]

4.9 Active not passive

Prefer the active to the passive voice.

The active is more concise and forceful.

Compare the following.

The outstanding balance should be confirmed by the debtor (9 words).	The debtor should confirm the outstanding balance (7 words).
The stocktake was attended by the internal auditor (8 words).	The internal auditor attended the stocktake (6 words).
A receipt was issued by the wholesaler (7 words).	The wholesaler issued a receipt (5 words).

In each case the second sentence is said to be 'active', i.e. 'something or someone does something'.
The first sentence is 'passive' in comparison, i.e. 'something or someone has something done to it '.
The passive takes more words to construct and, being clumsy, takes more effort to understand.

If you have a passive sentence try:

- changing 'X was done by Y' to 'Y did X'
- changing the verb e.g. 'profits were reduced by' to 'profits fell by'
- changing the subject e.g. 'these recommendations can be implemented in two ways' to 'there are two ways to implement these recommendations'.

Having said this, it is only fair to point out that some formal reports do require the passive, third person.

4.10 Short sentences

Shortening sentences can improve clarity.

Compare the following.

The completion of the report should be before 28 March 20X7 (8 words and date).	The report should be completed by 28 March 20X7 (6 words and date).
There is no availability of computer expertise (7 words).	Computer expertise is not available (5 words).
The practicality of using value-weighted selection is in doubt (10 words).	Value-weighted selection may not be practical (7 words).

In each case the second sentence is easier to read and comprehend. In the first sentences the words such as practicality, availability and completion are warning signs that the sentence is not as simple as it might be.

4.11 Economy with words

Use words economically.

Our language is cluttered with phrases that are best replaced by shorter expressions. Although the shorter forms may save only a word or two here and there, the cumulative savings over a long piece of writing can be significant. Some examples of long and short are:

Along the lines of	Like
For the purpose of	For
For the reason that	Because, since
In the near future	Soon
In short supply	Scarce
In accordance with	By
In several instances	Often
At this moment in time	Now
Prior to	Before
In very few cases	Seldom
A number of	Several
With regard to / in connection with	About
With the result that	So
With the minimum of delay	Quickly

4.12 Sentence length

Vary sentence length.

A sentence is a group of words that make complete sense. More than any other characteristic of a sentence, length is most clearly related to sentence difficulty. The longer a sentence is, the harder it is to understand.

When an excess of information is presented in a single package, the mind cannot grasp it all, at least on a single reading. Most current authorities agree that sentences aimed at the middle level of adult readers should average 16 to 18 words in length. For more advanced readers the average can be higher, and it must be lower for those of lower reading abilities. Of course, these figures do not mean that sentences of six or so words are taboo, nor do they mean that you should avoid long sentences of more than thirty words. It is the average that should be in keeping with the readability level of the reader.

4.13 Slang and foreign phrases

When we speak, we tailor our words to suit those to whom we speak; in writing, we address a wider audience and must use words which will be generally understood. It follows that certain words must be excluded from our written vocabulary since their meaning will not be clear to everyone. They fall into four classes.

Slang words are often vivid and effective in speech but should not be used in writing. Phrases such as 'get the push' and 'coming on heavy', should be replaced by standard English ones.

Words and phrases used only in certain districts are to be avoided for the same reason. They are excellent in speech, and often have more character than the corresponding words in standard English, yet, since they will not be generally understood, it is unwise to use them. The Scotsman may use 'wee' in speech, but he will use 'little' in written text.

Foreign words and phrases should be used as little as possible, unless they have already been absorbed into the language. Route, chef, chauffeur and matinee are French words that we could hardly do without, but you can usually avoid foreign phrases such as *inter alia, per annum, prima facie and carte blanche by writing among others, a year, at first sight and blank cheque or free hand.*

The UK and USA have been described as two countries divided by a common language. Not only does American spelling sometimes differ from ours but so do many expressions.

▷ ACTIVITY 2

Not at all obvious

Look at the following extract from a written report:

Ten newsagent shops in the Bristol area were selected to test the effectiveness of two different display stands in generating sales. For the purposes of the survey the shops were designated with the letters A–J.

During the period 15 March to 20 March the total sales for the three items were recorded. Two different stands were used to display those items for sale. Five of the stands were the traditional sloping top 5 ft wide stand made of formica with perspex divisions while the other five were the metal revolving type, 2 ft in diameter. Shops A, C, D, G, I, used the traditional stand and shops B, E, F, H, J, used the revolving stand.

Total sales of the items during the six-day test period (Monday to Saturday inclusive) were as follows: Shops E, F, G, H showed sales of 435, 475, 286 and 575 cards and Shop I 275 with Shop J at 525.

There is an obvious correlation between sales and type of display stand. This correlation is reflected in similar studies carried out in Manchester and Aberdeen.

This material is taken from a survey report. How well have you been able to assimilate the information? Was the correlation between the sales and the type of display stand quite as 'obvious' as the author suggests?

Required

(a) Your immediate superior, Mrs Jenkins, has asked you to rewrite this report in the short report format illustrated in an earlier section, presenting the facts in a more understandable manner.

(b) The second task is to write a memo to the author, Jo Bloggs, raising any further queries you may have about the survey report.

[Answer on p. 35]

4.14 The length of the report

To answer the question as to how long a report should be, we need to refer back to its purpose, which is to convey information to particular readers or to answer a question.

Obviously there is no 'right' answer as to length. Verbal reports can be just a few words long; for example 'his condition is stable'.
However, some academic works such as PhD theses may run to thousands of pages. The biggest indication of length should come in the specification of the request for the report, so the first general rule is:

- **Be sure you know what is expected of you before you begin.**

The **time allowed for the completion** of the report is another indication. If you telephone a hospital wanting a report on a sick relative you don't expect them to send you a dossier the following month. But if you are writing a project on alternative software for management information systems, your report is likely to cover at least a week's research and should reflect this.

The second general rule is only a clarification of the first and is to:

- **Confine yourself to the facts of the case you are reporting on.**

These two general rules, as well as those in the previous section on the language that you use, should give an indication of the length of the report required.

4.15 The style of the report

Style is the fashion of writing that transforms some collection of facts into a readable document.

Since reports tend to be quite formal, they are usually written in a **formal language.**

The **level of formality** may be due to the type of report. Although some insurance reports on car accidents are portrayed on walls of insurance brokers as highly amusing, they are not intended to be, as most are very serious. On the other hand, if the organisation is not one that demands formality, an academic piece of work may seem out of place.

A lack of formal style in a written report by a junior member of staff when the report is being read by the managing director or chairman may be seen as being too familiar, unless informality is customary within that organisation.

The essence of good style is to **avoid complex, stilted writing** and aim for a simple style that is the most clear and thus the most satisfactory.

5 Test your knowledge

1 What is the principal object of any report?

2 Give eight sections that might appear in a formal report.

3 How could you rewrite the following sentence to make it clearer and more concise?

'It is the policy of the company to tolerate, within reasonable constraints, a certain period of time of rehabilitation for an employee returning to their position after an extended absence.' [Answers on p. 37]

6 Summary

When writing any type of report the following matters should be considered:

- Who is the report for? – this will affect the style and language used in the report.
- What is the time scale for production of the report? – as well as ensuring that the report is completed on time this will also affect the length of the report.
- The overall structure of the report – it must have a beginning, a middle and an end.
- The clarity of the communication – ensure that detailed calculations are set out in the appendix not in the main body of the report and that the language used makes the message of the report quite clear.

Answers to chapter activities & 'test your knowledge' questions

△ ACTIVITY 1

Finding the right word

In the following sentences, the words printed in italics in the question have been replaced by more suitable words (usually to avoid malapropisms):

(a) One statesman thought the treaty derogatory to his country's honour.
(b) The Frenchman regards the observance of the Sabbath from a different standpoint.
(c) The town officials did their best to make the buses popular and profitable.
(d) Among the typists she raised such dissension that no pair of them remained on speaking terms.
(e) Your best plan is to treat him as contemptuously as you can.
(f) The body was so mangled that it could hardly be recognised as human.
(g) It seemed that the patient ought to die.
(h) The girl was nostalgic.
(i) By these remarks do you mean to imply that I know something about your savings?
(j) I have photographed the children of that school now for 30 years without a break.
(k) The island is famous for its luxuriant vegetation.
(l) The murderer was seen in the very act of firing his gun.
(m) After the discovery of chloroform surgical operations had a higher rate of success.

△ ACTIVITY 2

Not at all obvious

Part (a)

To: Mrs Jenkins

SURVEY REPORT COMPARING THE ABILITY OF TWO TYPES OF DISPLAY STAND TO GENERATE SALES OF CARDS

Introduction

The object of this report is to compare two types of display stand by analysing their ability to generate sales of cards in newsagents.

The first type of card stand is the traditional one. This is five feet wide, made from formica with sloping perspex divisions.

The second type is the revolving metal card stand. This is two feet in diameter.

For the purpose of this report we will call them Traditional and Revolving.

Procedure

The survey was carried out in three cities, Bristol, Aberdeen and Manchester. The results shown in this report are those from Bristol.

Ten newsagents from Bristol were studied over a period of six working days, the 15th to 20th March. Half of these newsagents have the traditional stand to display cards and the other half have the revolving card stand. Details of the names and addresses of all ten shops are in the Appendix. For easier comparison the shops have been allocated letters from A to J.

Findings

The following table shows the number of cards sold over the six days in Bristol:

Shop	Traditional card sales	Shop	Revolving card sales
A		B	
C		E	435
D		F	475
G	286	H	575
I	275	J	525

The findings were similar in the other two cities chosen for the survey.

Conclusion

The higher numbers of cards sold are all in shops which use the revolving card stands.

Part (b)

MEMORANDUM

To: Jo Bloggs **Date:**

From: A Clerk

Report on comparison of display stands and their ability to generate sales

Having read your survey report there are a number of questions that I would like you to answer:

1 How and why were the three cities chosen?

2 How and why were the ten newsagents in Bristol chosen?

3 Only six results are shown out of the ten shops studied. Where are the results from the others?

4 Are the figures for Aberdeen and Manchester available?

5 Have you considered exchanging Traditional for Revolving stands to determine whether the higher level of sales is a function of the type of stand or the size and location of the shop?

Test your knowledge

1 To communicate information.

2 Title page/summary/table of contents/introduction/main text/conclusions/recommendations/appendices/acknowledgements/references.

3 The company will allow a reasonable settling-in period when an employee returns to work after a long absence.

TABLES AND DIAGRAMS

INTRODUCTION

Most methods of data collection result in large amounts of data needing to be analysed in order to obtain relevant information. This will therefore involve organising the relevant data in order to obtain an overall impression. Organised data can be summarised using narrative, tables or diagrams. In this chapter we consider the ways in which data can be summarised into a table or presented in the form of a diagram (pictogram, pie chart and bar chart).

KNOWLEDGE AND UNDERSTANDING

- Tabulation of accounting and other quantitative information using spreadsheets (Elements 7.1, 7.2)
- Methods of presenting information: written reports; diagrammatic; tabular (Elements 7.1, 7.2)

CONTENTS

PERFORMANCE CRITERIA

- Prepare reports in the appropriate form and present them to management within the required timescales (Element 7.1)

1 Tables

1.1 Introduction

A **major drawback of summarising data using the narrative approach** is that the information required is not clearly presented and only a limited amount of data can be presented. A properly constructed table, however, gives the required information immediately and clearly.

EXAMPLE

A major bank is interested in the types of account held by its customers. The information below has recently been collected:

A sample of 5,000 accounts was taken, each account belonging to a different customer. 729 accounts were held by customers aged under 25 of whom 522 held current accounts, the remainder holding ordinary deposit accounts. 1,383 of the accounts were held by customers aged between 25 and 44, 1,020 being current accounts, 271 were ordinary deposit accounts and the remainder were high-interest deposit accounts. There were 1,621 accounts belonging to customers aged between 45 and 59, of these 61% were current accounts, 29% were ordinary deposit accounts and 10% high interest deposit accounts. Of customers aged 60 and over, 628 held current accounts, 410 held ordinary deposit accounts and the remainder held high interest deposit accounts.

Summarise the information contained in this narrative into a single table.

Solution

(a) **A simple one-way table**

A major point of interest in the given data is obviously the age breakdown of account holders. Working through the narrative, this could be presented as follows:

under 25	729
25 - 44	1,383
45 - 59	1,621
60 and over	1,267

The figure for the 60 and over group is given by 5,000 – (729 + 1,383 + 1,621) since there are a total of 5,000 accounts each held by different customers.

(b) **Title and headings**

The table in (a) gives us a clear breakdown of the ages of the customers but leaves the reader to guess what the columns mean. Clearly the left-hand column is age but it is better to label both columns clearly and to tell the reader what the subject of the table is. Also it is useful to show relevant totals, i.e. in this case the total number of accounts.

An improvement on the table given in (a) is thus as follows.

Age of customers

Age	*Number of customers*
under 25	729
25 – 44	1,383
45 – 59	1,621
60 and over	1,267
Total	5,000

(c) **Another one-way table**

The data also informs us of the number of accounts held of each type. A table of this information is more difficult to extract from the narrative and some steps of working may be helpful.

(1) There are three types of account: current accounts, ordinary deposit accounts and high interest deposit accounts.

(2) Current accounts:
522 (age under 25);
1,020 (aged 25–44);
989 (aged 45–59; 61% of 1,621 accounts = 0.61 x 1,621 = 988.81 or 989 accounts by rounding to nearest whole number of accounts);
628 (aged 60 and over).

(3) Ordinary deposit accounts:
207 (aged under 25; i.e. 729 minus the number of current accounts = 729 – 522);
271 (aged 25–44);
470 (aged 45–59; 29% of 1,621 accounts = 0.29 x 1,621 = 470);
410 (aged 60 and over).

(4) High interest deposit account:
0 (aged under 25; we must assume this since no other detail is given);
92 (aged 25–44; 1,383 minus the number of current and ordinary deposit accounts = 1,383 – (1,020 + 271) = 1,383 – 1,291);
162 (aged 45 – 59; 10% of 1,621 accounts = 0.10 x 1,621 = 162.1 or 162);
229 (aged 60 and over; total aged 60 and over minus number of current and ordinary deposit accounts = 1,267 (from (a)) – (628 + 410) = 229).

Summing the number of accounts in (2) to (4) gives the required table.

Number of different accounts held

Types of account	*Number of customers*
Current	3,159
Ordinary deposit	1,358
High interest deposit	483
Total	5,000

(d) **A two-way table**

Our objective at the start of this example was to construct a single table to summarise all the information contained in the narrative. Having carried out the simple calculations in (c) above, this is now easily done by employing a two-way table (sometimes called a cross-tabulation). In this example the two 'variables' are obviously age of customers and type of account held. These become the headings for the following required two-way table.

Ages and types of account held by sample of 5,000 customers

	Age				
Type of account	*under 25*	*25 - 44*	*45 - 59*	*60 and over*	*Total*
Current	522	1,020	989	628	3,159
Ordinary deposit	207	271	470	410	1,358
High interest deposit	0	92	162	229	483
Total	729	1,383	1,621	1,267	5,000

1.2 Guidelines for constructing tables

There are no set rules for constructing tables since tables often vary markedly in content and format. The following **guidelines** should however be adhered to:

- Always give the table a **title** and suitable **headings.**
- If the data contains a number of categories or sub-categories, use a **two-way table.**
- Give column and row **sub-totals** where appropriate.
- If the draft table contains too much detail, it will fail in its objective of summarising the data. **Further simplified tables** should then be constructed, each dealing with different aspects of the data.
- It is important to state the **source of the data.** This may be included in the title or given beneath the table.
- The **units in the table** should be 'manageable'. This can be accomplished by, for example, dividing particular column entries by 1,000 and including this fact in the column heading.

- It is sometimes useful to show **percentages** in the table in addition to the actual figures.

In analysing large amounts of data, tables similar to those already considered prove very useful. They simplify a mass of narrative into columns and rows of figures which are much easier to understand. Note that the use of computer spreadsheets can simplify the tabulation process, as illustrated in Chapter 7.

O EXAMPLE

Smith plc manufactures bed linen. In 20X2 its total sales were £126,000 and these sales increased by £28,000 in 20X3 and then again by £41,000 in 20X4. In comparison Brown plc, one of Smith's competitors, had total sales of £206,000 in 20X2 and their sales reduced by 10% each year in 20X3 and 20X4. Present this information in tabular form.

Solution

Step 1 It is useful in any problem where construction of a table is required to first write down the headings in the table. In this example this is easy:

Year *Sales of Smith plc* *Sales of Brown plc*

Step 2 The next stage in problems of this kind is to work out the individual entries in the table:

Smith plc:	20X2	£126,000
	20X3	£126,000 + £28,000 = £154,000
	20X4	£154,000 +£41,000 = £195,000
Brown plc:	20X2	£206,000
	20X3	£206,000 - (0.1 x £206,000) = £206,000 - £20,600 = £185,400
	20X4	£185,400 - (0.1 x £185,400) = £185,400 - £18,540 = £166,860

Step 3 The draft table is now easily formed:

Year	*Sales of Smith plc*	*Sales of Brown plc*
	£	£
20X2	126,000	206,000
20X3	154,000	185,400
20X4	195,000	166,860

Step 4 Since the units are all of the same order of magnitude, we can make the units more manageable by dividing by 1,000 although it might be acceptable to round Brown's figures to the nearest

£'000. Also a title should be added to the table. The final table might thus have the form:

Sales of Smith plc and Brown plc for 20X2 - X4

Year	*Sales of Smith plc*	*Sales of Brown plc*
	£000	£000
20X2	126	206
20X3	154	185
20X4	195	167

When planning your table try to minimise the number of columns across the page. Therefore in this example it is better to have the sales of Smith plc and Brown plc as the columns rather than to have a column for each year.

▷ ACTIVITY 1

Bunny and Hutch

The total number of employees of Bunny and Hutch Ltd on 31 December 20X4 was 3,984, of which 2,124 were men. During 20X4, 221 men had been engaged and 185 resigned. The corresponding figures for women were 97 and 108 respectively. Because of the different types of work done, the average wage rate paid to male employees in 20X4 was £121.32 and to female employees £87.93. The company worked for 50 weeks in 20X4. Tabulate this data, including in your table an estimate of the total wage bill.

[Answer on p. 70]

1.3 Analysis of tables

In some instances instead of drawing up a table you may be required to analyse or interpret the information in a table.

O EXAMPLE

The table below shows figures of employees in different types of employment for the years 20X2 to 20Y3. Interpret this data by commenting on the trend in employment in motor vehicle manufacturing and comparing it to what happened in 'manufacturing' and 'all industries and services'.

Total employees in employment

Year	*Motor vehicle manufacturing*	*Manufacturing*	*All industries and services*
	'000	'000	'000
20X2	490	7,779	22,121
20X3	510	7,830	22,663
20X4	497	7,873	22,790
20X5	457	7,524	22,710
20X6	448	7,281	22,543
20X7	464	7,328	22,619
20X8	471	7,290	22,777
20X9	459	7,258	23,158
20Y0	412	6,940	22,972
20Y1	355	6,221	21,871
20Y2	318	5,912	21,473
20Y3	306	5,641	21,210

Source: *Employment Gazette*

Solution

Questions of this type are a little vague in what is required. For each of the three columns of data on employment we could, for example, comment on every year to year change, e.g. employment in motor vehicle manufacturing increased by 20,000 from 20X2 to 20X3, fell by 13,000 from 20X3 to 20X4, etc. This is clearly a long-winded way of describing the trend in employment and should be avoided.

What is required is some comment on the general changes in employment, without too much detail. For all questions of this type this is best achieved by picking out the 'peaks' and 'troughs' in the data and also by commenting on the overall change in the data between the beginning of the period and the end. In this example, suitable comments might be as follows.

- The total number of employees in motor vehicle manufacturing has shown a decreasing trend over the period. It rose to a peak in 20X3, gradually fell until 20X6, increased slightly until 20X8 and then fell dramatically until 20Y3 when it was over 37% down on the 20X2 figure.
- The total number of employees in manufacturing industries also fell, on average, over the period. It rose slowly between 20X2 and 20X4 but then fell sharply until 20X6, when after a small increase in 20X7, it fell rapidly until 20Y3. Overall between 20X2 and 20Y3 there was a 27.5% fall in employment in manufacturing industries.

- The total number of employees in all industries and services showed far less fluctuation than the previous two sets of figure. The total rose between 20X2 and 20X4, fell back between 20X4 and 20X6, rose again to peak in 20X9 and then fell fairly sharply until 20Y3 when it was just over 4% below the 20X2 figure.

Workings

Percentage changes in employment between 20X2 and 20Y3:

Motor vehicle manufacturing $= \dfrac{490 - 306}{490} \times 100\% = 37.55\%$ fall

Manufacturing $= \dfrac{7,779 - 5,641}{7,779} \times 100\% = 27.48\%$ fall

All industries and services $= \dfrac{22,121 - 21,210}{22,121} \times 100\% = 4.12\%$ fall

It is also useful in questions of this type to give some overall comment about what appears to be happening (as indicated by the data).

In this example, there has obviously been a large movement of employees out of motor vehicle manufacturing between 20X2 and 20Y3. On the limited evidence available, this movement of employees does not seem to have been into other manufacturing industries since there has also been a 27.5% fall in employment in this area.

▷ ACTIVITY 2

Motor policies

The following table gives details of the motor insurance policies of an insurance company in 20X3.

Region	*Number of claims*	*Number of policies held*
North	1,330	16,223
Midlands	1,384	18,210
South	1,377	22,581
East Anglia	234	9,363
London	1,401	32,580
Wales	180	10,005
Scotland	118	7,388
Northern Ireland	659	6,276

Provide a brief interpretation of the information contained in this table.

[Answer on p. 71]

1.4 Averages

One of the statistics that will often be presented with a table of data is an average. The most commonly used will be the arithmetic **mean**, but you should also be aware of the other two types of average, the **mode** and the **median**, and the circumstances under which they may give additional useful information.

EXAMPLE

The manager of a sports shoe shop is preparing a report on buying patterns, and has compiled the following tally table of the sizes of ladies' shoes bought over a five day period:

Day/shoe size	*1*	*2*	*3*	*4*	*5*	*Total*
34	//	///		/	//	8
35	///	//	////	////	///	16
36	//	//	//	/		7
37	///	////	//	//	////	15
38	///// ////	///// /	///	////	///// /////	32
39	////	///	/////	///	/	16
40	///	//	///	///	////	15
41	///	/		//	/	7
42	/		//		/	4

Calculate the (i) mean, (ii) mode and (iii) median ladies' shoe size bought during this period.

Solution

The mean

If all the shoe sizes are added up, for all pairs sold, and the total divided by the number of pairs bought, the result will be the mean.

Sometimes the data will be presented as a set of individual item values, in which case you just need to add them up and divide by the number of items.

Here, the data is presented as a **frequency distribution**, showing how many items had each of the specified values. So we need to multiply out each shoe size by the number of pairs sold with that size to get the total of all the sizes of all shoes sold:

(34 x 8) + (35 x 16) + (36 x 7) + (37 x 15) + (38 x 32) + (39 x 16) + (40 x 15) + (41 x 7) + (42 x 4) = 272 + 560 + 252 + 555 + 1,216 + 624 + 600 + 287 + 168 = 4,534

We now need to add up the frequencies (the numbers of each size sold) to get the total number of pairs of shoes sold:

$$8 + 16 + 7 + 15 + 32 + 16 + 15 + 7 + 4 = 120$$

The mean shoe size bought is thus:

$$= 37.783$$

The points to note about this measure are:

- It is not an actual possible shoe size – so perhaps not very helpful when deciding on purchasing policies.
- It uses all the data.
- It can be fairly easily distorted by extreme values – if a tall lady with shoe size 45 had come in and bought 10 pairs of shoes on Day 3, say, the mean value would increase to 38.338, an increase of more than half a shoe size.

The mode

The mode is the most popular value – i.e. the value that occurs most often in the data.

In our case, this will be represented by the size with the highest frequency, i.e. 38.

The points to note about this measure are:

- It is an actual shoe size and thus may be more useful for planning purposes.
- It is not necessarily a unique value – if there had been 32 pairs of size 39 also sold, this would also be a modal size.
- It does not give any idea of the distribution of the other sizes.

The median

If all the pairs of shoes that were sold in the period were lined up in ascending order of size, the median value would be the value of the pair in the middle of the line.

In our example, there are 120 pairs and so there isn't a 'middle' pair. We would thus take the average of the 60th and the 61st pairs in the line.

To find these values, we need to add up the frequencies, from the top of the table until we reach the 60th/61st pairs:

34 to 37	8 + 16 + 7 + 15	=	46
34 to 38	46 + 32	=	78

So both the 60th and the 61st pairs must be size 38 which is thus the median value.

Points to note about this measure:
- It will often (though not necessarily) be an actual data value.
- It is not distorted by extreme values.

Note that in this case the mean, mode and median values are all very close (if not equal) to each other. This is because the distribution of shoe size sales was fairly symmetrical, i.e. evenly spread around the median value. This will not always be the case for a more skewed distribution.

2 Diagrams

2.1 Introduction

Presenting information as a diagram has greater visual impact, but less detail, than tabulation. There are a variety of different types of diagrams that can be used to illustrate data and the choice of the most appropriate type will depend upon:
- the type of data
- the amount of data
- the factors that you wish to emphasise.

In this chapter we will assume the diagrams are to be drawn by hand; in Chapter 7 we shall see how they may be produced as part of a spreadsheet program.

2.2 Pictograms

A pictogram is a simple diagram which uses pictures to represent numbers.

EXAMPLE

The number of letters received by five mail order firms in a year are given below:

Firm	*Annual number of letters*
Great Galaxy	3,475,000
Commonwealth	8,022,000
Largeforests	5,308,000
Ells	4,427,000
Berties	6,381,000

We could use a picture of a letter to represent a number of actual letters. In this case if we use a picture of a letter to represent 1,000,000 letters received, we obtain the pictogram below.

Annual number of letters

Firm

Great Galaxy

Commonwealth

Largeforests

Ells

Berties

Key Represents 1,000,000 letters

Always remember to include the **key** on your diagram.

As can be seen fractions in the pictogram are difficult to show accurately, but that is not the purpose of these diagrams. They are to give us a **quick, rough idea of relative size** and as such are fairly successful.

An alternative approach sometimes adopted is to magnify the picture so that its size represents the figure being illustrated as shown below.

Great Galaxy

Commonwealth

Largeforests

Ells

Berties

Key Represents 1,000,000 letters

O EXAMPLE

Draw an appropriate pictogram for the following beer sales figures.

Brewery	*Quarterly sales figure* (£)
Soprano	542,000
Blackdough	397,000
Empties	56,000
Browns	315,000

Solution

(Probably the easiest picture to use is a glass of beer.)

Soprano

Blackdough

Empties

Browns

Key: 1 glass = £100,000

2.3 Pie charts

A pie chart consists of a circle split into segments. The circle represents a total and the segments represent the parts which go to make up the total. The 360° of the circle is divided in proportion to the figures making the total.

O EXAMPLE

Suppose a family's income in 20X5 is £1,000 per month, and their expenditure splits down as follows.

	Amount £	Proportion %	Angle (degrees)	
Mortgage and insurance	300	30	108	(30% x 360)
Electricity and gas	50	5	18	(5% x 360)
Food and drink	200	20	72	etc
Clothes	40	4	14	
Car and petrol	150	15	54	
Telephone	10	1	4	
Savings	70	7	25	
Fares	60	6	22	
Miscellaneous	120	12	43	
	1,000	100	360	

Solution

The resulting pie chart would look like this:

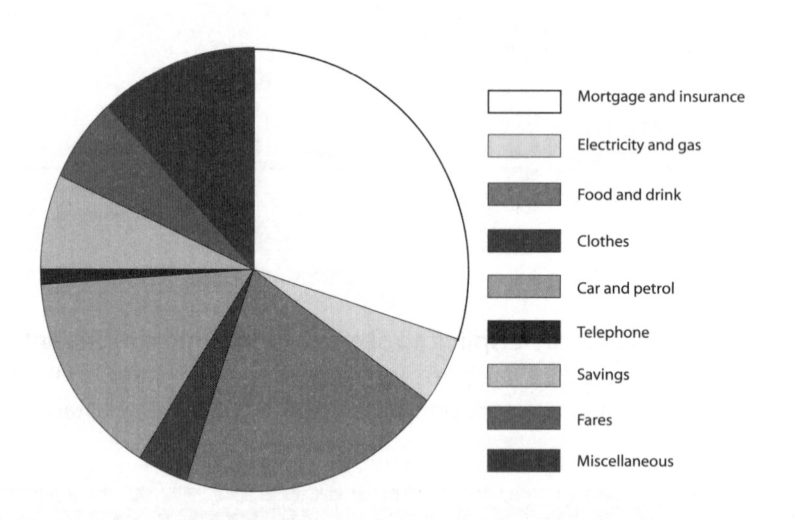

You can either use the names in the segments or represent each category by a different colour or shading, provided a key is given.
Again, we do not obtain a precise idea of expenditure on certain items or services, just an idea of their **relative proportions.**

EXAMPLE

Draw a pie chart for the following data.

Breakdown of grocery market share

Food Inc	29%
Grub plc	22%
Cookers	15%
Troughers	13%
Others	21%

Solution

Number of degrees:

	Percentage		*Angle*°
Food Inc	29%	360 x 0.29 =	104
Grub plc	22%	360 x 0.22 =	79
Cookers	15%	360 x 0.15 =	54
Troughers	13%	360 x 0.13 =	47
Others	21%	360 x 0.21 =	76
	100%		360

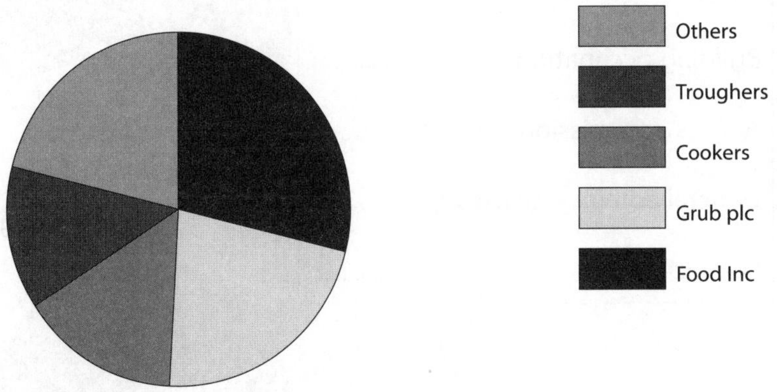

▷ ACTIVITY 3

WMSC (AAT CA D94 – amended)

The administration manager of WMSC, a charter shipping organisation, receives regular information on the analysis of the general expenses in the form of pie charts. He is having some difficulty in understanding the charts and, to make matters worse, when last month's charts were sent out, the 'key' was not completed.

Required

(a) Use the figures provided to complete the key to the pie charts by identifying which segment (labelled A to E) represents which expense. If you think A = Depreciation then write A opposite Depreciation in the letter column.

	November 20X6	*November 20X5*
	£000	£000
Wages and salaries	69	53
Building occupation costs	46	52
Agents' commission	58	42
General administration expenses	23	31
Depreciaiton	34	32
	230	210

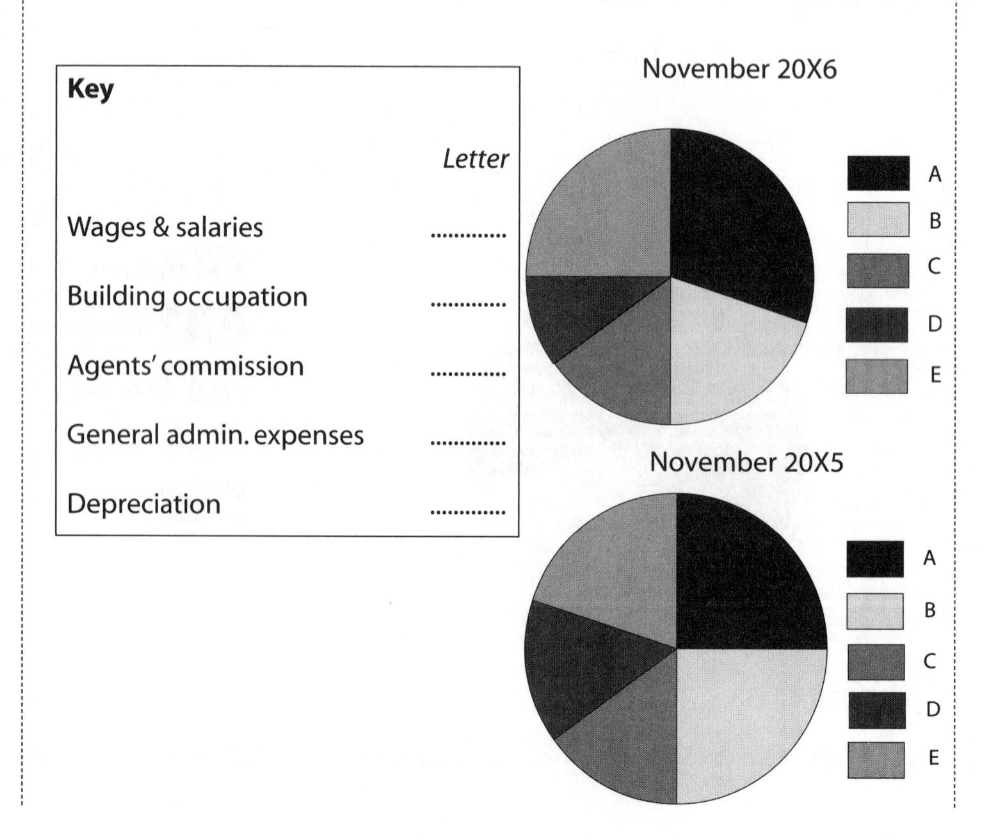

(b) Write a short report to the administration manager:
   (i) explaining the main points that are revealed by a comparison of the pie charts
   (ii) suggesting an explanation for the changes in the agents' commission and the general administration expenses.

[Answer on p. 71]

3 Bar charts

3.1 Introduction

One popular method of illustrating data in order to compare it or show its changes over time is to show it in the form of a bar chart. There are a number of different types of bar chart to consider:

- a simple bar chart
- a component bar chart
- a percentage component bar chart
- a compound bar chart.

We shall look at each type in turn.

3.2 Simple bar charts

In a simple bar chart the figures we wish to compare are represented by bars. These can either be drawn vertically or horizontally. The height or length of a bar is proportional to the size of the figure being illustrated.

EXAMPLE

The production figures of different car companies are given:

Firm	*Number of cars produced*
Ausota	180,000
Vauxsun	145,000
Moruar	165,000
Trihall	160,000
Fortin	170,000

Solution

A vertical bar chart can be prepared as follows:

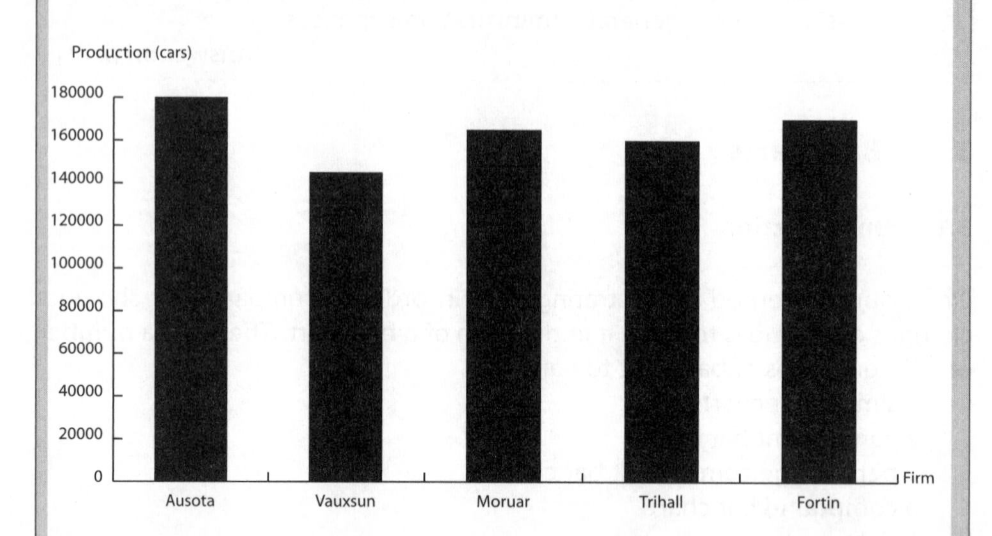

Alternatively the data could be shown in a horizontal bar chart.

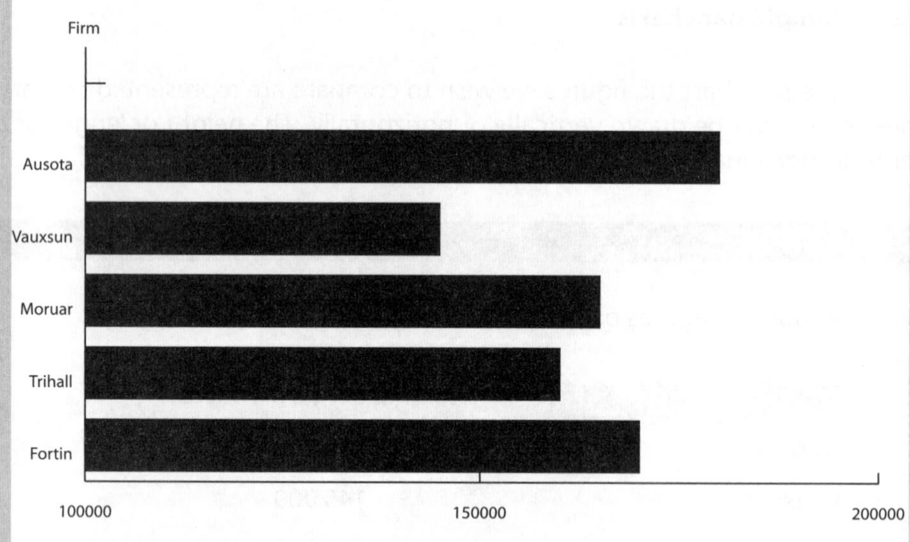

Vertical bar charts are much more commonly used than horizontal ones, therefore in an assessment produce the vertical version unless specifically asked for a horizontal one.

We can put the **appropriate identification** either in the bar itself, immediately adjacent to the bar, or use a key for shadings or colours. When drawing these charts it is very important to start the scale from zero. A misleading picture may be shown otherwise.

EXAMPLE

Draw a simple bar chart of the following figures for the number of branches of certain chain stores:

Chain store	*Branches*
AZX	360
Blazes	245
D & L	185
Cotton value	290
Allsorts	410

Solution

Bar chart showing the number of branches

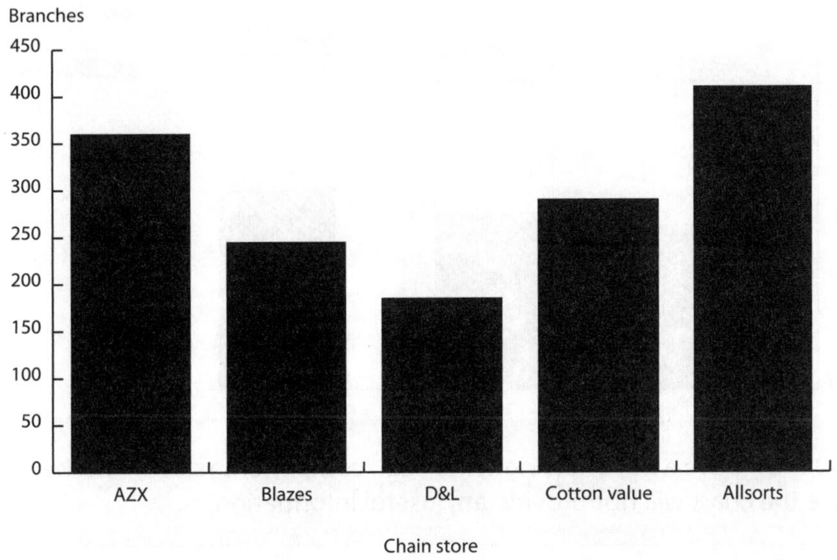

Branches
450
400
350
300
250
200
150
100
50
0
AZX Blazes D&L Cotton value Allsorts
Chain store

Always ensure that the bar chart has a title and that both axes are labelled to make it clear what the bar chart is illustrating.

3.3 Component bar charts

When we draw bar charts the totals we wish to illustrate can often be broken down into **sub-divisions or components.** These sub-divisions can be clearly illustrated using a component bar chart.

EXAMPLE

Wine consumption by type for a year is shown below.

Consumption figures (10,000 litres)				
	Red	White	Rose	Total
20X2	59.3	46.5	14.2	120.0
20X3	63.6	47.0	14.4	125.0
20X4	72.3	48.2	14.5	135.0

Solution

We start by drawing a **simple bar chart** of the total figures. The columns or bars are then **split up into the component parts.**

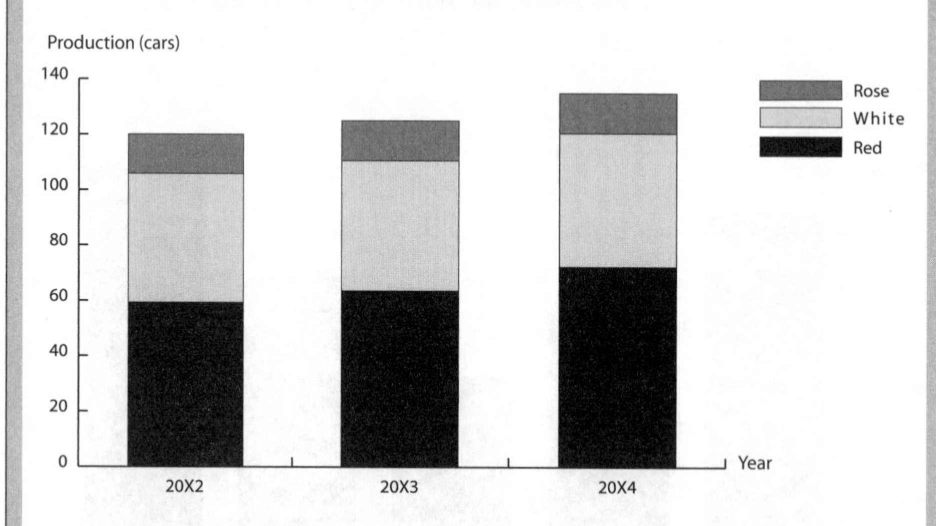

You must have a key showing what each component relates to otherwise the chart will not provide any useful information.

EXAMPLE

A shoe firm has three factories. The output of pairs of shoes by factory is:

	20X1	20X2	20X3	20X4
Leicester	350,000	300,000	550,000	400,000
Northampton	200,000	300,000	400,000	500,000
Nottingham	200,000	300,000	300,000	400,000

Draw a suitable diagram to illustrate this information.

Solution

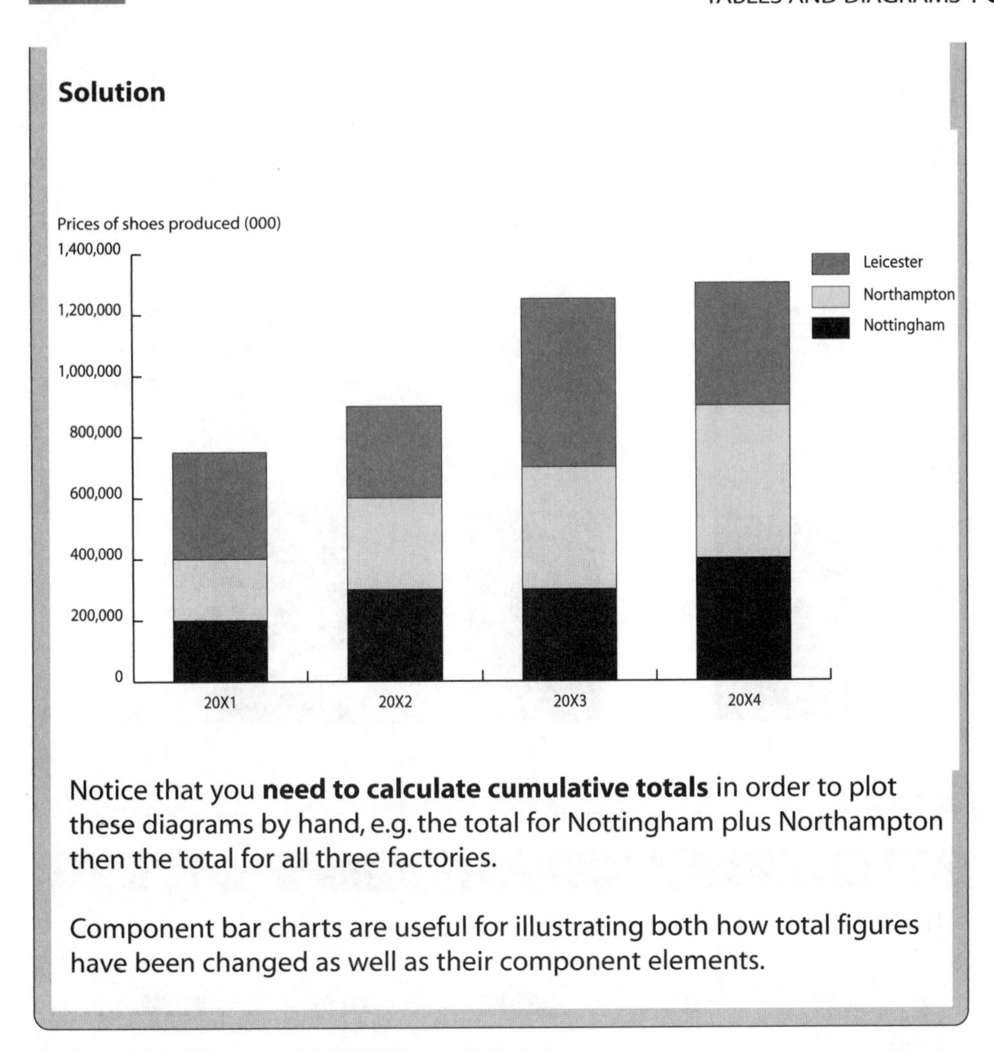

Notice that you **need to calculate cumulative totals** in order to plot these diagrams by hand, e.g. the total for Nottingham plus Northampton then the total for all three factories.

Component bar charts are useful for illustrating both how total figures have been changed as well as their component elements.

3.4 Percentage component bar chart

If we wish to know what proportion of a total each component represents, we can use a percentage component bar chart in place of a pie chart. All the columns of the bar chart are the same height or length representing 100%. These are then divided in the appropriate proportions.

EXAMPLE

Using the wine consumption figures again, the proportions for each type of wine consumption are calculated as:

	Red	White	Rose
20X2	$\frac{59.3}{120.0} \times 100 = 49.4\%$	$\frac{46.5}{120.0} \times 100 = 38.8\%$	$\frac{14.2}{120.0} \times 100 = 11.8\%$
20X3	$\frac{63.6}{125.0} \times 100 = 50.9\%$	$\frac{47.0}{125.0} \times 100 = 37.6\%$	$\frac{14.4}{125.0} \times 100 = 11.5\%$
20X4	$\frac{72.3}{135.5} \times 100 = 53.6\%$	$\frac{48.2}{135.0} \times 100 = 35.7\%$	$\frac{14.5}{135.0} \times 100 = 10.7\%$

Draw a percentage component bar chart.

Solution

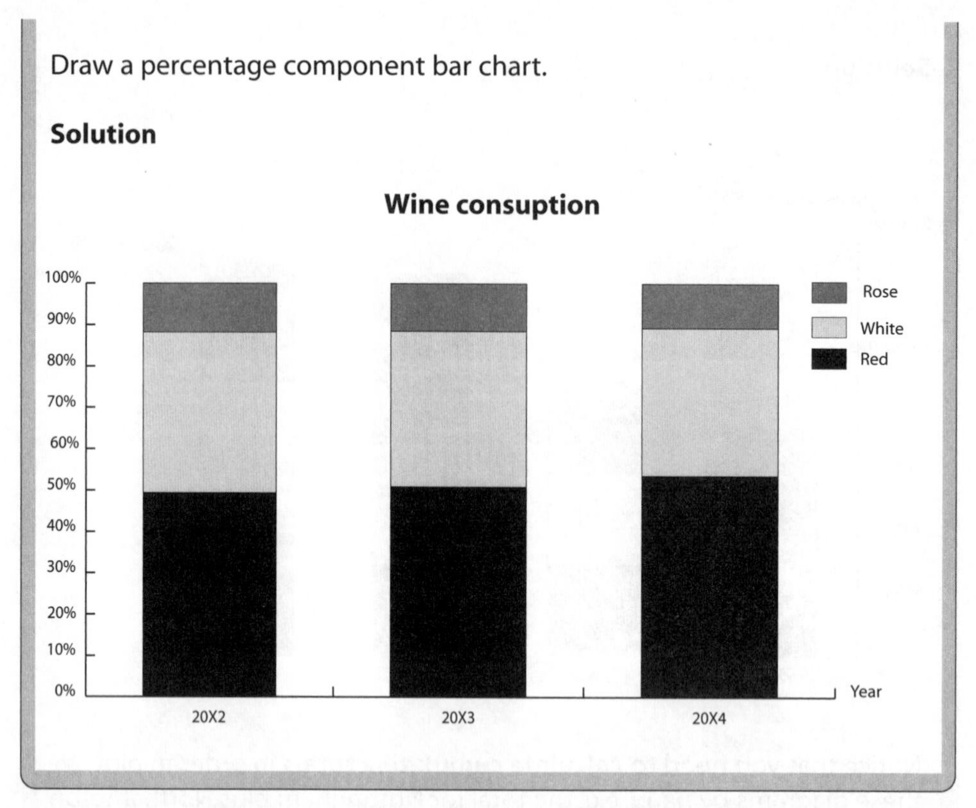

EXAMPLE

The shoe production figures are given again below.

	20X1	20X2	20X3	20X4
Leicester	350,000	300,000	550,000	400,000
Northampton	200,000	300,000	400,000	500,000
Nottingham	200,000	300,000	300,000	400,000

Draw a percentage component bar chart for the shoe production data.

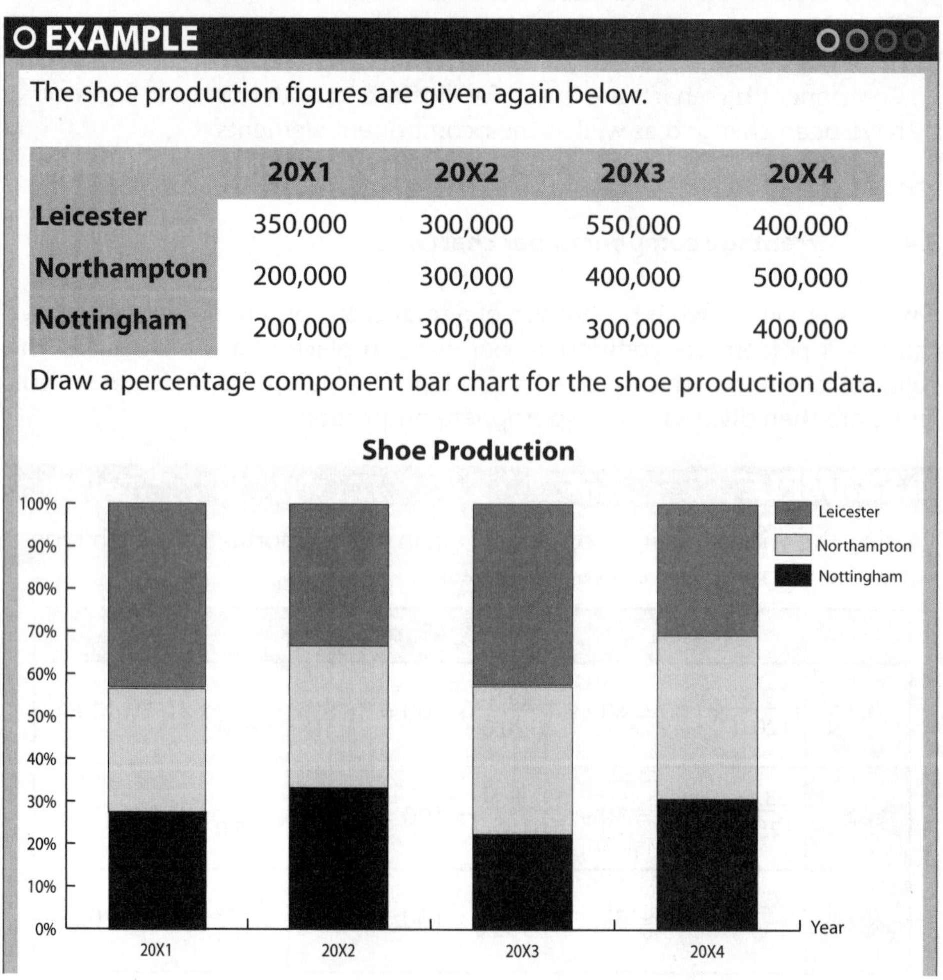

The proportions are worked out using the totals for each year, giving:

	Leicester	Northampton	Nottingham
20X1	$\frac{350,000}{750,000} \times 100 = 46.6\%$	$\frac{200,000}{750,000} \times 100 = 26.7\%$	$\frac{200,000}{750,000} \times 100 = 26.7\%$
20X2	$\frac{300,000}{900,000} \times 100 = 33.3\%$	$\frac{300,000}{900,000} \times 100 = 33.3\%$	$\frac{300,000}{900,000} \times 100 = 33.3\%$
20X3	$\frac{550,000}{1,250,000} \times 100 = 44.0\%$	$\frac{400,000}{1,250,000} \times 100 = 32.0\%$	$\frac{300,000}{1,250,000} \times 100 = 24.0\%$
20X4	$\frac{400,000}{1,300,000} \times 100 = 30.8\%$	$\frac{500,000}{1,300,000} \times 100 = 38.4\%$	$\frac{400,000}{1,300,000} \times 100 = 30.8\%$

Again the cumulative percentages must be calculated e.g. Nottingham plus Northampton then all three factories.

Percentage component bar charts do not illustrate how total figures have changed but they do clearly show how the elements of the total have changed.

▷ ACTIVITY 4 

Engineering assets

The accounts of an engineering company contain data on the value of its assets over the last five years as follows:

Asset	20X1	20X2	20X3	20X4	20X5
	£000	£000	£000	£000	£000
Property	59	59	65	70	74
Plant and machinery	176	179	195	210	200
Stock and work in progress	409	409	448	516	479
Debtors	330	313	384	374	479
Cash	7	60	29	74	74

Required

(a) Compare the values of the assets by constructing a component bar chart and a percentage component bar chart.

(b) Calculate the percentage increase in total value of assets over the five-year period.

(c) Comment on the movements in the assets over the five-year period in a short memorandum report to the manager, Mr Joseph.

[Answer on p. 72]

3.5 Compound bar charts

Our concern may not be with proportional comparisons but rather with **comparisons of the component figures themselves.** If this is the case we can use a **compound bar chart** where there is a bar for each component.

EXAMPLE

The wine data is given again below.

Consumption figures (10,000 litres)				
	Red	White	Rose	Total
20X2	59.3	46.5	14.2	120.0
20X3	63.6	47.0	14.4	125.0
20X4	72.3	48.2	14.5	135.0

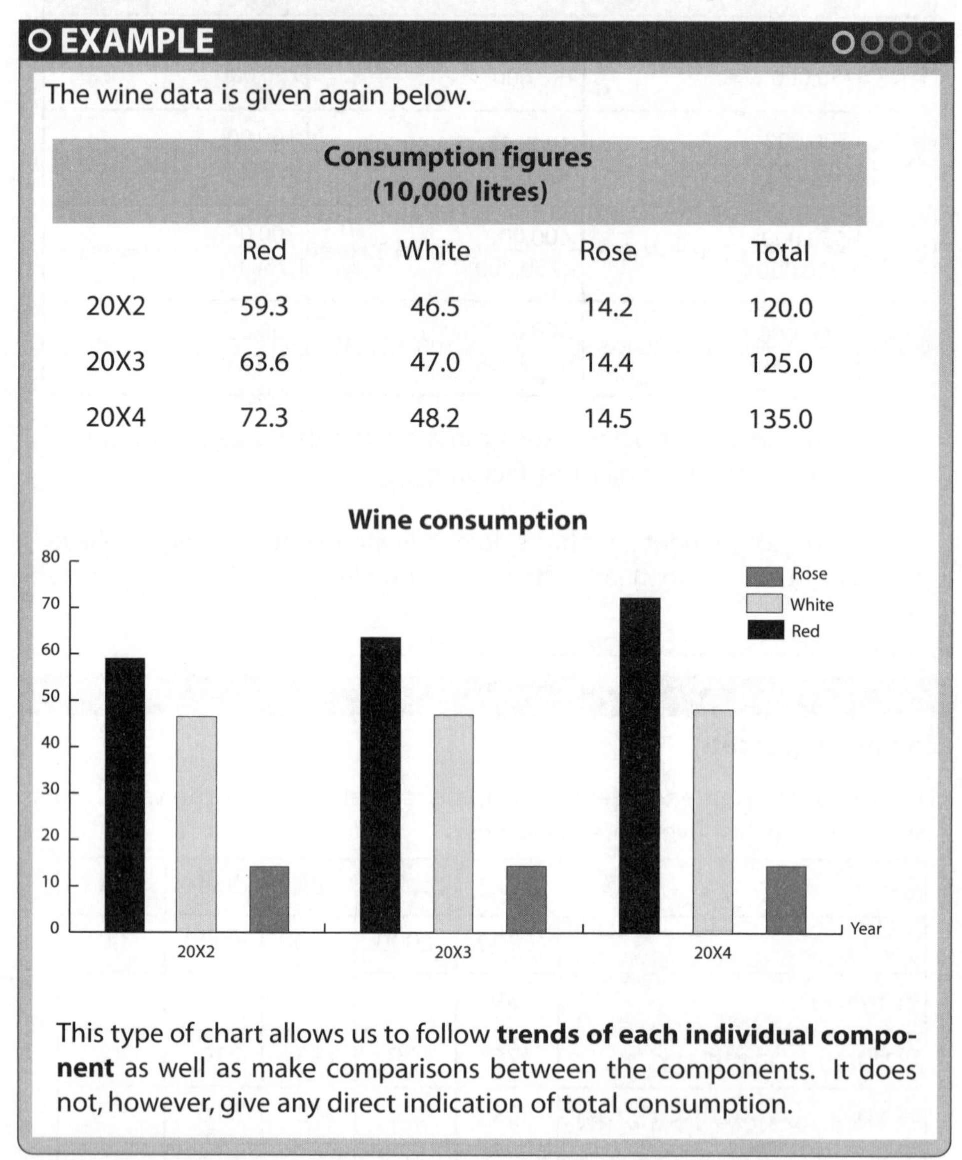

This type of chart allows us to follow **trends of each individual component** as well as make comparisons between the components. It does not, however, give any direct indication of total consumption.

EXAMPLE

The shoe production data is given again.

	20X1	20X2	20X3	20X4
Leicester	350,000	300,000	550,000	400,000
Northampton	200,000	300,000	400,000	500,000
Nottingham	200,000	300,000	300,000	400,000

Draw a compound bar chart for the shoe production data.

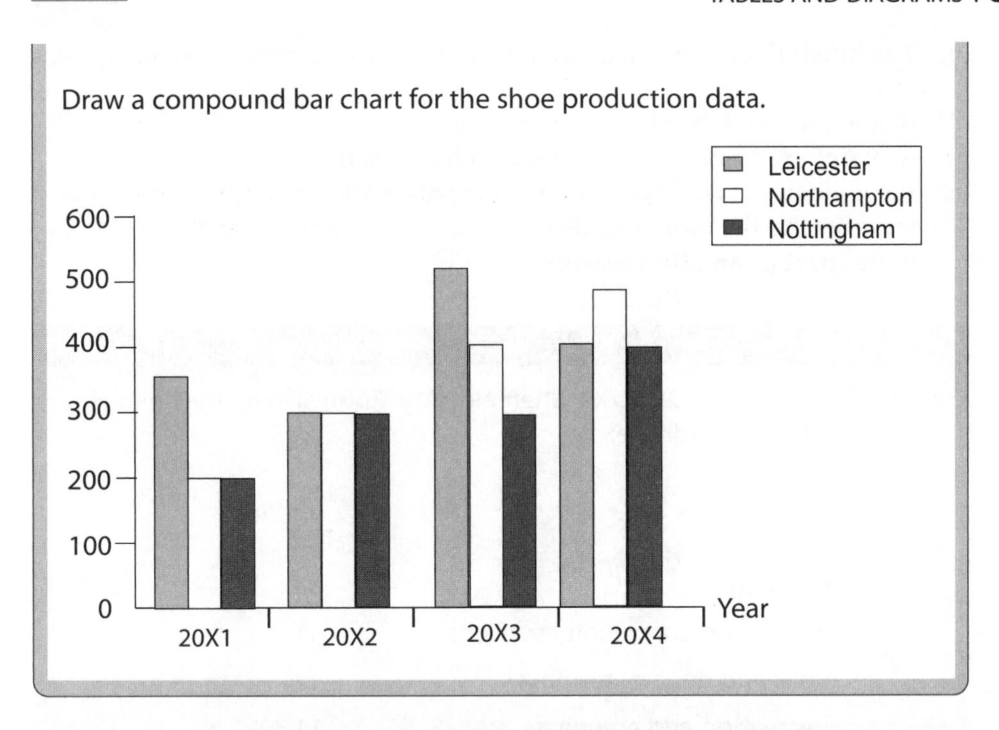

▷ ACTIVITY 5

Energy consumption

The table below shows the total UK inland energy consumption, measured in millions of tonnes of coal equivalent, for coal, petroleum and natural gas in the years 20X1 and 20X9.

Energy type	20X1	20X9
Coal	139.3	129.6
Petroleum	151.2	139.0
Natural gas	28.8	71.3

Illustrate this data pictorially using (a) a component bar chart and (b) a compound bar chart. Discuss the benefits in using each method.

[Answer on p. 74]

4 Rules for drawing charts and diagrams

4.1 Rules to follow

When drawing diagrams there are several points to consider:

(a) Try to make the diagrams **neat** and **uncluttered.** Use a **ruler.**

(b) If **graph paper** is available, use it.

(c) The diagram should have a **title.**

(d) The **variables and scales** should be shown on each axis.

(e) Set the scale so that you use **as much of the paper as you can** for the diagram; this will keep the diagram neater and assist accuracy.

(f) Units must be indicated on **both axes.**

(g) Where diagrams are combined or superimposed ensure that each is **recognisable separately** and suitably labelled.

(h) **Too much detail** on a diagram makes it confusing rather than enlightening.
(i) Remember the **key** where appropriate.
(j) Remember to **start scales at zero on bar charts.**
(k) Remember that **component and compound bar charts** become less and less effective the more sub-divisions you use. It is often worth considering **a pie chart as an alternative.**

EXAMPLE

In the financial year 20X3/X4 Sheffield City Council had the following major items of expenditure:

	£m
Education	175
Housing	84
Family and community services	41
Polic and general purposes	17
Recreation and amenities	11
Environmental health and clensing	11
Corporate estate	8

Illustrate this information.

Solution

Adding the figures up, the total expenditure was £347m. Given the number of categories, the clearest form for our illustration will be a pie chart. We must now work out the proportions of each category of expenditure and its angle.

	%	Angle
Education	$\frac{175}{347}$ x 100% = 51	$\frac{51}{100}$ x 360 = 184
Housing	$\frac{84}{347}$ x 100% = 24	$\frac{24}{100}$ x 360 = 86
Family & community services	$\frac{41}{347}$ x 100% = 12	$\frac{12}{100}$ x 360 = 43
Policy & general purposes	$\frac{17}{347}$ x 100% = 5	$\frac{5}{100}$ x 360 = 18
Recreation & amenities	$\frac{11}{347}$ x 100% = 3	$\frac{3}{100}$ x 360 = 11
Env. health & cleansing	$\frac{11}{347}$ x 100% = 3	$\frac{3}{100}$ x 360 = 11
Corporate estate	$\frac{8}{347}$ x 100% = 2	$\frac{2}{100}$ x 360 = 7
	100	360

The pie chart for the Sheffield City Council items of major expenditure is as follows.

Major expenditure of Sheffield City Council 20X3/X4

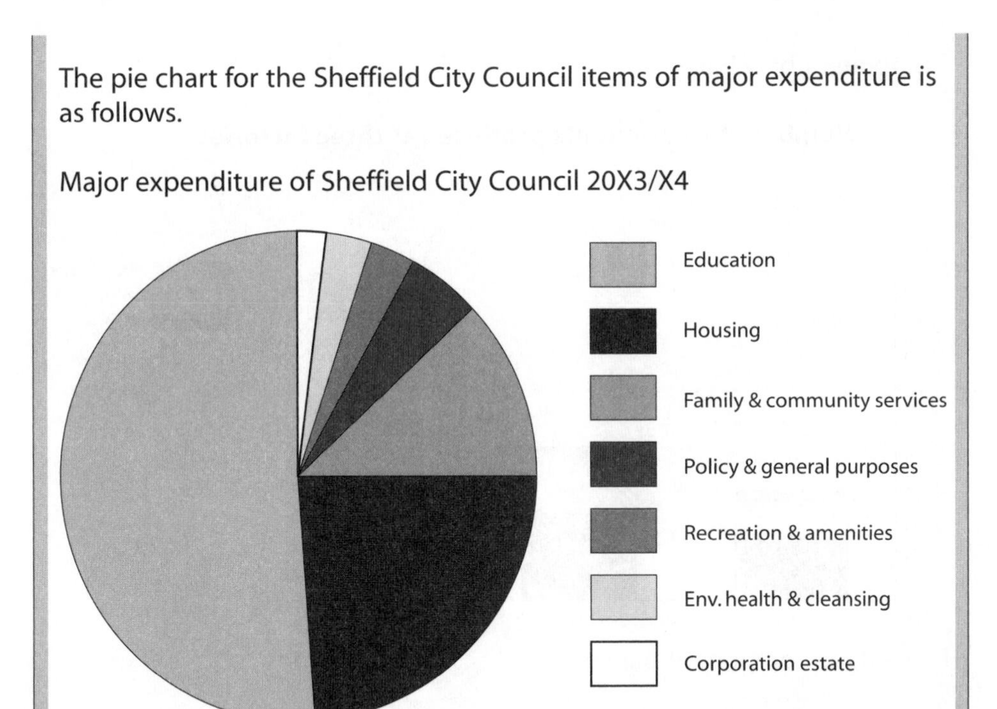

Note: This example is a good illustration of the problem of rounding errors. The % column originally added up to 99% (not 100%) and the angle column to 356° (not 360°), making the illustration only approximate. Education's percentage (50.43%) was rounded up to 51%. The angles were recalculated with these percentages and the problem disappeared.

4.2 Comment on diagrams

In some instances you may be required to comment upon or analyse the data shown in a diagram.

EXAMPLE

A computer company has three factories, located in Manchester, Bristol and Derby. The production records of each factory are as follows.

	Number of computers produced (hundreds)		
Factory	20X2	20X3	20X4
Manchester	3	5	14
Bristol	11	14	27
Derby	18	26	55
Total	32	45	96

Compare and contrast the production at the three factories using the component and percentage component bar charts given below (You do not need to calculate the percentages.)

Component bar chart

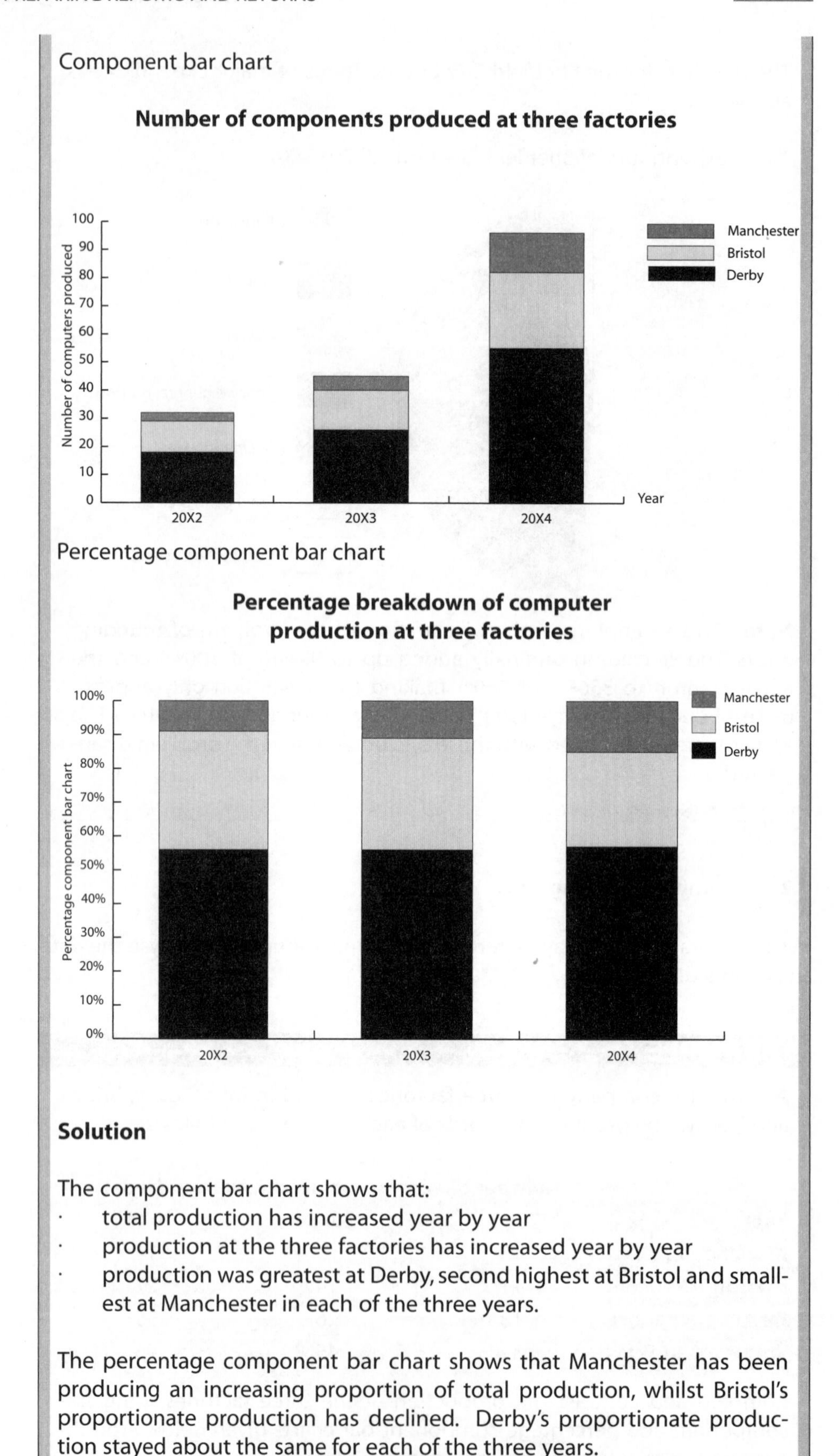

Percentage component bar chart

Solution

The component bar chart shows that:

- total production has increased year by year
- production at the three factories has increased year by year
- production was greatest at Derby, second highest at Bristol and smallest at Manchester in each of the three years.

The percentage component bar chart shows that Manchester has been producing an increasing proportion of total production, whilst Bristol's proportionate production has declined. Derby's proportionate production stayed about the same for each of the three years.

EXAMPLE

The following chart shows the average annual salaries of employees of BS Ltd for 20X2 to 20X4. List the major points of information shown by this diagram, and comment on its preparation.

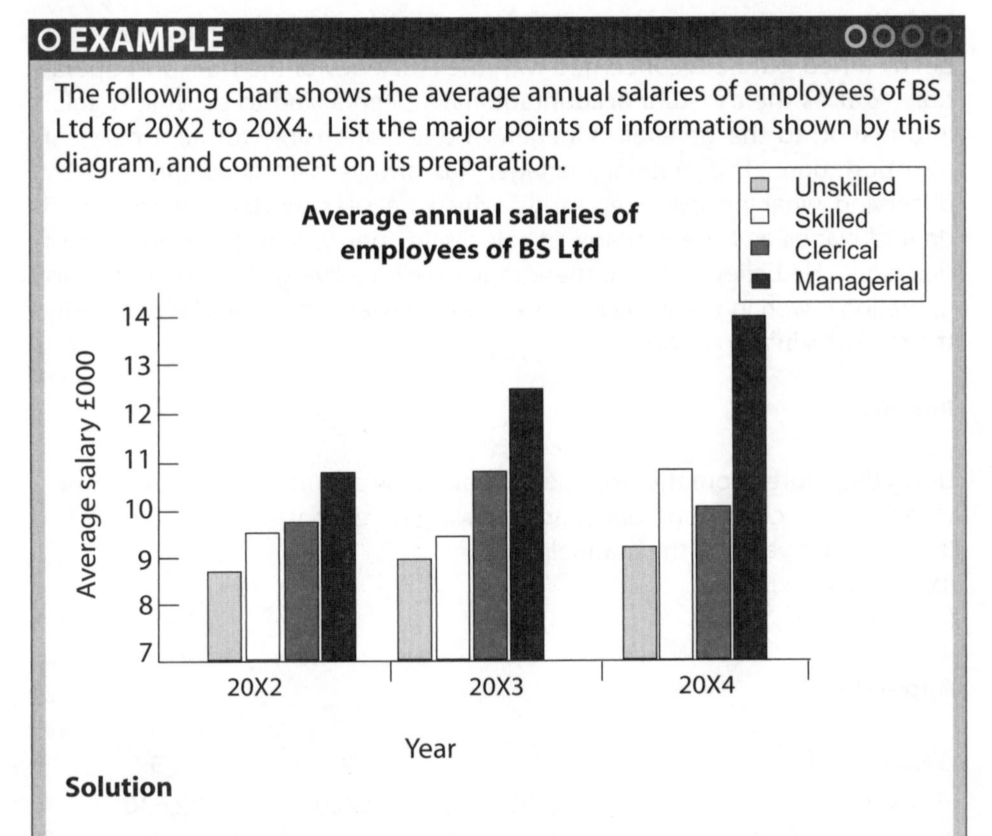

Solution

- The compound bar chart is misleading because the vertical scale does not start from zero (starts presumably from £7,000).
- BS Ltd employees are assumed to fall into four categories: unskilled, skilled, clerical and managerial.
- All categories of employees had a salary increase each year, except clerical staff in 20X3 when their salaries fell from the previous year. No account was taken of inflation.
- The chart is limited in the amount of information it gives since no percentage figures are given. Year to year percentage increases could be calculated for each category by reading figures from the diagram. However, it appears that unskilled and skilled employees have seen about the same percentage increases whilst managerial staff have had much larger percentage increases in salaries.

ACTIVITY 6

BTC (AAT CA J94)

Until three years ago, BTC, an accountancy training organisation, ran its own fleet of vans and delivered manuals to retailers and colleges. The decision was taken to concentrate on core activities and so several organisations were carefully considered before RD plc was selected to take on the responsibility for storing and delivering the manuals. It was agreed that RD would purchase the manuals from BTC at the recommended selling price, less an agreed discount. This ensured that RD would automatically benefit from future increases in the selling price of the manuals. The arrangement has worked well for both organisations and a good relationship has been established.

The managing director of RD has been satisfied with the profits that have been earned, but he is concerned with the efficiency of the transport operation. You, as the assistant accountant, have been asked to provide regular information to the general manager, who is responsible for all aspects of transportation. The general manager has always controlled this area by observing what he calls 'key ratios' which he sees as delivery costs and drivers' wages as a percentage of sales, sales per van and the number of deliveries. He believes that, if these ratios are improving, then the transport operation is working well. He is also a great believer that graphs help to clarify the statistics in any report.

Required

Using the figures from the Appendix below, draw a multiple bar chart (sometimes called a compound bar chart) showing for each year:

(a) the sales value of the manuals sold

(b) the van expenses

(c) the drivers' wages.

Appendix

Years	**1**	**2**	**3**
Sales (£)	200,000	222,200	272,630
Van expenses (£)	14,000	15,000	18,000
As percentage of sales	7	6.7	6.6
Drivers' wages (£)	52,000	56,600	68,150
As percentage of sales	26	25.5	25
Number of vans	3	3	4
Sales per van (£)	66,667	74.067	68,158
Number of deliveries	1,000	1,100	1,400

[Answer on p. 76]

5 Test your knowledge

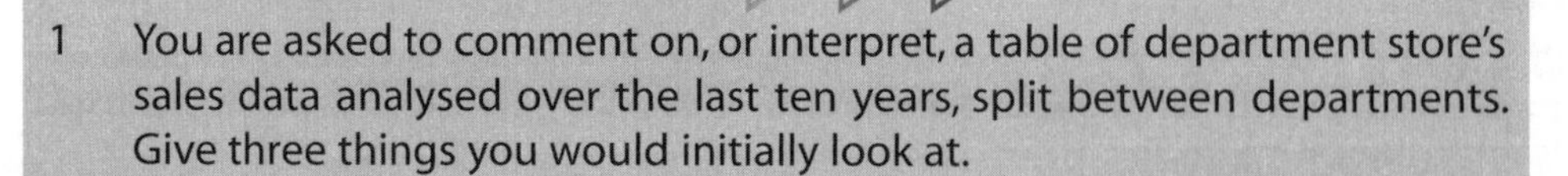

1 You are asked to comment on, or interpret, a table of department store's sales data analysed over the last ten years, split between departments. Give three things you would initially look at.

For the following presentation methods, give one relative advantage and one relative disadvantage of the first over the second:

2 Table, pictogram.

3 Simple bar chart, pie chart.

4 Component bar chart, compound bar chart.

[Answers on p. 76]

6 Summary

When data is given in narrative form it is often difficult to analyse and understand. However if the narrative data can be shown in tabular form it is often much clearer and easier to understand. Spreadsheets may be used in the tabulation process – see Chapter 7.

When presenting data in a report it is often appropriate to show the data in the form of a diagram in order that trends or comparisons of component elements can be seen more clearly. Diagrams do not provide precise details of figures but they are useful in providing useful visual information for comparing relative size.

There are a variety of different types of diagram that can be used and the one chosen will depend upon the type of data, the size of the figures and the information that you wish to convey. If the total figures are important a pie chart or percentage component bar chart would not be appropriate but if only the make up of the totals is important then these would be suitable. Therefore care should be taken when choosing which form of diagram to use to illustrate data.

Answers to chapter activities & 'test your knowledge' questions

△ ACTIVITY 1

Bunny and Hutch

Employees and wages of Bunny and Hutch Ltd 20X4

	Number of employees		*Average weekly wage*	*Total annual wage*
	1 Jan	31 Dec	£	£
Men	2,088	2,124	121.32	12,774,996
Women	1,871	1,860	87.93	8,201,671
Total	3,959	3,984	105.64	20,976,667

Number of women employed at 31 December	=	3,984 - 2,124 = 1,860
Number of men employed at 1 January	=	2,124 - 221 + 185 = 2,088
Number of women employed at 1 January	=	1,860 - 97 + 108 = 1,871
Total number employed at 1 January	=	2,088 + 1,871 = 3,959
Average number of men in year	=	(2,088 + 2,124) ÷ 2 = 2,106
Average number of women in year	=	(1,871 + 1,860) ÷ 2 = 1,865.5
Total annual wage bill for men	=	2,106 x 121.32 x 50 = £12,774,996
Total annual wage bill for women	=	1,865.5 x 87.93 x 50 = £8,201,671
Total annual wage bill	=	12,774,996 + 8,201,671 = £20,976,667

These estimates of the annual wage bill can be obtained in other ways. We could alternatively have used the 1 January figures of number employed or 31 December figures.

To calculate the total average weekly wage we could simply add £121.32 to £87.93 and divide by two. However, this assumes an equal number of men and women employees. Alternatively, since we now have an estimate of the total wage bill, the average weekly wage can be calculated as:

$$\frac{£20,976,667}{3,971.5 \times 50} = £105.64$$

△ ACTIVITY 2

Motor policies

The region with the highest number of policies held was London and this region also had the largest number of claims made in 20X3. The region with the smallest number of policies held was Northern Ireland, although this region had the fifth highest number of claims of the eight regions. The smallest number of claims made was in Scotland which had the second smallest number of policy-holders.

Since the number of policies held in the different regions varies, more information can be gained by calculating the percentage number of claims per policies held for the eight regions.

Region	Claims per policies held
	(%)
North	8.2
Midlands	7.6
South	6.1
East Anglia	2.5
London	4.3
Wales	1.8
Scotland	1.6
Northern Ireland	10.5

From this table we can see that, although London had the highest actual number of claims, it is only the fourth highest in terms of claims as a proportion of policies held. In fact, Northern Ireland has the highest number of claims per policies held, whereas Scotland has the lowest number of claims per policies held.

△ ACTIVITY 3

WMSC

Part (a)

		November			
Key	Letter	20X6		20X5	
		%	angle°	%	angle°
Wages and salaries	A	30	108	25	90
Building occupation costs	B	20	72	25	90
Depreciation	C	15	54	15	54
General admin expenses	D	10	36	15	54
Agents' commission	E	25	90	20	72
		100	360	100	360

Part (b)

To: Admin Manager

From: Assistant accountant

Subject: November pie charts Date: 6 December 20X6

(1) It is important to stress that in this comparison it is the relative size of the expenses that we are comparing.
(2) Wages and salaries with building occupation costs amount to 50% of the total expenditure for each year but the proportion has changed by wages increasing and building costs reducing.
(3) The proportion of agents commission has increased in November 20X6 and general admin expenses has reduced.
(4) Depreciation is the same proportion in both years.
(5) The agents' commission may have increased because the volume of sales increased (a variable expense). The general administration expenses may have reduced due to more work being tackled in-house rather than by a bureau, e.g. computing. (This is backed-up by an increase in wages and salaries in 20X6.)

(Other reasons could be stated in answer to 5 above.)

△ ACTIVITY 4

Engineering assets

Part (a)

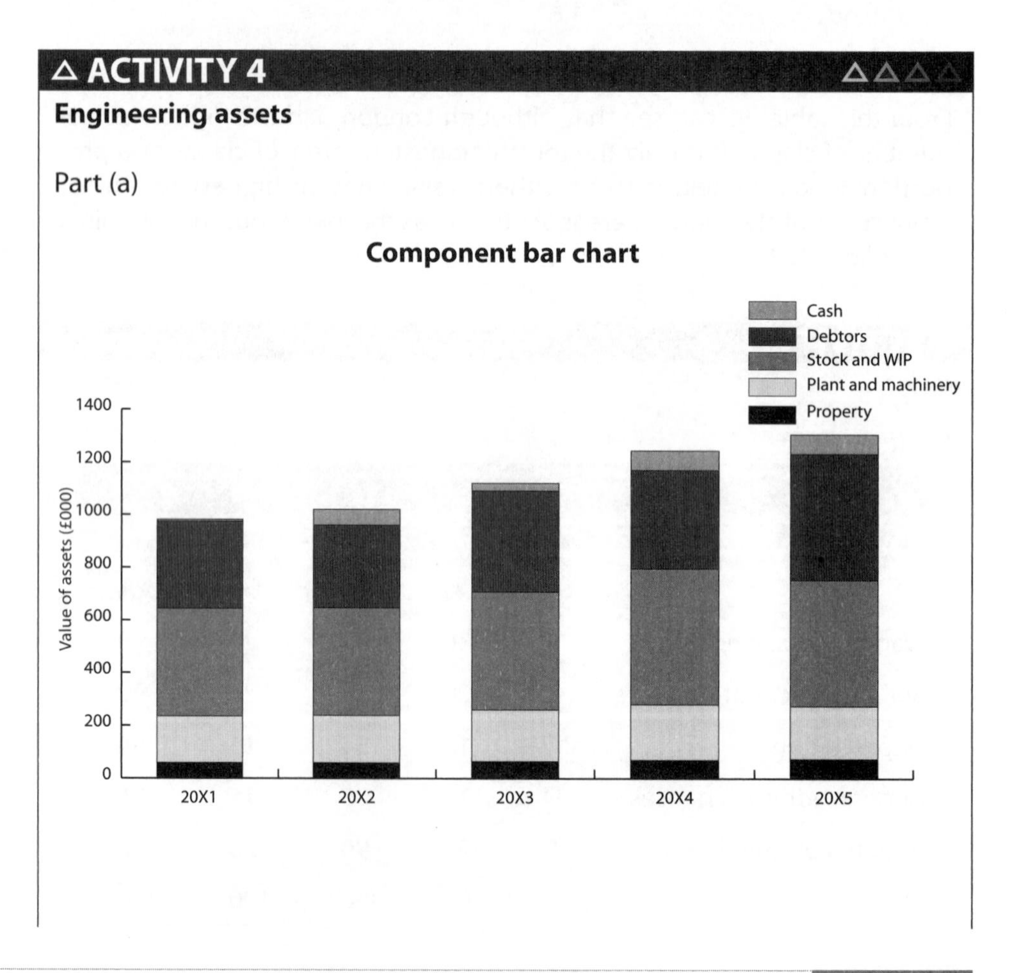

To construct a percentage component bar chart, we need to calculate the value of each of the assets as a percentage of the total, as follows.

Asset	20X1		20X2		20X3		20X4		20X5	
	£000	%	£000	%	£000	%	£000	%	£000	%
Property	59	6.0	59	5.8	65	5.8	70	5.6	74	5.7
Plant and machinery	176	17.9	179	17.5	195	17.4	210	16.9	200	15.3
Stock and WIP	409	41.7	409	40.1	448	40.0	516	41.5	479	36.7
Debtors	330	33.6	313	30.7	384	34.2	374	30.1	479	36.6
Cash	7	0.8	60	5.9	29	2.6	74	5.9	74	5.7
	981		1,020		1,121		1,244		1,306	

Percentage component bar chart

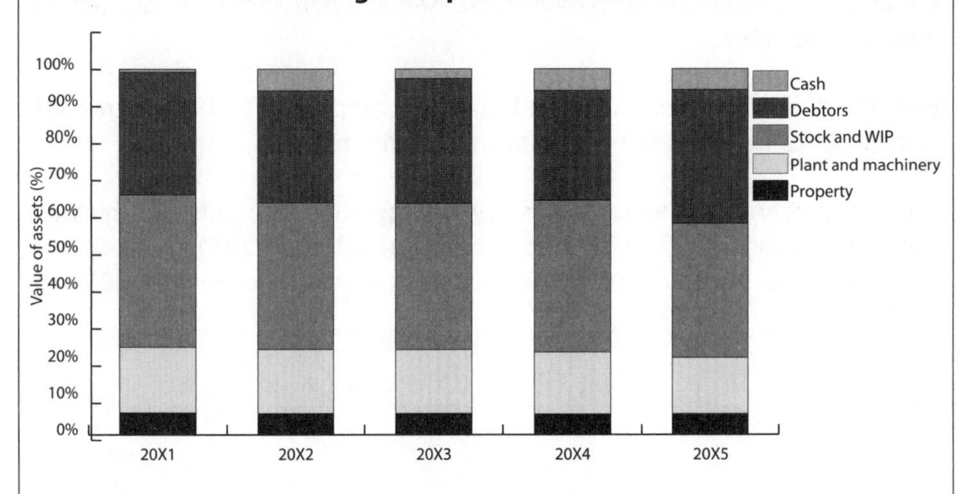

Part (b)

The total value of assets in 20X1 is £981,000

The total value of assets in 20X5 is £1,306,000.

This represents an increase in the five-year period of £325,000. The percentage increase in the total value of assets

$$= \frac{325,000}{981,000} \times 100 = 33.1\%$$

Part (c)

Memorandum

To: Mr Joseph

From: A Clerk Date:

Subject: Movements in the assets over the five-year period

From the bar chart it is evident that there has been a yearly increase in total assets over the five-year period.

There have been some very small increases in the property component (1) and this component has remained a similar percentage of the total assets throughout the period.

The plant and machinery component (2) shows an increase over the first four years and a decrease in the fifth year. The stock and work in progress component (3) is larger than the plant and machinery component, but behaves in a similar way. Both have decreased as a percentage of total assets over the five years.

Both the debtor component (4) and the cash component (5) have increased since 20X1 but there is some variation in the figures.

Both debtors and cash increased as a percentage of total assets, but this was not a steady increase. The debtors percentage fell from 20X1 to 20X2 and then again from 20X3 to 20X4 whilst the cash percentage fell from 20X2 to 20X3.

△ ACTIVITY 5

Energy consumption

We first need to calculate the total energy consumption for each year (in millions of tonnes of coal equivalent).

20X1 Total consumption = 139.3 + 151.2 + 28.8 = 319.3
20X9 Total consumption = 129.6 + 139.0 + 71.3 = 339.9

Part (a)

Component bar chart

UK Inland energy consumption 20X1 and 20X9

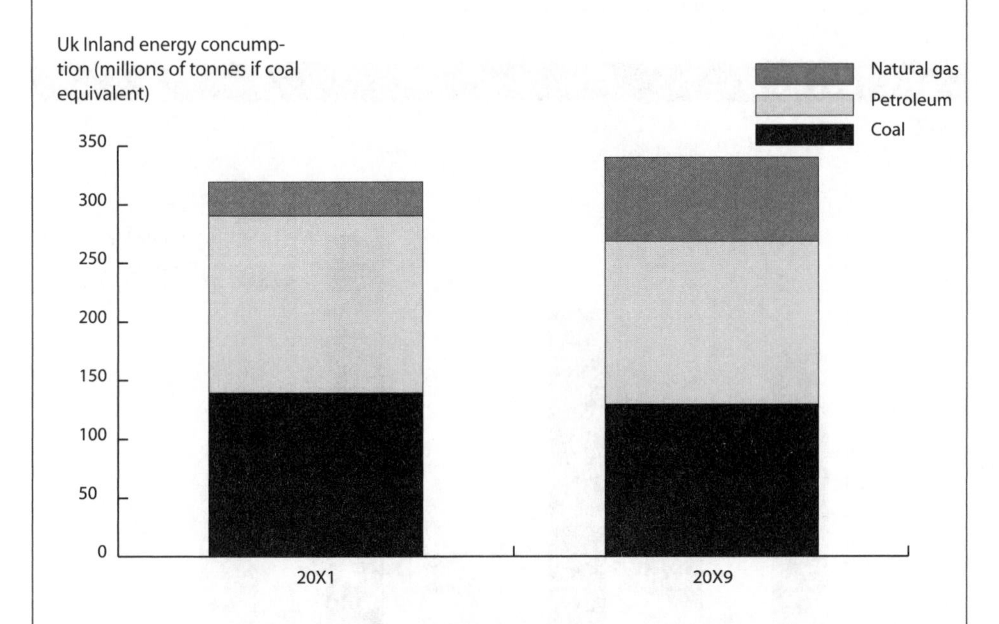

Part (b)

Compound bar chart

UK Inland energy consumption 20X1 and 20X9

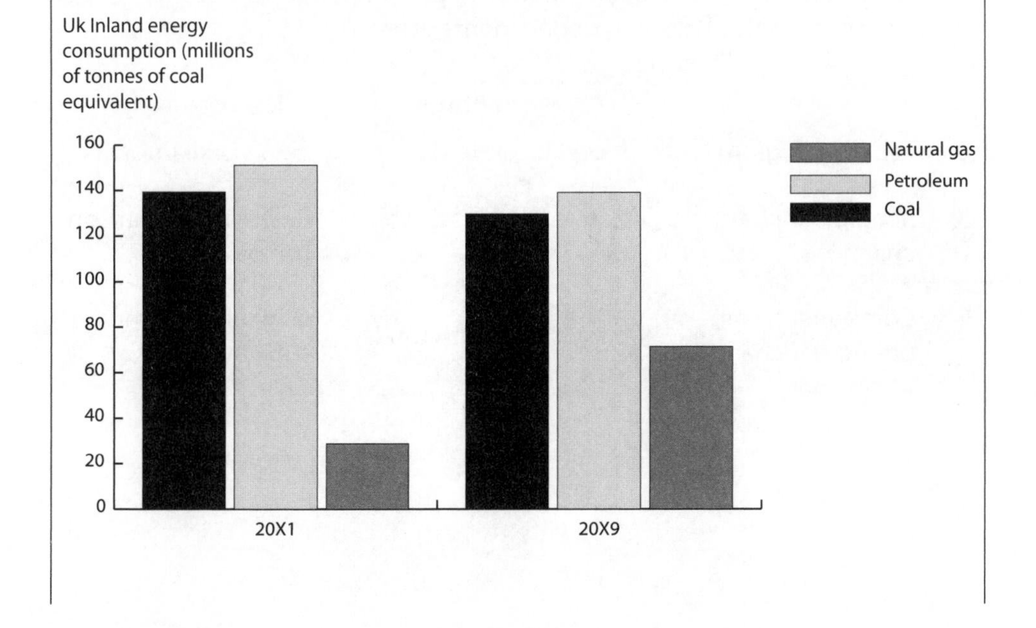

The benefits of the diagrams are:

(1) (a) shows total energy consumption for each year but (b) does not.
(2) (b) allows us to use a larger vertical scale than (a), giving increased accuracy.
(3) (b) shows the trend or change between the years for each energy product. [(a) also shows this trend but not as clearly.]

△ ACTIVITY 6

BTC

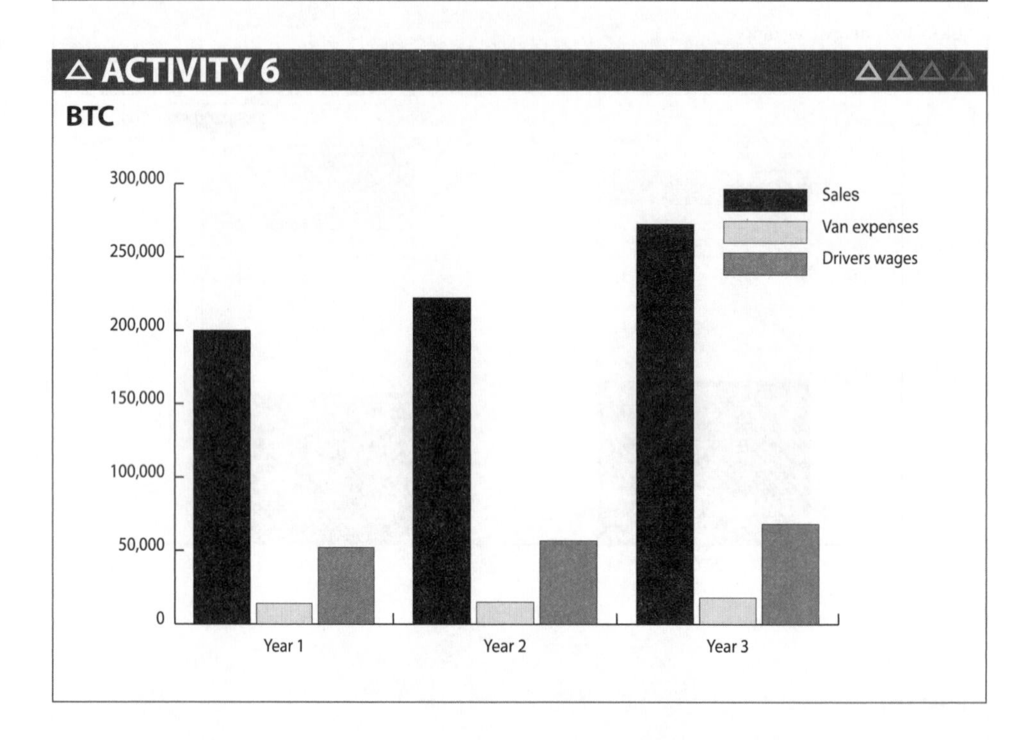

Test your knowledge

1 Total store sales – trend over period. Departmental sales – trend over period. Split of sales between departments year-by-year.

		Advantage	Disadvantage
2	Table, pictogram	More accurate data.	Less visual impact
3	Simple bar chart, pie chart	Can read off total values	Relative comparison not so clear
4	Component, compound bar chart	Shows category totals	Difficult to compare sub categories

GRAPHS, TIME SERIES AND INDEX NUMBERS

INTRODUCTION

In the previous chapter we looked at the ways in which data can be presented in the form of tables and diagrams. In this chapter, we are going to start by looking at the use of graphs as a means of presenting data and how to go about drawing them in an assessment. We are then going to turn our attention to the way in which a series of values recorded over a period of time can result in a time series (and when these values are plotted on a graph, this graph is known as a time series graph). Finally, we will be looking at a standardised way of comparing data over time by the use of index numbers. The techniques covered in this chapter are commonly tested in Unit 7 assessments.

KNOWLEDGE AND UNDERSTANDING

- Time series analysis (Element 7.1)
- Use of index numbers (Element 7.1)

CONTENTS

PERFORMANCE CRITERIA

- Compare results over time using an appropriate method that allows for changing price levels (Element 7.1)

1 Graphs

1.1 Introduction

Graphs are very useful as a means of presenting and interpreting data. Graphs are also very important in **economics** for illustrating, for example, cost and profit functions, and they are often used as a starting point in more **complex statistical analysis.** They are also useful methods of illustrating how costs or revenues have changed over time.

Frequently in tests you are asked to draw a graph to illustrate data. In particular you may have to graph the results or costs of a business over a number of time periods (a time series) and possibly to find the trend of this series.

1.2 Straight-line graphs

A **straight-line graph** is illustrated below.

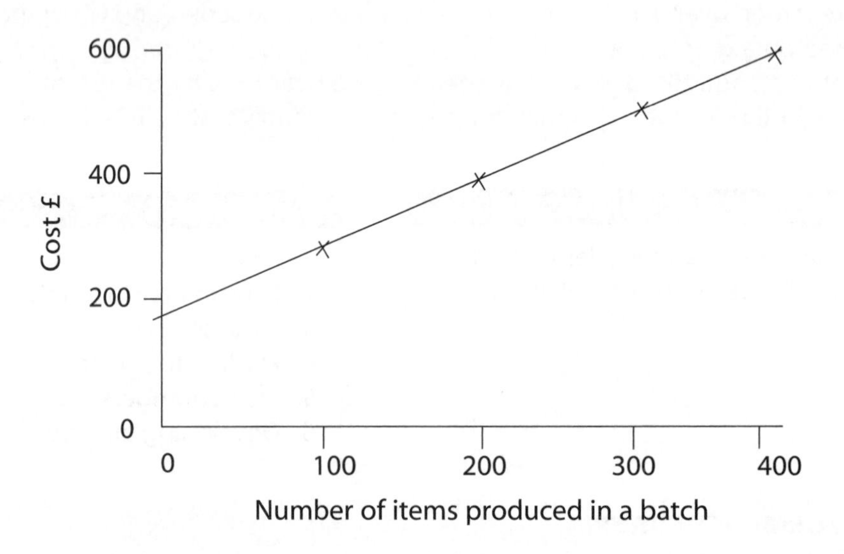

This straight-line graph shows the cost of producing a number of items on a production line. It shows that, even if no items are produced, there is a cost of about £190 to 'set up' the production line. After that, costs increase as production increases at a steady rate.

1.3 Time series

DEFINITION

A time series is a series of figures given for costs or revenues at regular intervals over time, e.g. monthly, quarterly, annually. A time series graph is illustrated below.

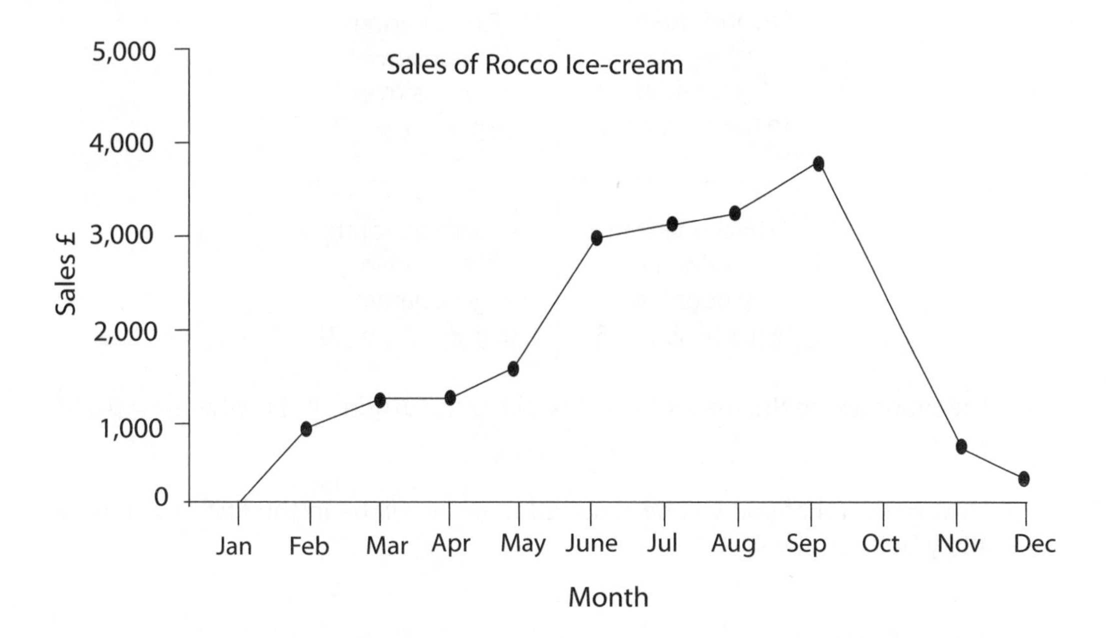

This illustrates the sales of Rocco Ice-cream for the 12 months of a particular year. It shows that, as expected, sales increase over the summer months. The data in such a graph is called a time series and is considered in detail later.

The two graphs shown here are significantly different.

- The **straight–line graph** has a clear, direct relationship from which it would be fairly easy to obtain an expression explaining how costs and number of items produced were related.
- The pattern shown in the **time series** is more complicated and it would be very difficult to obtain a relationship in this case.

2 How to draw a graph

2.1 Variables

A graph will have just **two variables, x and y,** which are related. The major points to be remembered when drawing such graphs are given below.

Since there are two variables, two axes are required. The vertical axis is used to represent y, the **dependent variable** in the relationship. The **x variable** is represented on the horizontal axis, this being the **independent variable.** The independent variable is either the time scale with a time series or the factor which causes the change in the dependent variable e.g. quantity of production.

2.2 Axes

The horizontal and vertical axes are used to represent **both positive and negative values.** This is done by dividing the graph into four quadrants as shown below.

Second quadrant x negative y positive (e.g. x = -2, y = 3)	First quadrant x positive y positive (e.g. x = 2, y = 3)
Third quadrant x negative y negative (e.g. x = -2, y = -3)	Fourth quadrant x positive y negative (e.g. x = 2, y = -3)

The point where the axes intersect is called the **origin** and is where x = 0 and y = 0.

Most graphs that you will be required to draw will be in the first quadrant (x and y both positive).

2.3 Scale

Choosing **suitable scales** for the axes is very important. When using graph paper, the squares are divided up in multiples of ten and it is therefore logical to use multiples of ten for the intervals on the scale. It is not practical to use intervals of, say, three or seven on an axis.

The **intervals for the scales need not be the same** for both the x and y axes. For example, an interval of five units on the x-axis and 100 units on the y-axis is permissible. Care should, therefore, be taken to examine the scales of the x and y axes when interpreting a graph.

2.4 Labelling the axes

Always remember to **label the axes** on a graph. The minimum requirement is to label them x and y (or some other letters). If the graph has a practical meaning, then label the axes with the actual title of the variable e.g. production in units on the x axis and total cost on the y axis.

EXAMPLE

Draw a graph of the following values:

x	5	–10	–5	–2	10	15
y	50	–100	–50	20	75	25

Solution

In this data, the x values range from –10 to +15, while the y values range from –100 to +75. Our scales, logically based on intervals of a multiple of 10, must therefore cover these ranges. It would not be sensible in this example to use the same scale for both the x and y axes because of the very different ranges.

A suitable graph is shown below.

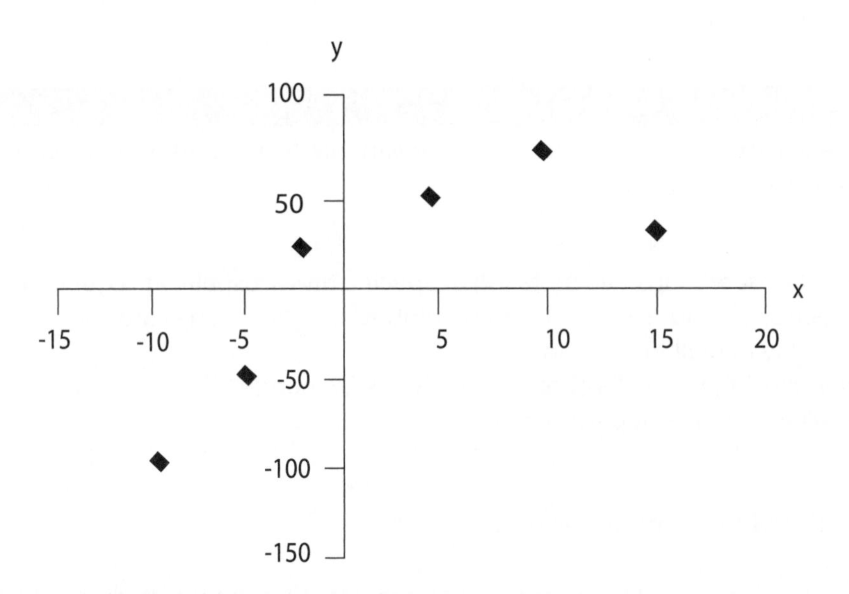

Take care when planning a graph. Your aim should be to use as much of the page as possible so think carefully about the scale to be used on each axis.

▷ ACTIVITY 1

Video v DVD

The following data is the number of video recorders/players sold in the United Kingdom from 20X4 to 20X9 inclusive:

Year	*20X4*	*20X5*	*20X6*	*20X7*	*20X8*	*20X9*
Number of video players (millions)	10.61	9.38	8.43	7.37	6.52	5.56

Required

(a) Plot this data on a graph and comment on the pattern observed.

(b) The data below gives the number of DVD players sold over the same period:

Year	*20X4*	*20X5*	*20X6*	*20X7*	*20X8*	*20X9*
Number of DVD players (millions)	6.82	8.29	9.57	10.72	11.97	12.71

Is there any evidence to support the statement that the rate of decrease in video players has been compensated for by the increase in DVD players? [Answer on p. 103]

3 Time series

3.1 Introduction

☐ DEFINITION

A **time series** is a set of values for some variable (e.g. monthly production) which varies with time.

The set of observations will be taken at specific times, usually at regular intervals. Examples of figures which can be plotted as a time series are:

(a) monthly rainfall in London

(b) daily closing price of a share on the Stock Exchange

(c) weekly sales in a department store.

3.2 Drawing a time series graph

Given below is a typical time series graph representing the quarterly birth rate in the Netherlands over a four-year period.

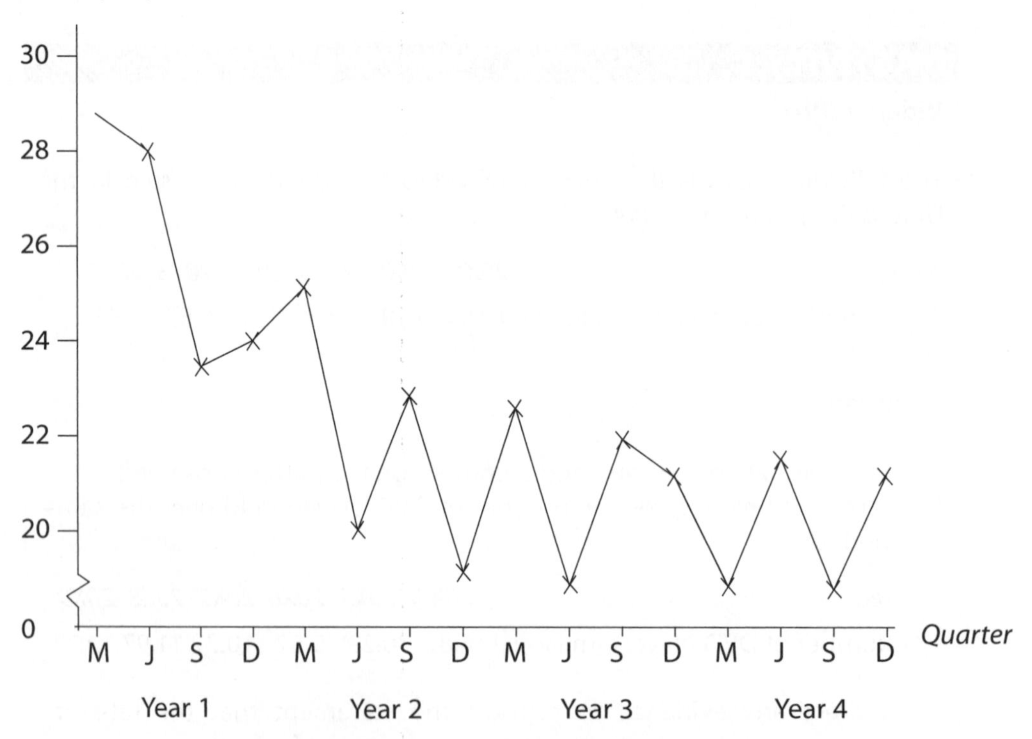

In such a graph, **each point is joined to the next by a straight line,** hence the typically 'jagged' appearance.

Do not make the mistake of trying to construct a smooth curve which will pass through all the points on a time series graph. You will find it practically impossible and, in any case, it is not necessarily correct to do so. In fact, the only reason for joining the points at all is to give a clearer picture of the pattern, which would be more difficult to interpret from a series of dots.

3.3 Use of a time series graph

The graph of a time series may be useful for investigating what happened in the past but the real importance of studying a time series is trying to use it to **forecast** what will happen in the future. In other words the past information is recorded, analysed and projected into the future to help with production planning, staff recruitment, etc.

3.4 Characteristic movements of a time series

Analyses of time series have revealed certain characteristic movements or variations, some or all of which are present to varying degrees. These movements are sometimes called the components of the time series. Analysis of these components is essential for forecasting purposes. The four main types of components are:

(a) long-term movements or **basic trend** (see below)

(b) **cyclical** movements – long term swings about the trend line or curve, e.g. caused by the trade cycle – prosperity/recession/depression/recovery.

(c) **seasonal** movements – shorter term patterns followed by the time series, e.g. due to changing seasons/days of week, etc.

(d) irregular or **random** movements – due to chance events such as floods, strikes, elections, etc.

In this Unit we will concentrate on the extraction of the trend.

3.5 Basic trend

DEFINITION

The **basic trend** refers to the general direction in which the graph of a time series appears to be going over a long interval of time.

The movement can be represented on the graph by a **trend curve or line.** The trend line is effectively a line of best fit. It is a straight line or curve which best fits the general movement in the time series.

Some common basic trends are illustrated below:

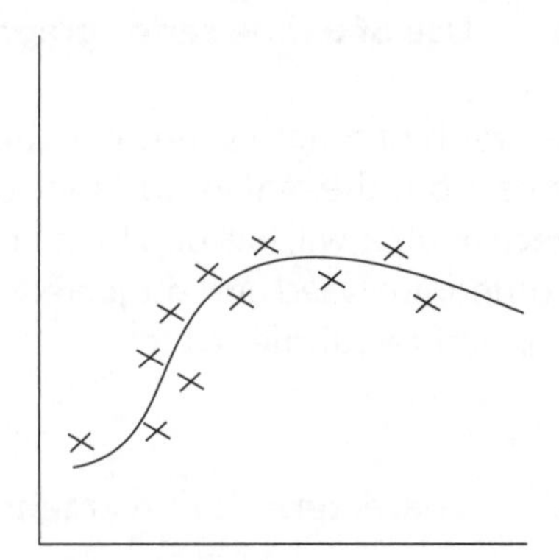

▷ ACTIVITY 2

Trends

In what order should the following be placed to show movements that can be described as a trend, seasonal variation, cyclical variation and random variation respectively?

1 The pattern of the number of bed-nights sold by Brighton bed and breakfast establishments.
2 The steady decline in the infant mortality rate due to improvements in intensive care treatment.
3 Changes in house prices in the North relative to the Retail Price Index.
4 The increase in buildings insurance claims due to the worst storms to hit England in history.

A 2, 3, 1, 4
B 2, 1, 3, 4
C 3, 4, 1, 2
D 3, 1, 2, 4

[Answer on p. 104]

4 Finding the trend

4.1 Introduction

One way, admittedly not very scientific, of isolating the trend is **simply to draw it in freehand on the graph** (as with the trend illustrations shown earlier).

This is not usually good enough for assessment purposes and the two more objective methods are:
(a) using **moving** averages

(b) calculating the least squares line of best fit using **regression analysis.**

However, regression is not needed for this Unit and is not covered in this textbook. This section concentrates on the method of **moving averages** which can be used whether the trend is linear or not. This is all that is required for Unit 7.

4.2 Moving averages

DEFINITION

A moving average is an average of each consecutive set of time series figures e.g. the average of each successive three-month period.

By using **moving averages** of **appropriate order,** the variations in a time series can be eliminated leaving a 'smoothed' set of figures which is taken as the trend.

EXAMPLE

Given below are the sales figures for a business for the last year.
You are required to calculate a three month moving average for these figures.

Month	Time series sales
	£000
1	300
2	500
3	500
4	500
5	700
6	900
7	900
8	900
9	1,100
10	1,300
11	1,300
12	1,300

Step 1

Calculate the total of the sales for the first three months (month 1 to 3).

$300 + 500 + 500 = 1,300$

Step 2

Find the average sales for this three-month period by dividing by 3.

$$\frac{1,300}{3} = 433.33$$

Step 3

Repeat the process for the next three-month period moving on just one month (months 2 to 4).

$$\frac{500 + 500 + 500}{3} = 500.00$$

Step 4

Repeat the calculation for each successive three-month period.

Month 3 to 5 $\frac{500 + 500 + 700}{3} = 566.66$

Month 4 to 6 $\frac{500 + 700 + 900}{3} = 700.00$

and so on.

Step 5

List the moving averages on the original time series with each moving average being shown against the middle one of the three months used.

Month	Time series sales	3-month moving average
	£000	£000
1	300	
2	500	433.33
3	500	500.00
4	500	566.66
5	700	700.00
6	900	833.33
7	900	900.00
8	900	966.66
9	1,100	1,100.00
10	1,300	1,233.33
11	1,300	1,300.00
12	1,300	

This three-month moving average is the trend of the sales showing a general (and very large) increase over the year.

A three-month moving average would be appropriate where the data appears to have a seasonal pattern (cycle) repeating itself every three months. Each group of three months' data used in the averaging process will contain a representative month from each part of the cycle (e.g. an average month, an above average month and a below average month). Averaging these removes the seasonal effects and shows the general data movement.

4.3 Centred moving averages

In the previous example the period for the moving average was an odd number i.e. a three-month moving average. This meant that it was possible to place each moving average against the central month for each calculation.

However if the moving average is taken with an even number of periods e.g. a four-year moving average then there is no central period. Instead the moving average total must be shown in the middle of the period which will be between the second and third years of each calculation. This makes it impossible to plot the moving average or trend on a graph.

Therefore a further average must be taken known as the **centred moving average.** This is done by taking each successive pairs of moving average figures and finding their own average which is then placed in the middle of their figures. This is the trend figure.

This will all be seen more clearly in the next example.

O EXAMPLE

Given the following production costs for 20W7–20X7, calculate the four-year moving averages and four-year centred moving averages.

Year	Data
	£000
20W7	50.0
20W8	36.5
20W9	43.0
20X0	44.5
20X1	38.9
20X2	38.1
20X3	32.6
20X4	38.7
20X5	41.7
20X6	41.1
20X7	38.8

Step 1

Calculate the four-year moving average for each successive period:

20W7 to 20X0 $\frac{50 + 36.5 + 43 + 44.5}{4} = 43.5$

20W8 to 20X1 $\dfrac{36.5 + 43 + 44.5 + 38.9}{4}$ = 40.73

20W9 to 20X2 $\dfrac{43 + 44.5 + 38.9 + 38.1}{4}$ = 41.13

and so on.

Step 2

Place each of these figures in the central point of the four-year period on

Year	Data	Four-year moving average
	£000	
20W7	50.0	
20W8	36.5	
		43.50
20W9	43.0	
		40.73
20X0	44.5	
		41.13
20X1	38.9	
		38.53
20X2	38.1	
		37.08
20X3	32.6	
		37.78
20X4	38.7	
		38.53
20X5	41.7	
		40.08
20X6	41.1	
20X7	38.8	

Step 3

Calculate the centred moving average by taking each successive pairs of four-year moving averages and finding their average:

$$\frac{43.50 + 40.73}{2} = 42.12$$

$$\frac{40.73 + 41.13}{2} = 40.93$$

$$\frac{41.13 + 38.53}{2} = 39.83$$

and so on.

Step 4

Show each of these centred moving averages in the centre of the two four-year figures used – this is effectively against year 3 of each of the original four year's figures used.

Year	Data	Four-year moving average	Centred moving average trend
	£000		
20W7	50.0		
20W8	36.5		
		43.50	
20W9	43.0		42.12
		40.73	
20X0	44.5		40.93
		41.13	
20X1	38.9		39.83
		38.53	
20X2	38.1		37.81
		37.08	
20X3	32.6		37.43
		37.78	
20X4	38.7		38.16
		38.53	
20X5	41.7		39.31
		40.08	
20X6	41.1		
20X7	38.8		

The final column, the centred moving average is the trend of the data. The reason for calculating the centred moving average is so that the trend line can now be plotted on a graph together with the original figures.

Production costs 20W7 to 20X7 and trend

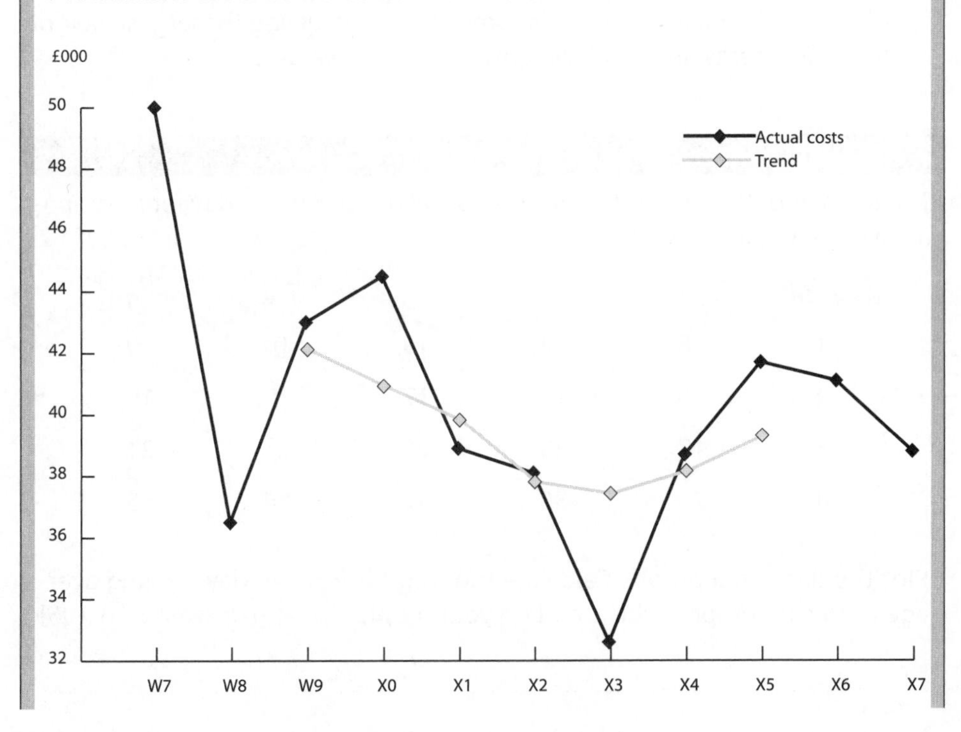

Note that the vertical axis does not start at zero as the figures are so far above zero. This is perfectly acceptable on a graph provided that the break in the axis shown as above.

The trend line now clearly depicts what is happening in general with these costs. They fell fairly dramatically and have then started to rise again.

▷ ACTIVITY 3

Moving average

Sales in £s of a particular product for the last five years have been:
100, 110, 108, 112, 107

Calculate three-year moving averages to the nearest £. [Answer on p. 104]

4.4 Disadvantages of moving averages

Although an extremely simple method of finding the trend, moving averages have certain **disadvantages.**

(a) **Data at the beginning and end of the series is lost** – therefore the moving averages do not cover the complete period.
(b) The moving averages may generate **cycles or other movements** that were not present in the original data.
(c) The averages are **strongly affected by extreme values.** To overcome this a 'weighted' moving average is sometimes used giving the largest weights to central items and small weights to extreme values.

▷ ACTIVITY 4

The following data shows the number of cash receipts per day for a company over four working weeks:

Week/day	1	2	3	4	5
1	8	12	15	10	9
2	10	13	17	15	16
3	17	23	25	21	21
4	26	30	32	34	35

Plot the data on a graph. Calculate the trend using five-day moving averages and superimpose this trend on your graph. [Answer on p. 105]

4.5 Making a forecast using a time series

If you are required to forecast a figure for the future given a time series, there are three main ways of doing it:

- drawing the time series, drawing in a trend line and extending it in the direction it appears to be going
- looking at the increment between trend values and seeing if there is a pattern; if there is, add on values for this pattern until your required date in the future is reached
- if there is no patterns in the increment, calculate an average increment and add these on until you reach the date.

Note that however you use a time series to predict a value in the future, you cannot predict very far ahead.

5 Index numbers

5.1 Introduction

DEFINITION

An **index number** is a means of explaining changes over time in economic variables such as prices, wages, output, etc.

It shows how these items **change with time** and can be divided into three types:

(a) **price index numbers,** which measure changes in prices
(b) **quantity index numbers,** which measure changes in quantity
(c) **value index numbers,** which measure changes in the value of services or activities of goods.

5.2 Using an index

An index is a useful method of comparing figures over time by simplifying them to a single index figure that can be compared to a base year which is given an index of 100. The index then shows the change in the figures each year comparison to that base year

EXAMPLE

Given here are the production cost figures for a business for the last eight years:

Year	Cost
	£000
20X0	138
20X1	149
20X2	158
20X3	130
20X4	136
20X5	150
20X6	154
20X7	162

You are to calculate an index for these costs using 20X0 as the base year.

Solution

The formula for calculation of each year's index is $\frac{\text{Current year costs}}{\text{Base year costs}} \times 100$.

We can now calculate the index for each year:

Year	Cost	Calculation	Index
	£000		
20X0	138	138/138 X 100	100.0
20X1	149	149/138 X 100	108.0
20X2	158	158/138 X 100	114.5
20X3	130	130/138 X 100	94.2
20X4	136	136/138 X 100	98.6
20X5	150	150/138 X 100	108.7
20X6	154	154/138 X 100	111.6
20X7	162	162/138 X 100	117.4

The indices that are above 100 show that the costs have increased over the 20X0 costs in that year. The indices that are below 100 show that the costs are lower in that year than in 20X0.

We can now see clearly from the index figures that costs rose for two years then fell below 20X0 levels for two years before continuing to rise substantially.

6 Developing an index

6.1 Introduction

The general problems found in developing an index are as follows:

- selection of items to be included
- choice of base year
- choice of weights if the index is an aggregate.

6.2 Items to be included

The items to be included in the index should be: **(1) relevant, (2) representative, (3) reliable and (4) comparable over time.**

(1) Items must be **relevant,** e.g. a producers' price index should be composed of wholesale prices, whereas a cost of living index should comprise retail prices.

(2) An index number is generally based on a sample. For example, it would be impossible to include prices for every type of food in an index of food prices. The items chosen should be adequate in number and importance and **representative of the whole.** Generally the index will be more reliable the more items there are, as abnormal movements in one or two commodities will not unduly affect it.

(3) It is essential for the data to **be accurate.** Preference should be given to items for which reliable quotations can be obtained with confidence.

(4) One of the greatest difficulties is **variation in quality or situations** where the classification of the item has changed.

6.3 Base period

Because the trend represents a movement in prices there has to be a **base period** to compare with. The year or period chosen for a base must be 'normal', e.g. if constructing an index to measure the volume of motor car production, the base month should not be one in which there was a major strike. This would give a misleading impression of the prosperity of the motor industry if the months following the strike showed a substantial increase.

The base period may be a single date, a month or a year. The length of the base period usually depends on the interval at which the index number is to be calculated. The index number for the base period is given the value 100 and this might be allocated to :

- a year – 20X5 = 100
- a month – August 20X5 = 100
- a single date – 16 August 20X5 = 100.

6.4 Relatives, or one item index numbers

If the price of one item is recorded at different times, then an index number can be constructed to show **changes in price.**

The index number, or price relative is $\frac{\text{Current price of item}}{\text{Base price of item}}$ x 100.

O EXAMPLE

Year	Price of car service
20X0	£36.50
20X1	£39.20
20X2	£44.70
20X3	£51.40
20X4	£52.50

Taking 20X1 as the base year calculate an index for these prices.

Solution

The index for 20X0 is:

$$\frac{36.50}{39.20} \times 100 = 93.1$$

Similarly, for 20X2:

$$\frac{44.70}{39.20} \times 100 = 114.0$$

and if the other years' index numbers are calculated:

20X3 $\frac{51.40}{39.20} \times 100 = 131.1$

20X4 $\frac{52.50}{39.20} \times 100 = 133.9$

6.5 Using the index

The figures obtained are index numbers and often called **price relatives.** All the figures are calculated as percentages of the figure for 20X1 and so they show percentage changes from 20X1 (e.g. the price for 20X3 is 31.1% higher than that in 20X1).

However, you cannot say the percentage rise from 20X3 to 20X4 is:

133.9 – 131.1 = 2.8%

It is in fact:

$$\frac{52.50}{51.40} \times 100 = 102.1$$

so a 2.1% increase has occurred. We could use the appropriate index numbers to find this increase from 20X3 to 20X4:

$$\frac{133.9}{131.1} \times 100 = 102.1 \text{ (as before)}$$

6.6 Quantity index

The idea of a relative or single item index is not limited to prices. Suppose the number of cars serviced at a garage is known. Then, an index with base year 20X1 is calculated as:

Year	Number of cars	Index number	
20X0	2,138	$\frac{2,138}{2,210} \times 100 =$	96.7
20X1	2,210		100.0
20X2	2,356	$\frac{2,356}{2,210} \times 100 =$	106.6
20X3	2,199	$\frac{2,199}{2,210} \times 100 =$	99.5
20X4	2,056	$\frac{2,056}{2,210} \times 100 =$	93.0

This is called a quantity index.

6.7 Aggregates, or weighted index numbers

The more complex situation is where **several items need to be combined into a single index number.**

O EXAMPLE

A firm's production involves three raw materials, the unit costs of which are:

	Costs (per kg) 20X3	Costs (per kg) 20X4
Steel	£2.00	£2.50
Plastics	£1.50	£1.50
Wood	£0.50	£0.60

To compare costs we would average these costs and then work out an index number comparing those average costs. This, however, does not take account of the fact that different quantities of each raw material may be required. If 3 kg of steel, 2 kg of plastic and 1 kg of wood are used, then a weighted index is found using the quantities as weightings.

The formula for a weighted index is:

$$\text{Combined index number} = \frac{\text{Weighted average for given period}}{\text{Weighted average for base period}} = 100$$

and the weighted average is calculated in the usual way as:

$$\text{Weighted average} = \frac{\sum WX}{\sum W}$$

where X denotes costs and W denotes weights.

Calculate an index for 20X4 with 20X3 as the base year (20X3 index = 100).

Solution

Raw material	w	20X3 costs	wx_3	20X4 costs	wx_4
		£	£	£	£
Steel	3	2.00	6.00	2.50	7.50
Plastic	2	1.50	3.00	1.50	3.00
Woods	1	0.50	0.50	0.60	0.60
Σw	6	Σwx_3	9.50	Σwx_4	11.10

Weighted average (20X3) $= \frac{£9.50}{6} =$ £1.5833

Weighted average (20X4) $= \frac{£11.10}{6} =$ £1.8500

The index is then:

20X3 = 100.0

20X4 $\frac{1.8500}{1.5833} \times 100 = 116.8$

This could also be computed as:

$$\frac{\Sigma wx_4}{\Sigma wx_3} \times 100 = \frac{11.10}{9.50} \times 100 = 116.8$$

This is known as an aggregative approach to calculating a weighted index.

EXAMPLE

(a) Find an index number for 20X3 and 20X4 with 20X2 as base period for average pay using the figures in the table and an aggregative approach.

	Average par (£)		
	20X2	20X3	20X4
	£	£	£
Non-skilled	110	115	123
Semi-skilled	128	145	162
Skilled	150	162	180

There are 25 non-skilled, 15 semi-skilled and 10 skilled employees.

(b) What is the percentage rise in average pay from 20X2 to 20X3 and from 20X3 to 20X4?

Solution

(a) Using the numbers of employees as weights the calculations are:

	W	Pay (20X2)	W x pay
		£	£
Non-skilled	25	110	2,750
Semi-skilled	15	128	1,920
Skilled	10	150	1,500
	50		6,170

20X2 weighted average = $\frac{£6,170}{50}$ = £123.4

	W	Pay (20X3)	W x pay
		£	£
Non-skilled	25	115	2,875
Semi-skilled	15	145	2,175
Skilled	10	162	1,620
	50		6,670

20X3 weighted average = $\frac{£6,670}{50}$ =£133.4

	W	Pay (20X4)	W x pay
		£	£
Non-skilled	25	123	3,075
Semi-skilled	15	162	2,430
Skkilled	10	180	1,800
	50		7,305

20X4 weighted average = $\frac{£7,305}{50}$ = £146.1

The index number is then (using 20X2 as base year = 100):

Year	Index
20X2	100.0
20X3	$\frac{133.4}{123.4} \times 100 = 108.1$
20X4	$\frac{146.1}{123.4} \times 100 = 118.4$

(b) To find the percentage increase from 20X2, the base year, simply take the difference in the index number value. For 20X3 it is:

% Rise from 20X2 to 20X3 = 108.1 – 100 = 8.1%

However, to find the change from 20X3 to 20X4, as 20X3 is not the base year, work out the index number ratio and subtract 100, ie:

% Rise from 20X3 to 20X4 = $\frac{118.4}{108.1} \times 100 - 100 = 109.5 - 100 = 9.5\%$

▷ ACTIVITY 5

WBA

The cost of the materials used in the manufacturing of a technical manual, WBA, is:

	20X3			20X3		
	Quantity	Price	Total (Pence)	Quantity	Price	Total (Pence)
Cover	1	10.8p	10.8	1	10.6	10.6
Paper	230	30p/100	69	250	31p/100	77.5
Ink	5	1p	5	6	1p	6
Bindings	1	2p	2	1	3p	3
			86.8			97.1

Calculate an index number which indicates the overall change in prices in 20X4 (20X3 = 100). Use 20X3 quantities as the basis for the calculation.

[Answer on p. 106]

6.8 Retail Prices Index (RPI)

One of the most commonly used indices is the Retail Prices Index. This is an index compiled by the Department of Employment and published monthly in the Department of Employment Gazette and Monthly Digest of Statistics.

DEFINITION

The **general index of retail prices** measures the percentage changes month by month in the average level of prices of commodities and services purchased by the great majority of households in the UK, including practically all wage earners and most small and medium salary earners.

The RPI is often used as a measure of general inflation in the country.

6.9 Industry sector average index

(a) An industry sector average is simply an average figure for a particular variable that is measured for a particular sector of industry for a particular period.
For example the average may be calculated for prices in retail male clothing for the year ended 31 December 19X8.
There are clearly millions of possible industry averages that can be calculated. The index above could be divided into several averages by distinguishing between male children's clothing and male adult clothing.

(b) An industry sector average index is an index that compares the average over a period of time. Thus the industry average of prices of men's clothing could be turned into an index using the techniques we have already studied.

EXAMPLE

The hourly wage for agricultural workers in Wiltshire for 20X4 was found by sending a questionnaire to a sample of 2,000 farms asking for the number of agricultural workers employed and their average hourly wage for each farm. The figures were collected and a weighted average produced for all 2,000 farms.

The results for 20X4 showed that the average hourly wage was £8.75.

The results for the previous three years were:

Year	Average hourly wage
	£
20X1	7.50
20X2	8.10
20X3	8.50

Calculate the average hourly wage index using 20X1 as the base year.

Solution

Year	Average hourly wage		Index
	£		
20X1	7.50	(7.50/7.50) × 100	100.0
20X2	8.10	(8.10/7.50) × 100	108.0
20X3	8.50	(8.50/7.50) × 100	113.3
20X4	8.75	(8.75/7.50) × 100	116.7

6.10 Deflating a series using the Retail Prices Index (RPI)

If a series of figures is concerned with **sums of money and recorded through time** then it will be affected by **inflation** and so changes can be misleading. One often hears comments such as '£1.50 for a pint of beer! It was only 2s 4d when I was a boy'. The important factor is, how long did someone have to work to earn the 2s 4d to buy the original pint and how long does he now have to work to buy the current pint?

To overcome this, **'real prices' are found by deflating the original series.** This is effectively changing the money values to values at one point in time, the base time, and so making the figures directly comparable.

EXAMPLE

Consider the following table of average weekly pay and the RPI, by year:

Year	Average weekly wage	RPI
	£	
20X5	69.50	91.0
20X6	78.40	98.6
20X7	90.10	111.8
20X8	108.60	131.9
20X9	120.30	145.9

The 'real' value of earnings in relation to 20X5 would be calculated as:

$$\text{Average wage for year} \times \frac{\text{RPI for 20X5}}{\text{RPI for year}}$$

This gives for 20X6, a deflated figure of:

$$£78.40 \times \frac{91.0}{98.6} = £72.36$$

Similarly, for 20X7 the deflated figure is:

$$£90.10 \times \frac{91.0}{111.8} = £73.34$$

For 20X8 the deflated figure is:

$$£108.60 \times \frac{91.0}{131.9} = £74.92$$

and for 20X9 the deflated figure is:

$$£120.30 \times \frac{91.0}{145.9} = £75.03$$

Bringing this information together in one table, gives:

Year	Average weekly wage	RPI	'Real' weekly wage (20X5)
	£		£
20X5	69.50	91.0	69.50
20X6	78.40	98.6	72.36
20X7	90.10	111.8	73.34
20X8	108.60	131.9	74.92
20X9	120.30	145.9	75.03

Looking at the change from 20X5 to 20X9 shows that the purchasing power of average wages has risen by:

$$\frac{75.03 - 69.50}{69.50} \times 100 = \frac{5.53}{69.50} \times 100 = 7.96\%$$

Use of the RPI to deflate figures for costs or revenues is often used in assessments in order to give a more realistic picture of any changes in costs and revenues.

▷ ACTIVITY 6

Energy supplies

Given below is the sales revenue of a business from 20X1 to 20X5 and the average RPI for each year.

Year	Sales	RPI
	£	
20X1	486,000	111.8
20X2	521,000	131.9
20X3	562,000	145.9
20X4	604,000	150.3
20X5	683,000	156.3

Required

(a) Deflate the sales revenue using the RPI to show all revenue in terms of 20X1 prices.

(b) Comment on your results.

[Answer on p. 106]

7 Test your knowledge

1. For each of the four components of a time series, explain how they may arise in the case of sales for a particular product.
2. Why might it be necessary to calculate centred moving averages?
3. What is the purpose of the weights when computing a weighted average index number?
4. If a ream of inkjet printer paper costs £7.99 in 20X5 (RPI = 112.3), has its real cost gone up or down since 20X1 (RPI = 104.5) when it cost £7.60?

[Answers on p. 107]

8 Summary

In this chapter we have been considering cost and revenue information over a period of time. This is known as a **time series** and the costs or revenues can be illustrated on a **graph.**

Further analysis can then be made of this time series by isolating the basic **trend** by calculating **moving averages.** The basic trend line can then be drawn onto the time series graph to indicate how the figures are generally moving over time.

When comparing a list of figures for costs, revenues or quantities over time it is not always easy to determine how these figures are moving. Use of an index for each period's figures compared to a base period index of 100 shows quite clearly whether each period's figures are increasing or decreasing compared to the base period.

One further specific use of an index is to use the Retail Prices Index, the general measure of price inflation, to deflate a time series in order that any real increase or decrease in costs or revenues can be clearly seen.

Answers to chapter activities & 'test your knowledge' questions

△ ACTIVITY 1

Video v DVD

Part (a)

Graph of number (in millions) of video recorder/players sold.

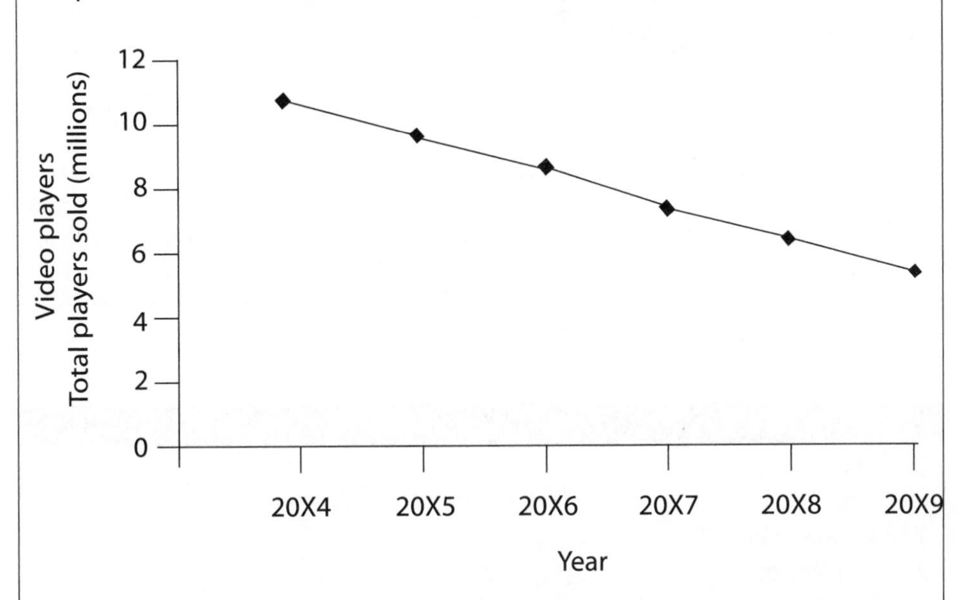

The graph shows that there has been a regular decline in the number of video players sold over the period. The data follows an almost perfect straight line.

Part (b)

The best way of answering this question is to find the total number of players sold each year and plot this on a graph.

Year	20X4	20X5	20X6	20X7	20X8	20X9
Sales (millions)	17.43	17.67	18.00	18.09	18.49	18.27

As the graph indicates, the total number of players sold increased fairly steadily up to 20X8, then fell again in 20X9. Thus it would appear that up to 20X8 the fall in sales of video players was compensated by an increase in sales of DVD players.

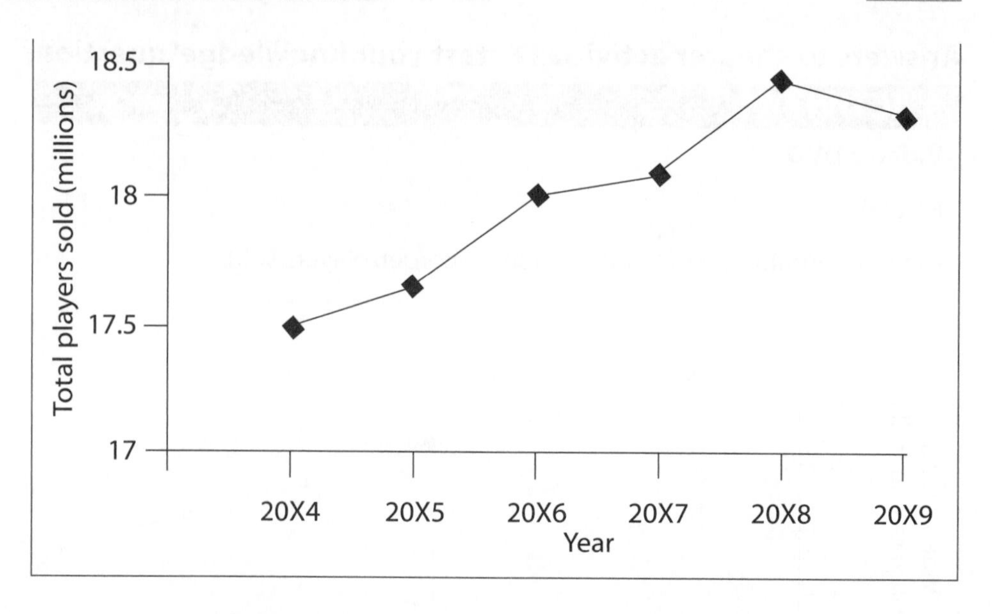

ACTIVITY 2

Trends

1. is seasonal
2. is a trend
3. is probably (arguably) cyclical
4. is random

To rank these trend, seasonal, cyclical, random would mean:
2, 1, 3, 4 (answer B)

ACTIVITY 3

Moving average

	Three-year total	Three-year moving average
£	£	£
100		
110	318	106
108	330	110
112	327	109
107		

△ ACTIVITY 4

The five-day moving average trend is simply found by adding up the figures in fives and dividing by five. No centring is required as the moving average is based on an odd number.

Week/day		Data	5-day moving average trend
1	1	8	
	2	12	
	3	15	10.8
	4	10	11.2
	5	9	11.4
2	1	10	11.8
	2	13	12.8
	3	17	14.2
	4	15	15.6
	5	16	17.6
3	1	17	19.2
	2	23	20.4
	3	25	21.4
	4	21	23.2
	5	21	24.6
4	1	26	26.0
	2	30	28.6
	3	32	31.4
	4	34	
	5	35	

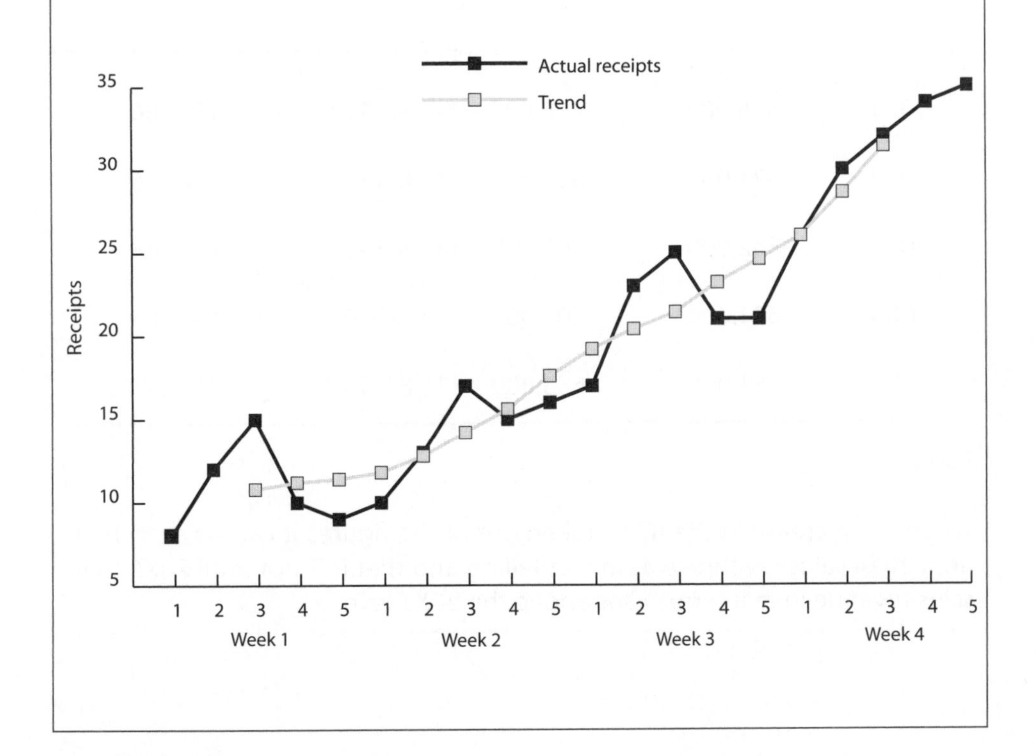

△ ACTIVITY 5

WBA

20X4	Sales revenue	Calculation	Deflated sales revenue
Cover	1	10.6p	10.6
Paper	230	31p/100	71.3
Ink	5	1p	5
Binding	1	3p	3
			89.9

$$\text{Index} = \frac{89.9}{86.8} \times 100 = 103.6$$

△ ACTIVITY 6

Energy supplies

Part (a)

Year	Sales revenue	Calculation	Deflated sales revenue
	£	£	£
20X1	486,000	486,000 x 111.8/111.8	486,000
20X2	521,000	521,000 x 111.8/131.9	441,606
20X3	562,000	562,000 x 111.8/145.9	430,648
20X4	604,000	604,000 x 111.8/150.3	449,283
20X5	683,000	683,000 x 111.8/156.3	488,544

Part (b)

When the increase in the RPI is taken out of the figures it can be seen that until 20X4 sales revenue was in fact falling and that it is not until 20X5 that sales revenue in real terms rises above the 20X1 level.

Test your knowledge

1. **Trend** – over a long period of time, sales may initially increase as the product gets introduced into the market, then remain reasonably static once accepted, then decline as fashions change or alternatives enter the market.

   Cyclical movements – the effects on medium-term sales (year on year) of a changing economy.

   Seasonal movements – short-term fluctuations (by quarter, month or even days of week) in sales brought about by time of week/year – depends upon nature of product.

   Random variations – effects on sales of unexpected events, such as tax changes, climate factors, strikes, etc.

2. Where moving averages are computed with an even number of periods, each average falls between two actual data values. Centring allows the average to be realigned with an actual data value, necessary for extraction of seasonal variations.

3. The weightings allow the relative significance of the component items to be reflected in the index number. When comparing input materials costs over time, for example, we do not want the result to be distorted by a 100% increase in price of a material which only comprises 0.1% of our total usage.

4. In 20X1 pounds, the 20X5 ream costs £7.99 x $\frac{104.5}{112.3}$ = £7.435. Thus, it is cheaper in real terms than in 20X1.

PERFORMANCE ASSESSMENT

INTRODUCTION

Many internal management reports are related to performance, for example, they may be measured in terms of profitability or productivity. Similarly, returns to outside agencies might require you to calculate various ratios, percentages and other performance indicators for the returning organisation. This chapter looks at the most common performance indicators and considers how they might be applied to different businesses in order to assess performance.

In your assessment you are likely to have to produce a number of performance indicators for different organisational units. You may also have to deal with the simple consolidation of figures for different divisions within an organisation and we will therefore also be looking at how to consolidate the figures for these different divisions.

KNOWLEDGE AND UNDERSTANDING

- Use of standard units of inputs and outputs (Elements 7.1, 7.3)
- Relevant performance and quality measures (Element 7.1)
- Main types of performance indicators: productivity; cost per unit; resource utilisation; profitability (Element 7.1, 7.2)
- Ratios: gross profit margin; net profit margin; return on capital employed (Elements 7.1, 7.2)

CONTENTS

PERFORMANCE CRITERIA

- Consolidate information derived from different units of the organisation into the appropriate form (Element 7.1)
- Reconcile information derived from different information systems within the organisation (Element 7.1)
- Account for transactions between separate units of the organisation in accordance with the organisation's procedures (Element 7.1)
- Calculate ratios and performance indicators in accordance with the organisation's procedures (Element 7.1)
- Ensure calculations of ratios and performance indicators are accurate (Element 7.2)

1 Analysing performance

1.1 Types of analysis

Examples of performance analyses might include the following:

- **Performance of individual units within the business** – divisions, departments, services, products, processes or sales areas.

  Performance indicators will depend upon the nature of the unit. For example, divisions and products may be measured in terms of profitability, services and processes in terms of costs per unit, productivity and/or resource utilisation measures.

- **Overall performance of the organisation as a whole,** in comparison with budgeted targets, previous years and/or other organisations in the same business sector.

  Performance indicators in this instance will commonly be in terms of profitability and resource utilisation. Measures will often be in the form of **ratios.**

In addition, **returns to outside agencies,** such as trade associations, will often require various ratios, percentages and other performance indicators for the returning organisation (see next chapter).

1.2 Performance indicators

This chapter looks at the most **common performance indicators** and how they might be applied to various types of business. The performance indicators to be covered are:

- cost per unit
- productivity
- resource utilisation
- profitability.

1.3 Organisational units

The Standards of Competence for Unit 7 also require you to be able to deal with different units within an organisation e.g. divisions, subsidiary companies. Therefore we will consider how to consolidate the figures for different organisational units.

2 Cost per unit

2.1 Introduction

If costs can be individually attributed to a particular business activity or process (cost centre), its performance may be measured by **cost per unit.**

2.2 Cost units

The determination of an **appropriate cost unit** for the particular activity or part of the business being assessed can be difficult, but is key to giving a meaningful measure. The cost unit chosen should relate to the relevant output or activity in such a way that it is clear that levels of costs will in some way be dependent upon the volume of cost units.

We will now think about examples for different types of business and activity.

2.3 Manufacturing businesses or processes

Production and related costs will invariably be related to the **products being produced/sold.** Thus the cost unit will also be directly derived from the product units themselves.

Business /process	Cost unit
Book publisher	Book
Printing process	1,000 pages printed
Brewing	Barrel
Electricity	kWh (i.e. kilowatt hour)
Timber mill	100 ft of wood

2.4 Non-manufacturing businesses/activities

Business/activity	Cost unit
Accountants	Chargeable hour
College	Enrolled student
Hotel	Bed-night
Hospital	Patient-day
Credit control	Customer account
Selling	Orders taken / £ sales made
Maintenance	Man-hours

These present greater problems in determining a suitable standard measure of output or activity. Some examples of commonly used cost units for **service industries, or service departments** within a business, are given; however, there will often be equally useful alternatives.

2.5 Allocation of costs to cost units

To determine the cost per unit, the particular product, area of business or activity will need to have **costs attributed to it,** both direct costs and overheads. The process of tracing costs to cost units via these cost centres will include **overhead allocation, apportionment and absorption,** as assessed in Unit 6.

You are unlikely to be asked to get involved in complex cost-tracing exercises for this unit; you may, however, have to decide upon an appropriate cost unit over which to spread given costs.

O EXAMPLE

A production process has incurred costs of £124,000 for the week ending 30 September 20X0. During that week it produced 200,000 of its single product.

What is the cost per unit produced?

Solution

$$\text{Cost per unit} = \frac{£124{,}000}{200{,}000} = 62 \text{ pence per unit}$$

▷ ACTIVITY 1 

Haulage accounting unit

Suggest suitable cost units appropriate to the following:

(a) a road haulage business

(b) a firm of solicitors

(c) a hospital.

[Answer on p. 142]

3 Productivity

3.1 Introduction

Productivity is a measure of the efficiency of the production process or service provision within an organisation. It can be measured in a variety of ways but is normally measured as a ratio.

3.2 Labour productivity

One common method of measuring the productivity of the labour force is to calculate the number of units produced for each direct labour hour and then to compare this to the budgeted production per labour hour. The units per direct labour hour can also be compared over time by looking at the productivity in each period.

EXAMPLE

The budget for a factory is to produce 120,000 units of its single product in a week using 24,000 direct labour hours The actual production in the week was 116,000 units and this took 24,500 hours.
What is the actual level of output per direct labour hour for the week and how does this compare to the budgeted level of output?

Solution

Actual output per direct labour hour = $\frac{116,000}{24,500}$ = 4.73 units per hour

Budgeted output per direct labour hour = $\frac{120,000}{24,000}$ = 5 units per hour

Therefore the productivity of the factory for the week is lower than the budgeted productivity.

3.3 Labour efficiency

The efficiency of the labour force can be measured by comparing the expected hours for the actual production to the actual hours worked. This is normally expressed as a percentage.

$$\text{Efficiency} = \frac{\text{Budgeted hours for actual production}}{\text{Actual hours for actual production}} \times 100$$

EXAMPLE

The budget for a factory is to produce 120,000 units of its single product in a week using 24,000 direct labour hours. The actual production in the week was 116,000 units and this took 24,500 hours.
What is the labour efficiency measure for the week?

Solution

$$\text{Efficiency} = \frac{\text{Budgeted hours for actual production}}{\text{Actual hours for actual production}} \times 100$$

As it was budgeted that 5 units should be produced each hour then the budgeted hours for the actual production of 116,000 units should be:

$\frac{116,000}{5}$ = 23,200 hours

Efficiency = $\frac{23,200}{24,500} \times 100$

= 94.7%

As this figure is less than 100% it shows a lack of efficiency from the workforce compared to the budgeted figures.

3.4 Machine productivity

In a machine intensive production environment it may also be useful to calculate the number of units produced per machine hour. This can then be compared to the budgeted production per machine hour or to the production levels of earlier periods.

EXAMPLE

A machine production line was in operation for 48 hours in the week ending 24 July 20X0 and 1,200 units were produced. In the previous week the production line was in operation for 45 hours and 1,150 units were produced.

Compare the machine productivity for the two weeks.

Solution

Week ending 24 July	$\frac{1,200}{48}$	=	25 units per machine hour
Previous week	$\frac{1,150}{45}$	=	25.5 units per machine hour

The current week's production is less efficient than the previous week.

3.5 Non-manufacturing organisations

Productivity measures can also be used in non-manufacturing organisations or business units. For example in a firm of accountants the number of chargeable hours per professional staff member may be calculated and monitored. In a sales department the number of sales orders taken per sales staff each week may be calculated.

It is important to realise that the calculation of any of these performance indicators on their own is not enough. The performance indicators are only of use if they are compared either over time or between divisions or to budgeted figures.

ACTIVITY 2 

The Snowy Ski Company

Data

The Snowy Ski Company manufactures skis and related equipment. Charles O'Hagan is manager of the main factory based in South Wales. There is a second factory in Yorkshire, England. The production department is made up of the following sections:

- Moulding
- Assembly
- Finishing

Mr O'Hagan has become concerned about the performance of his work-force compared with the factory in Yorkshire. He has collected performance data from the two factories and produced a spreadsheet model to analyse the data. The results of this data are given below.

You are an accounting technician, assisting Mr O'Hagan in the South Wales factory.

Performance Analysis

Ski Units Completed:	*Week 1*	*Week 2*	*Week 3*	*Week 4*
South wales	1,200	1,350	1,400	1,300
Yorkshire	1,000	1,050	1,150	1,100
Budgeted labour hours per ski unit				
(the same for each factory)				
Moulding	3.4			
Assembly	4.3			
Finishing	6.4			
Actual hours worked				
South Wales:				
Moulding	4,200	4,320	4,760	4,940
Assembly	4,950	5,795	5,995	5,724
Finishing	7,432	8,745	9,315	8,562
Yorkshire:				
Moulding	3,600	3,570	4,025	3,810
Assembly	4,213	4,530	5,120	4,875
Finishing	6,457	7,021	7,765	6,912
Standard hours produced				
(Ski units completed x budgeted hour per ski unit				
South wales:				
Moulding	4,080	4,590	4,760	4,420
Assembly	5,160	5,805	6,020	5,590
Finishing	7,680	8,640	8,960	8,320
Yorkshire:				
Moulding	3,400	3,570	3,910	3,740
Assembly	4,300	4,515	4,945	4,730
Finishing	6,400	6,720	7,360	7,040
Variance (hours worked)				
(Standard hours – actual hours)				
South Wales:				
Moulding	(120)	270	0	(520)
Assembly	210	10	25	(134)
Finishing	248	(105)	(355)	(242)
Total	338	175	(330)	(896)
Yorkshire:				
Moulding	(200)	0	(115)	(70)
Assembly	87	(15)	(175)	(145)
Finishing	(57)	(301)	(405)	128
Total	(170)	(316)	(695)	(87)

Required

(a) Calculate the total actual hours worked in each factory and the actual hours per ski unit produced (to one decimal place). Present your results in the table below.

	Week 1	Week 2	Week 3	Week 4
Total Actual Hours				
South Wales				
Yorkshire				
Ski Unit Completed				
South Wales	1,200	1,350	1,400	1,300
Yorkshire	1,000	1,050	1,150	1,100
Hours per Unit				
South Wales				
Yorkshire				

(b) Write a report for Mr O'Hagan which compares the efficiency of the two factories and highlights any problem areas. The report should also consider the limitations of the analysis carried out and possible reasons for the differences in performance. [Answer on p. 142]

4 Resource utilisation

4.1 Introduction

DEFINITION

Resource utilisation is a measure of the extent to which resources were used in relation to resources available.

4.2 Manufacturing operations

Machine and labour utilisation can be measured as the ratio of hours spent in production (productive hours) to hours available (i.e. machine capacity or labour hours paid).

EXAMPLE

Example: resource utilisation in manufacturing

A printing machine has the capacity to print 5,000 A4 pages per hour. During one 40-hour week, 120,000 pages were printed. The labour force spent 140 hours that week working on products although 160 hours were paid for. Calculate the machine and labour utilisation.

Solution

The machine must have been used for 120,000/5,000 = 24 hours in the week. Thus the machine utilisation in the week was 24/40 = 60%. (This could equally well be measured as 120,000/(5,000 x 40).)

Labour utilisation 140/160 = 87.5%.

The low labour utilisation is probably due to idle time.

4.3 Non-manufacturing operations

Examples of suitable utilisation measures for various types of **service activities** are as follows:

Professional	Chargeable hours: total hours paid
Public transport	Passenger miles: total miles run
Hotel	Rooms occupied: rooms available (occupancy rate)

5 Profitability

5.1 Introduction

The profitability of an organisation can be assessed by looking at the gross profit margin, net profit margin and return on capital employed.

These figures will be illustrated in the following example using the figures given below for GJ Ltd.

Summarised balance sheet at 31 December 20X1

	£000	£000
Fixed assets		2,600
Current assets		
Stocks	600	
Debtors	900	
Cash at bank and in hand	100	
	1,600	
Current liabilities	800	
		800
Capital employed		3,400

Summarised profit and loss account for the year ended 31 December 20X1

	£000
Sales	6,000
Cost of sales	4,000
Gross profit	2,000
Administrative expenses	(1,506)
Distribution and marketing	(74)
Net profit before interest and tax	420

5.2 Return on capital employed (ROCE)

Capital employed represents the long-term investment in the business by the owners in the form of equity (sole trader, partners or shareholders) and other investors in the form of debt (e.g. providers of long-term loans). In the case of GJ Ltd, there being no long-term loans, capital employed is just represented by owners' capital and is equivalent to net assets.

Return on capital employed is frequently regarded as the best measure of profitability, indicating how successful a business is in utilising its assets. There are a number of ways that ROCE may be calculated; the basic formula is as follows:

$$\text{ROCE} = \frac{\text{Net profit before interest and tax}}{\text{Capital employed}} \times 100$$

O EXAMPLE

What is the return on capital employed for GJ Ltd?

Solution

$$\text{ROCE} = \frac{420}{3{,}400} \times 100 = 12.35\%$$

5.3 Return on equity

Return on equity (RoE) measures the profitability of the equity investment in the business. It would be expressed simply as:

$$\text{RoE} = \frac{\text{Net profit after interest}}{\text{Equity}} \times 100$$

It is important to ensure that you use the correct combination of profit and capital employed:

- profit before interest – can be combined with all capital (equity + debt)
- profit after interest – can be combined with equity alone

O EXAMPLE

A business has profit before interest of £160,000 and an interest charge of £20,000. The capital of the business is made up of a long-term loan of £200,000 and equity funds of £1,000,000.

What is the return on capital employed and the return on equity for the business?

Solution

$$\text{ROCE} = \frac{\text{Profit before interest}}{\text{Equity + debt}} \times 100$$

$$= \frac{160,000}{1,200,000} \times 100$$

$$= 13.3\%$$

$$\text{RoE} = \frac{\text{profit after interest}}{\text{Equity}} \times 100$$

$$= \frac{160,000 - 20,000}{1,000,000} \times 100$$

$$= 14\%$$

5.4 Net profit margin (on sales)

A **low margin** indicates low selling prices or high costs or both. Comparative analysis will reveal the level of prices and costs in relation to competitors.

$$\text{NPM} = \frac{\text{Net profit}}{\text{Sales}} \times 100$$

EXAMPLE

What is the net profit margin for GJ Ltd?

Solution

$$\text{NPM} = \frac{420}{6,000} \times 100 = 7.0\%$$

5.5 Gross profit margin

The gross profit margin isolates the pure 'nuts and bolts' of a business, i.e. ignoring indirect expenses and sundry income. It considers the profitability of the actual production or trading element of the business.

$$\text{GPM} = \frac{\text{Gross profit}}{\text{Sales}} \times 100$$

EXAMPLE

What is the gross profit margin for GJ Ltd?

Solution

$$\text{GPM} = \frac{2,000}{6,000} \times 100 = 33\tfrac{1}{3}\%$$

5.6 Asset turnover

Asset turnover could be described as a measure of resource utilisation and is sometimes called capital productivity. It is a measure of how much turnover or sales is being earned by each £ of capital employed and is calculated as:

$$\text{Asset turnover} = \frac{\text{Sales}}{\text{Capital employed}}$$

5.7 Breakdown of ROCE

Return on capital employed is made up of two figures – the net profit margin and asset turnover:

$$\text{ROCE} = \text{net profit margin x asset turnover} = \frac{\text{Net Profits}}{\text{Sales}} \times \frac{\text{Sales}}{\text{Capital employed}}$$

$$= \frac{\text{Net profit}}{\text{Capital employed}}$$

So in any analysis of return on capital employed it is worth breaking down the ratio into these two component parts and analysing each separately.

EXAMPLE

What is the asset turnover for GJ Ltd?

Show how the ROCE is made up of asset turnover and net profit margin.

Solution

$$\text{Asset turnover} = \frac{6,000}{3,400}$$

$$= 1.7647$$

This indicates that every £1 of capital employed by GJ Ltd is earning £1.76 of turnover. It is a measure of how hard the assets of the business are being worked.

ROCE = asset turnover x net profit margin

= 1.7647 x 7% = 12.35%

6 Interpretation of ratios

6.1 Introduction

We shall now look at why **care needs to be taken in interpreting ratios.**

First a couple of general points to bear in mind when looking at a set of accounts with a view to commenting on the position they indicate:

- Before you start calculating ratios, **read the accounts** to identify any obvious points. You do not need a ratio to tell you that sales levels have doubled, for example.
- **Try to look at ratios in groups** rather than in isolation; a group of ratios may provide a clearer indication of where the cause lies. Group together the ROCE, net and gross profit margins and asset turnover to try to get a picture of what is happening in the business.

6.2 Inter-firm comparison of ROCE

As we have seen, the aim of the ROCE is to see how effectively the business is using the money invested in it. This can be compared to a target figure or to ROCE for earlier periods.

It may be valid to compare this ratio with that of our rivals, but some care needs to be taken here.

EXAMPLE

Z Ltd, a recently formed company, has ROCE of $\frac{£5,000}{£50,000} = 10\%$.

Z Ltd's main rival is A Ltd, a long-established company. A Ltd has the same profit as Z Ltd and has capital employed of only £40,000. Compare the ROCE of the two companies.

Solution

A Ltd's ROCE is $\frac{5,000}{40,000} = 12.5\%$.

Clearly, the two different figures for ROCE do not imply that A Ltd is necessarily a better company than Z Ltd.

- Be aware of the **age structure of companies' capital** before comparing them. A Ltd's fixed assets will be older and having been depreciated longer will have a lower net book value therefore a lower capital employed.
- Often **new investment does not bring immediate profits.** This may be for a number of reasons. It may take time for the company's employees to learn to use the new equipment. Alternatively, it may take the company time to obtain enough orders to use the new facilities to the full. (This may result in a temporary reduction in the ROCE.)

6.3 Interpretation of gross and net profit margins

By looking at these two ratios together, we can determine whether a change in the net profit margin can be explained by deteriorating trade success or other expense charges.

O EXAMPLE

	20X1	20X0
	£000	£000
Sales	100	100
Cost of sales	82	80
Gross profit	18	20
Overheads	11	10
Net profit	7	10

Compare the gross and net profit margins of the business for the two years.

Solution

	20X1	20X0
GPM	18%	20%
NPM	7%	10%

The net profit margin has fallen fairly dramatically this year. This can partly be explained by a decrease in gross profit margin but also by an increase in overheads.

This is an illustration of using more than one ratio to guide our thoughts.

▷ ACTIVITY 3

Business Computers Ltd

Data

Business Computers Ltd is a computer company specialising in the manufacture of hardware, software and the provision of related consultancy services. The company is split into three divisions:
Hardware – Commercial
Hardware – Government
Software services and consultancy services

The company has traditionally traded in the hardware market, selling computers to business and government organisations. However, in recent years an increasing amount of business is being done in software services for the company's own products and related consultancy provision.

The company is now reviewing its products, services and markets. The commercial hardware market is likely to become more competitive with development costs rising. The government hardware market will be restricted by government spending limits over the next three years.

However, the long-term projection is that more government departments and organisations will adopt more commercial practices and demand products the company produces. The software services and consultancy division work originated from government contracts and most of the company's work comes from this source.

You work in the finance department of the company as an Accounting Technician and you have been given a number of tasks by the Financial Accountant in order to provide information for the review.

Results for the 20X4/X5 financial years were as follows.

Year		Hardware - Commercial	Hardware - Government	Software & Consultancy
		£	£	£
20X5	Sales	15,957,000	24,768,000	11,368,000
20X5	Development costs	6,376,000	7,832,000	2,134,000
20X5	Other costs	7,215,000	8,150,000	3,716,000
20X5	Number of employees	831	607	423
20X4	Sales	17,643,000	25,974,000	9,276,000

Note: It is company policy to write off development costs in the year of expenditure because of the pace of technological change within the industry.

Task 1

Complete the following table of ratios for 20X5. The ratios for 20X4 are given.

Business Computers Limited

Table of ratios

Division	Ratio	20X4	20X5
Hardware - Commercial	Net profit/sales	17.5%	
	Development costs/sales	34.7%	
	Sales per employee	£22,107	

Division	Ratio	20X4	20X5
Hardware - Government	Net profit/sales	36.6%	
	Development costs/sales	30.9%	
	Sales per employee	£41,200	
Software & Consultancy	Net profit/sales	39.4%	
	Development costs/sales	21.7%	
	Sales per employee	£23,614	

Task 2

Write a detailed report to the financial accountant using the report format below, comparing divisional performance between 20X4 and 20X5 and giving recommendations for the company's future division.

BUSINESS COMPUTERS LTD
REPORT ON DIVISIONAL PERFORMANCE

To:

From:

Date:

[Answer on p. 143]

7 Analysis of results by organisational unit

7.1 Introduction

Whilst most outside users of financial accounts will be concerned only with the performance of the organisation as a whole, this will not generally give useful information to the **managers** of the organisation, unless it is a small, one product/service business.

Many organisations will therefore generate additional information from their accounting and administrative systems that breaks down the **overall revenues and costs between the organisational units** within the business, as defined by management.

7.2 Organisational units

The term **organisational units** is used here to cover all of the following:

- divisions
- departments (productive and service/support)
- sales areas
- processes
- products/services.

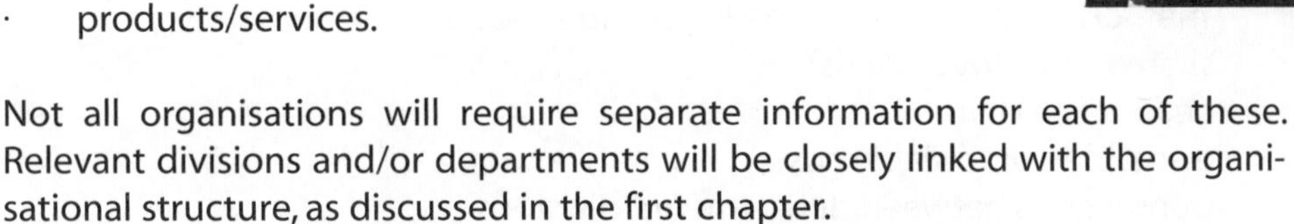

Not all organisations will require separate information for each of these. Relevant divisions and/or departments will be closely linked with the organisational structure, as discussed in the first chapter.

Management will need to know how these units are performing individually as part of the responsibility accounting system – **unit managers being held responsible** for revenues and costs under their control attributable to their unit.

Even if there are no separately operating divisions or departments, a business that has **more than one type of output** (different products or services) will inevitably wish to assess the separate costs/profitability of these.

For Unit 7 you need to be able to carry out simple analyses of given revenue and/or cost figures between divisions, products, etc. and to assess the results. Once the results are split, much of the performance appraisal process will be exactly as discussed earlier in this chapter.

7.3 Divisions and departments

The divisions or departments within an organisation will often be accounted for as **profit centres** – that is, both revenues and costs can be traced to them, allowing the calculation of an individual profit figure for each centre.

Examples of divisionalised/departmentalised businesses include the following:

- organisations operating through **branches** (banks, travel and estate agents, retail shops/stores, etc)
- organisations operating on a **regional basis** (utilities, health authorities, manufacturers/ wholesalers, etc)
- organisations split into **separate departments within the same location** (department stores, accountants/solicitors firms, local authorities, etc).

All of these types of individual units will be centrally controlled via a **head office** or central board.

With careful use, these individual profit figures can be analysed in order to allow assessment of the performance of both the division/department itself and the **manager responsible for it.** There will generally be departmental targets set for this purpose.

The separate results will be combined or **consolidated** within the overall financial/ management accounts for the organisation as a whole.

7.4 Problem areas

In setting up **accounting and performance appraisal systems** for separate divisions/departments, consideration must be made of the best method for dealing with the following aspects:

- shared costs (overheads)
- head office costs
- traceable/controllable costs
- transactions between departments/divisions
- consolidation of results.

7.5 Shared costs

In many departmentalised businesses, costs will be incurred that relate to **more than one department,** for example:

- buildings costs where a building is occupied by more than one department
- shared support/service departments (e.g. maintenance, canteen, accounts)
- advertising and marketing costs.

Each department should generally be held responsible for a **share of these costs,** on the basis that, if the department did not exist, the level of costs incurred would generally be lowered.

An appropriate basis for apportioning each shared cost between the departments needs to be established.

Shared cost	Basis for apportionment
Buildings cost (rent, rates, heat/light, etc)	Floor area
Maintenance	Maintenance hours
Canteen	Number of employees
Accounts	Volume of transactions
Advertising and marketing	Revenue

The process of allocation and apportionment of such costs is principally assessable in Unit 6.

7.6 Head office costs

The **head office,** or other **central management unit** for a departmentalised/divisionalised business will incur its own costs – management salaries, administrative costs, premises costs, etc. Unless these costs can be identified with the organisational units in a meaningful way, resulting divisional net profit figures can be misleading in assessing performance.

It is therefore usual to **omit head office costs** from individual units' results analyses, including them as a total figure only when consolidating the results for the overall accounts.

7.7 Traceable/controllable costs

In assessing the results of a department/division, all revenues and costs that are **traceable to that unit** will generally be included.

DEFINITION

Traceable costs are those costs which are incurred as a result of the department/division being in operation.

For example, this will include wages and salaries of the unit's employees, variable costs of production/service and other overheads (variable and fixed) that relate directly to the unit. This may include apportioned costs, if the basis used gives a fair indication of the cost that would be saved if the unit were to close.

To assess the manager of the unit, however, only the traceable costs that are **controllable** by him/her should be included in the profit figure used to assess performance.

Thus, although the **manager's salary** is traceable to the unit, the manager is unlikely to have control over its level! Additionally, the depreciation and other **costs of fixed assets** that were acquired through head-office decisions should be excluded from managerial assessment.

EXAMPLE

A summary divisional report might appear as follows:

	Division X	Division Y	Total
	£000	£000	£000
Controllable elements			
Sales	820	510	1,330
Variable costs	(460)	(340)	(800)
Contribution	360	170	530
Fixed costs	(125)	(54)	(179)
Controllable profit	235	116	351
Other traceable costs (including apportioned costs	(240)	(72)	(312)
Traceable/(loss)	(5)	44	39
Head office costs			(12)
Profit			27
Contribution/sales (%)	43.9%	33.3%	39.8%
Controllable profit margin	28.7%	22.7%	26.4%
Traceable profit/(loss) margin	(0.6%)	8.6%	2.9%

Comment on the position shown by this divisional report.

Solution

The **controllable contribution and profit lines** should be used in the **assessment of the managers.** Division X's contribution margin is considerably better than that of Division Y, although this advantage is lessened at the controllable profit level. Division X's manager perhaps needs to review his fixed costs to ensure they are all necessary and being properly controlled (although the two divisions' cost structures may be expected to be different if they are concerned with different lines of business).

The contribution line may also be used in the **assessment of the division,** as it is likely to be the traceable as well as controllable contribution; most variable costs will be under the control of the manager. Both divisions have a generally healthy operational performance, i.e. on a short-term basis.

However, the **traceable profit/(loss) line** indicates that Division X does not appear to have a longer-term future, unless fixed costs can be reduced. The validity of this conclusion will depend upon the proportion of traceable fixed costs that are apportioned and the extent to which this apportionment reflects the true use of the resources by the divisions and thus the costs that may be saved if the division were to close.

7.8 Transactions between departments/divisions

In some departmentalised/divisionalised organisations, **units will use each other's products or services.**

For example, a manufacturer's production process may be split between machining, assembly and packing units and products are passed from one unit to another; a tuition college may have a printing department which is used by the publishing and courses department, etc.

How should such transactions be accounted for in a divisional/departmental accounting system? This will depend to a certain extent upon **how the units are structured**. Possibilities include the following:

- One unit may be treated as a **'subsidiary'** of another, as in a cost centre being part of a profit centre. In this case, all the costs of the cost centre will be charged to the profit centre as with any other cost.
  An example would be an alterations department within a clothing department of a shop/store.
- If the cost centre provides goods/services to more than one profit centre (as in the printing department of the tuition college), the costs of that department could be **split between the profit centres** using a basis that reflects the degree of usage by each profit centre (as in the allocation and apportionment of costs of a service department).

Thus the printing department's costs may be split between publishing and courses according to the volume of work carried out for each.

- If all units involved are to be treated as profit centres, then some form of charge for goods/services provided from one unit to another will need to be recorded in each unit's accounts. Such a charge would be known as a **transfer price.**

7.9 Setting a transfer price

Possible **bases for setting a transfer price** are as follows.

(i) **Actual cost:** If goods/services were transferred at actual cost (marginal or full), the supplying unit will not record a profit as such. It will also provide no incentive for cost control.

(ii) **Standard cost:** This will help to contain cost variances within the responsible unit and will encourage cost control.

(iii) **Cost plus:** Transfers recorded at cost plus an allowance for contribution/profit will share the final profit between the contributing units.

(iv) **Market price:** If the supplying unit could sell its output to other organisations as well as to units within its own, the transfer price may be based upon the outside market price. Adjustments may be made to allow for differences in packaging/distribution costs, credit terms, etc.

Each unit will then be assessed upon revenues and costs that are commercially based, i.e. that imitate the situation if each unit were selling/buying to/from the outside market. This will generally promote decisions re output levels, etc. that are optimum for the organisation as a whole.

8 Consolidation of results

8.1 Introduction

When **consolidating the results** from different operating units to give an overall result for the organisation, care must be taken to ensure that the figures have been prepared on a **comparable basis.** Problems in this respect will arise mainly in combining divisions that are largely operated independently of each other, with managers given a high degree of responsibility. Examples of the sort of problems that may arise include the following:

- costs being categorised differently
- different accounting policies being used (e.g. for depreciation, stock, research and development expenditure, etc.)
- differing attitudes being used in determining the level of bad debt provision, stock write-downs, etc
- inter-departmental transfers being recorded at different amounts in the books of the units involved.

These problems can largely be overcome by **setting up standard organisational policies and procedures,** but this will remove a degree of the autonomy of the units.

If the individual units are to be allowed some freedom in deciding policies, etc, there will need to be a **reconciliation exercise** carried out at head office to bring the results in line with each other for consolidation.

8.2 Consolidating revenue

A business is often divided into a number of separate divisions, typically a sales division and one or more production divisions. The production division will transfer goods to the sales division at a value agreed between the divisions and may or may not also sell on its own account to external customers.

When you consolidate the results, you will have to avoid double counting the internal sales made by the production division to the sales division. You will therefore need to know the value of products transferred.

Consider the following figures

Division A	**Division B**		
Total £000	To division A £000	To external customers £000	Total £000
500	250	50	300

The total external sales will be

	£000
Division A	500
Division B	50
	550

The external sales are not 500 + 300 = 800 because 250 of the division B's sales are internal transfers to the Division A.

EXAMPLE

Anderson Ltd has two divisions, a sales and a manufacturing division. The manufacturing division sells goods to the sales division at cost and to external customers at full price. The sales division sells to external customers at full price.

Consolidate the sales of Anderson including only the external sales.

All figures in £000s

	Sales division	**Manufacturing division**		
	Total	To sales division	To external customers	Total
January	356	235	98	333
February	369	244	95	339
March	245	162	86	248
April	267	176	82	258
May	246	162	65	227
June	156	103	62	165
July	178	117	67	184
August	146	96	52	148
September	246	162	64	226
October	278	183	75	258
November	378	249	78	327
December	389	257	87	344

Solution

All figures in £000s

	Sales division	**Manufacturing division**	**Total**
	Total	To external Customers	
January	356	98	454
February	369	95	464
March	245	86	331
April	267	82	349
May	246	65	311
June	156	62	218
July	178	67	245
August	146	52	198
September	246	64	310
October	278	75	353
November	378	78	456
December	389	87	476

8.3 Consolidating sales and cost of sales

In the above example, we only considered the consolidation of sales and simply deducted internal sales from the sales of the production division.

We shall now consider the effect on the cost of sales as well as the effect on sales by repeating the example in 8.2 but adding the cost of sales figures.

Repeating the example from 8.2, Divisions A and B have the following results

	Division A £000	Division B £000
Sales	500	300
Cost of sales	200	120
Gross profit	300	180

Division B transferred goods which cost £50,000 to Division A at a price equal to the cost of the goods.

If you now consolidate the results and simply added the two sales and cost of sales figures, the total sales and the total cost of sales would both be overstated by £50,000, the transfer price. You have to reduce B's sales by £50,000 to remove the internal transfer from the sales figures, and you have to reduce A's cost of sales by £50,000 to remove the internal transfer from the cost of sales figures.

The result of the consolidation is therefore as follows;

	Division A £000	Division B £000	Adjustment £000	Total £000
Sales	500	300	(50)	750
Cost of sales	200	120	(50)	270
Gross profit	300	180		480

Note that the gross profit is not affected because both sales and cost of sales are reduced by the same amount.

However the gross profit percentage will be affected because sales have been reduced by £50,000.

Note also that it doesn't matter what the cost or value of the goods that are transferred is. You always adjust the figures by the price agreed between the divisions. If B had transferred the goods to A at £100,000, the figures would be:

	Division A	Division B	Adjustment	Total
	£000	£000	£000	£000
Sales	500	300	(100)	700
Cost of sales	200	120	(100)	220
Gross profit	300	180		480

8.4 Consolidations involving sales, purchases and stock

A further complication may arise if goods are transferred between divisions but are still in transit at the year end.

Consider the following example. You are told that during the period, B transferred goods valued at their cost of £30,000 to A, of which £2,000 were still in transit at the period end and were not in A's stock. You are given the following figures which include the divisions' stock figures.

	Division A		**Division B**	
	£000	£000	£000	£000
Sales		500		300
Opening stock	150		100	
Purchases	200		175	
	350		275	
Closing stock	(130)		(90)	
Cost of sales		220		185
Gross profit		280		115

The consolidated figures will be:

	Division A		**Division B**		**Adjust**	**Total**	
	£000	£000	£000	£000	£000	£000	£000
Sales		500		300	(30)		770
Opening stock	150		100			250	
Purchases	200		175		(28)	347	
	350		275			597	
Closing stock	(130)		(90)		(2)	(222)	
Cost of sales		220		185			375
Gross profit		280		115			395

Note that you have to reduce both sales and the cost of sales by £30,000. However because only £28,000 has been included in A's purchases you cannot reduce those purchases by the full £30,000. You therefore have to treat the £2,000 of goods in transit as if they are in A's stock and increase the closing stock by £2,000 (which is shown as a negative figure because it is deducted from the purchases to give the cost of sales).

EXAMPLE

Austin Ltd is divided into two divisions, the North and South.
It is preparing its accounts for the 3 months to 31 March 20X8.
The two divisions sell directly to external customers and in addition the North division sells some goods to the South.

The following figures show the sales and purchases of the two divisions for the three months to 31 March 20X8.

	North			**South**	
	External sales	Internal sales	Purchases	Sales	Purchases
	£000s	£000s	£000s	£000s	£000s
January	345	57	150	380	135
February	267	63	130	276	157
March	298	48	90	298	128

The stock of the two divisions is as follows

	Opening stock	Closing stock
	1 Jan 20X8	31 March 20X8
North	140	130
South	120	125

At the end of March, North had despatched £5,000 of goods to South which were in transit at the 31 March and were not included in South's books of account.

Task 1

Calculate the internal and external sales figures for North and South for the three months

Task 2

Calculate the purchases for North and South for the three months

Task 3

Prepare the consolidated profit and loss account down to the figure for gross profit for the three months

Solution

Task 1

External and internal sales for the three months to 31 March 20X8

	North		South
	External sales	Internal sales	Sales
	£000s	£000s	£000s
January	345	57	380
February	267	63	276
March	298	48	298
	910	168	954

Task 2

Purchases for the three months to 31 March 20X8

North Purchases	South Purchases
£000s	£000s
150	135
130	157
90	128
370	420

Task 3

Consolidated profit and loss account to 31 March 20X8

	North	South	Adjustments	Consolidated
	£000s	£000s	£000s	£000s
Sales	910	954	(168)	1,696
Opening stock	140	120		260
Purchases	370	420	(163)	627
	510	540		887
Closing stock	(130)	(125)	(5)	(260)
Cost of sales	380	415		627
Gross profit	530	539		1,069

8.5 Transfers between divisions

As we have seen it is often the case in a divisionalised organisation that there will be transfers of goods or services between divisions and these will be charged to the receiving division at a transfer price.

This means that this transfer price will be included in the 'selling' division's sales figure and in the 'purchasing' division's cost of sales. When consolidating the divisions' performance these transfers must be excluded in order to give a true figure for the sales to external organisations and purchases from external organisations.

EXAMPLE

A business has two divisions with the following summarised results for the last month:

	Division A	Division B
	£	£
Sales	108,000	155,000
Cost of sales	63,000	89,000
	45,000	66,000
Less: expenses	23,000	34,000
Net profit	22,000	32,000

During the month Division B transferred goods to Division A at a transfer price of £16,000.

Prepare the consolidated results for the month.

Solution

	Division A	Division B	Adjustments	Total
	£	£		
Sales	108,000	155,000	(16,000)	247,000
Cost of sales	63,000	89,000	(16,000)	136,000
	45,000	66,000		111,000
Less: expenses	23,000	34,000		57,000
Net profit	22,000	32,000		54,000

The interdivisional sale must be excluded from both sales and cost of sales as it has been recorded as a sale in Division B's books and as a purchase in Division A's books.

▷ ACTIVITY 4

Grand Hotel Group

Your company, the Grand Hotel Group, operates a chain of three hotels in Southern England. The group has been affected in recent years by the recession. The management of the group have been rather worried by the recent downturn in profitability and called in a firm of management consultants in mid 20X1.

As a result of the review by the management consultants, a programme was undertaken to restore profitability. This included the following actions:

(1) a reduction in the number of part-time staff with remaining staff put on a full-time basis

(2) a planned reduction in fixed charges (i.e. administrative expenses, rent, rates, etc)

(3) an organised marketing campaign to increase revenue from weekend and mid-week bargain breaks and conferences. The campaign was to emphasise the competitive pricing of such services and the campaign costs are included in other variable operating expenses.

The programme was implemented in the Autumn of 20X1 and the first results of it are shown in the 20X2 accounts. A summary of the accounts is given on the following page.

You have been asked by the hotel management to evaluate the success of the programme put forward by the management consultants' review.

Assume the hotels are open for 365 days each year and work to the nearest £.

Assessment tasks

Task 1

Calculate for 20X0, 20X1 and 20X2:

(a) net profit

(b) net profit as a percentage of turnover

(c) average staff costs

(d) turnover at year 1 (20X0) prices.

Write a short report highlighting any significant trends and drawing management's attention to items you consider worthy of consideration.

Task 2

(a) Calculate four different ratios for 20X0, 20X1 and 20X2 to evaluate the effectiveness of the programme implemented as a result of the management consultant's review summarising your findings in the form of a short report.

(b) What further information would help you to quantify the success of the programme introduced by the group?

The Grand Hotel Group

	20X0	20X1	20X2
	£	£	£
Turnover	3,200,000	2,910,000	3,600,000
Costs			
Food and beverages	240,000	220,000	400,000
Payroll and related expenses	720,000	680,000	660,000
Other variable operating expenses	220,000	200,000	380,000
Fixed charges (admin. expenses, rent, rates, etc)	1,800,000	1,800,000	1,700,000
Other information			
Number of employees (full-time equivalent)	140	130	115
Number of rooms	120	120	120
Number of rooms let	28,400	26,400	35,300
Retail Price Index	100	107	111
UK unemployment	5.3%	6.8%	9.2%
Average household disposable income	£19,050	£18,750	£18,250

[Answer on p. 145]

▷ ACTIVITY 5

BTC

Until three years ago, BTC, an accountancy training organisation, ran its own fleet of vans and delivered manuals to retailers and colleges. The decision was taken to concentrate on core activities and so several organisations were carefully considered before RD plc was selected to take on the responsibility for storing and delivering the manuals. It was agreed that RD would purchase the manuals from BTC at the recommended selling price, less an agreed discount. This ensures that RD would automatically benefit from future increases in the selling price of the manuals. The arrangement has worked well for both organisations and a good relationship has been established.

The managing director of RD has been satisfied with the profits that have been earned, but he is concerned with the efficiency of the transport operation. You, as the assistant accountant, have been asked to provide regular information to the general manager, who is responsible for all aspects of transportation. The general manager has always controlled this area by observing what he calls 'key ratios' which he sees as delivery costs and drivers' wages as a percentage of sales, sales per van and the number of deliveries. He believes that, if these ratios are improving, then the transport operation is working well. He is also a great believer that graphs help to clarify the statistics in any report.

Appendix 1

Years	**1**	**2**	**3**
Sales (£)	200,000	222,200	272,630
Van expenses (£)	14,000	15,000	18,000
As percentage of sales (%)	7	6.7	6.6
Drivers' wages (£)	52,000	56,600	68,150
As percentage of sales (%)	26	25.5	25
Number of vans	3	3	4
Sales per van (£)	66,667	74,067	68,158
Number of deliveries	1,000	1,100	1,400
Sales per delivery (£)	200	202	195

The accountant, although very interested in performance measures, is worried about the information in Appendix 1. His main concern is that the selling prices of the manuals have increased dramatically over the last two years. This was due to BTC's policy of initially pricing below the normal market price and then, once the manuals had been accepted by the market, increasing prices quite sharply. The accountant wants to remove these specific price rises from the figures before calculating the 'key ratios' and has produced the following index numbers of price changes based on Year 1.

Years	1	2	3
Sales	100	110	137
Van expenses	100	104	106

Drivers' wages have shown very little change during these years and can remain as per Appendix 1.

Task 1

Complete Appendix 2 below by:

(a) converting the actual figures for Years 2 and 3 (from Appendix 1) to Year 1 prices by using the price index given (calculations to the nearest £)

(b) calculating the 'key ratios' including sales per delivery £s (calculations to one decimal place).

Appendix 2

Years	**1**	**2**	**3**
Sales (£)	200,000		
Van expenses (£)	14,000		
As percentage of sales (%)	7		
Drivers' wages (£)	52,000	56,600	68,150
As percentage of sales (%)	26		
Number of vans	3	3	4
Sales per van (£)	66,667		
Number of deliveries	1,000	1,100	1,400
Sales per delivery (£)	200		

Task 2

Write a report to the general manager commenting upon the performance of the transport operation. The report should be in three sections.

Section 1: should explain whether the 'key ratios' in Appendix 1 support the general manager's opinion

Section 2: should explain whether the 'key ratios' in Appendix 2 indicate an efficient operation

Section 3: (a) should state whether you consider that the transport operation is efficient and whether Appendix 1 or Appendix 2 should be the basis of future reports, giving reasons for your decisions

(b) should also suggest one other 'key ratio' that should be observed (no calculation is required) and say how often this type of information should be presented.

[Answer on p. 146]

9 Test your knowledge

1. How might you measure the productivity of a customer complaints department?
2. What is the ratio standard hours : actual hours measuring?
3. How might you measure the utilisation of a gym in a health club which contains various aerobic machines such as treadmills, rowing machines, etc?
4. If a return on capital measure included profit before tax and interest as the numerator, what would you expect to see as the denominator?
5. If ROCE = 24.8% and net profit margin is 10 1/3 %, what is asset turnover?
6. Company A acquires part of Company B's manufacturing business in May 20X0. Company A makes up its accounts to 30 June. What impact might this acquisition have on Company A's ROCE?
7. What is the significance of the difference between traceable and controllable costs in performance evaluation?
8. Division A makes Product X at a cost of £5; it can then sell it to external customers (with unlimited demand) at £12 including post and packing of £2.50, or it can transfer it to Division B. At what price should the transfer be made to promote optimum decisions for the company as a whole?

[Answers on p. 148]

10 Summary

This chapter has covered all areas of internal reporting for organisational units. We started by looking at performance indicators covering cost per unit, productivity, resource utilisation and profitability. In particular we considered gross and net profit margins, return on capital employed and asset turnover and how these are all related.

The performance indicators considered can be calculated for an organisation as a whole or for separate areas or divisions of an organisation. If an organisation is divisionalised then this will provide further problems to consider. The assessment of a divisional manager's performance must be carefully assessed excluding head office costs and non-traceable or uncontrollable costs.

A final problem that was considered was the issue of transactions between divisions. If a transfer price is charged by one division providing goods or services to another then when the divisional results are consolidated the amount of the goods transferred in the period must be deducted from both sales and cost of sales.

Answers to chapter activities & 'test your knowledge' questions

△ ACTIVITY 1

Haulage accounting unit

(a) Tonne/mile or tonne/kilo
(b) Client hour charged
(c) Bed day; patient

△ ACTIVITY 2

The Snowy Ski Company

Part (a)

	Week 1	Week 2	Week 3	Week 4
Total actual hours				
South wales	16,582	18,860	20,070	19,226
Yorkshire	14,270	15,121	16,910	15,597
Ski units completed				
South Wales	1,200	1,350	1,400	1,300
Yorkshire	1,000	1,050	1,150	1,100
Hours per unit				
South Wales	13.8	14.0	14.3	14.8
Yorkshire	14.3	14.4	14.7	14.2

Part (b)

REPORT

To: Mr O'Hagan

From: An Accounting Technician

Subject: The efficiency of the South Wales and Yorkshire Factories

Performance was analysed over a four week period.

With the exception of week 4 the South Wales factory was consistently more efficient than the Yorkshire factory, generally taking 3% fewer hours overall to produce one ski unit. However, it should be pointed out that this 3% may not be significant if there are cost differences between the two factories, or indeed differences in equipment used.

The Yorkshire factory's actual labour hours also generally exceeded standard hours produced, the only exceptions being the Moulding

Department in week 2, the Assembly Department in week 1 and the Finishing Department in week 4.

The South Wales factory worked well in weeks 1 and 2 with overall favourable variances, but adverse variances for Moulding (week 1) and Finishing (week 2). Week 3 saw an overall adverse variance caused by a very high adverse variance in the finishing department. Week 4, however, saw extremely serious problems with large adverse variances in all departments. Clearly the large adverse variances require some explanation throughout, however, some measure of significance is required to judge which variances are large. 5 per cent of budget may be a suitable figure in this case.

In particular, the very high adverse variances in week 4 in South Wales require explanation. Was there a power failure or machine breakdown? Have labour conditions changed, or is there a regular monthly cycle of this nature? An explanation is also required into why Yorkshire seems to be relatively consistently worse than South Wales. Is it reasonable that the same budgeted labour hours apply to both factories or are conditions in each slightly different? Are the standards set in the Yorkshire factory correct or is the training regime different in Yorkshire?

The figures alone are insufficient to judge the overall performance of the factories. Qualitative information is also necessary.

△ ACTIVITY 3

Business Computers Ltd

Task 1

Business Computers Ltd
Table of ratios

Division	Ratio	20X4	20X5
Hardware - Commercial	Net profit/sales	17.5%	14.8%
	Development costs/sales	34.7%	40.0%
	Sales per employee	£22,107	£19,202
Hardware - Government	Net profit/sales	36.6%	35.5%
	Development costs/sales	30.9%	31.6%
	Sales per employee	£41,200	£40,804
Software & Consultancy	Net profit/sales	39.4%	48.5%
	Development costs/sales	21.7%	18.8%
	Sales per employee	£23,614	£26,875

Task 2

BUSINESS COMPUTERS LTD
REPORT ON DIVISIONAL PERFORMANCE

To: Financial Accountant

From: A Technician

Date: 18 June 20X6

The revenue for the Hardware Commercial division in 20X5 has declined from 20X4 as has the net profit/sales ratios. The development costs have risen and the sales per employee gone down.

Overall the results of the Hardware Commercial Department are alarming as each indicator is worse in 20X5 than in 20X4. The increase in the development/sales ratio and the decrease in the sales per employee show there is a pressure upon costs whilst the ability of staff to generate revenue is decreasing. This seems to be reflective of the increasingly changing and competitive nature of the market the company operates in.

The revenue for the Hardware Government division has declined in 20X5, as has the net profit/sales ratio slightly. The development costs over sales have increased and the sales per employee have gone down slightly. Overall the results for 20X5 are disappointing compared to 20X4, however, the changes are not as severe as the Hardware Commercial Department. Also analysis must be tempered by two factors; firstly that government spending restrictions might have cut back performance and secondly this division can be seen to act as a loss leader for the innovative software and consultancy division.

The Software and Consultancy division has had a good year. Sales are up, as is the net profit/sales ratio, development costs per sales are down and there is a marked improvement in sales per employee. The indicators are good but could they have been better?

Overall the company should concentrate upon the hardware government division which is connected to the highly profitable Software and Consultancy division. Long-term prospects also look good given government intentions. Looking at the financial data, the company should keep only a nominal presence in the Hardware Commercial market.

△ ACTIVITY 4

Grand Hotel Group

Task 1

	20X0	20X1	20X2
(a) Net profit (£)	220,000	10,000	460,000
(b) Net profit %	6.9%	0.3%	12.8%
(c) Average staff costs (£)	5,143	5,231	5,739
(d) Turnover at year 1 prices (£)	3,200,000	2,719,626	3,243,243

Report to the directors on recent financial trends

Net profit has moved from £220,000 in 20X0 to £10,000 in 20X1 through to a figure of £460,000 in 20X2. The net profit ratio has moved from 6.9% of sales in 20X0 through to a negligible 0.3% in 20X1 and on to a 12.8% net profit in 20X2.

The implementation of the programme does seem to have had a very beneficial effect upon profitability in 20X2. This can partly be explained by the fact that fixed costs seem to be recovered and any pricing policy above marginal cost will add to profit.

Average staff costs have moved gradually up from 20X0/X1 whilst there is nearly a 10% jump in 20X2 on the 20X1 figure (£5,231 to £5,739). It does seem that the rise in 20X1 might have initially been caused by a lack of control over labour costs and then maybe by higher rates for full-time employees for 20X2.

Sales in real terms have increased. The increase in sales in real terms in 20X2 compared with 20X0 is commendable given that average disposal income has fallen over the period and the unemployment rate has increased.

Task 2

Report to the directors on ratio analysis within the Grand Hotel Group

Part (a)

Total revenue	20X0	20X1	20X2
Room occupancy %	64.8%	60.3%	80.6%
Revenue per employee	£22,857	£22,385	£31,304
Profit before fixed charges as a percentage of revenue	63.1%	62.2%	60.0%
Average revenue per room let	£113	£110	£102

The programme does seem to have met its objectives as total revenue in 20X2 has increased by 24% over 20X1 and the net profit percentage has moved upwards to 13%. Also, whilst room occupancy fell from 64.8% in 20X0 to 60.3% in 20X1, it rose to 80.6% in 20X2.

Sales activity has increased in 20X2 whilst revenue per room has decreased, reflecting discounted tariffs. There appears to be a more efficient utilisation of staff as, whilst their basic rates have increased by just over 11% between 20X0 and 20X2, the sales per employee have gone up from £22,857 in 20X0 to £31,304 in 20X2.

Fixed costs have gone down by £100,000 which has increased profitability in 20X2. This could have been brought about by decreasing administration overheads. The profit before fixed charges as a percentage of revenue has declined from 63.1% in 20X2 to 62.2% in 20X1 and 60.0% in 20X2. This seems to be caused by the competitive pricing policy which had led to an increase in sales as stated above.

Part (b)

Additional useful information which could be provided includes the following:

- How is the hotel competing against industry average?
- What is the performance compared with budget?
- Information about how staff have adapted to change.
- Information about perception of services by customers.
- What are the results of the individual hotels?
- Break-down of revenue and costs for rooms and food and beverages

△ ACTIVITY 5

BTC

Task 1

Years	1	2	3
Sales (£)	200,000	202,000	199,000
Van expenses (£)	14,000	14,423	16,981
As percentage of sales	7	7.1	8.5
Drivers' wages (£)	52,000	56,600	68,150
As perentage of sales	26	28	34.2
Number of vans	3	3	4
Sales per van (£)	66,667	67,333	49,750
Number of deliveries	1,000	1,100	1,400
Sales per delivery (£)	200	183.6	142.1

Task 2

To: General Manager

From: Assistant Accountant

Subject: Transport operation **Date:** June 20X4

Section 1

(Note Appendixes 1 and 2 are in the question and answer to Task 1 and are not added to this report.)

1.1 In Appendix 1, attached to this report, are details of sales and main cost items relating to the above operation. 'Key ratios' have been calculated to assist in interpreting the performance.

1.2 Most of the 'key ratios' have improved: sales have increased and van expenses are down from 7% to 6.6% of sales, drivers' wages have similarly reduced from 26% to 25% and the number of deliveries has increased. The only hiccup is in the sales per van for year 3. However, as the new van was purchased during the year, a full year's use was not achieved.

1.3 On the basis of Appendix 1, the operation is working efficiently.

Section 2

2.1 In Appendix 2, also attached to this report, the same 'key ratios' were calculated and a different picture emerged. The reason for the difference from Appendix 1 is that specific price rises have been removed from the figures.

2.2 Sales have hardly changed during the three years. Van expenses and drivers' wages have both increased as a percentage of sales. Sales per van have fallen, indicating that the utilisation of vans is not as good as it used to be. The new 'key ratio' of sales per delivery is interesting as it indicates that smaller deliveries are being made than previously.

2.3 On the basis of Appendix 2, the operation is not working as efficiently as in year 1.

Section 3

3.1 The transport operation is not as efficient now as it used to be. There is a need to control van expenses and drivers' wages carefully. The fall in sales per delivery could mean that customers are ordering less (although sales have remained steady) or that we are not as efficient in planning our deliveries as we were. Did we need to buy the new van? Static sales could mean a lack of future potential in this sector.

3.2 I believe that, in the future, information of this nature should be produced regularly, at least monthly. Appendix 2 is the model that we should follow as it indicates the underlying quantity changes. One extra 'key ratio' that should be studied is miles per gallon achieved by the vans. This would indicate whether the vans were being efficiently maintained and driven and would also provide a deterrent to anyone attempting to steal petrol.

3.3 This report indicates areas that need investigation.

Test your knowledge

1 Complaints resolved: complaints received.

2 Efficiency (e.g. of labour).

3 Machine hours used: machine hours available (machines available x gym opening hours).

4 Total capital employed, i.e. equity + debt, as profit before interest will be split between these providers of capital.

5 ROCE (24.8%) = net profit margin ($10^1/_3$ %) x asset turnover.
Asset turnover = $24.8/10^1/_3$ = 2.4 times.

6 The capital employed is likely to rise with the increased asset base; however, there will only be one month's worth of profits included in the return. Thus, the ROCE is likely to fall.

7 Traceable costs, being all costs directly attributable to an organisational unit's existence, are used for unit appraisal; however, of these, only those controllable by the unit manager should be included in an appraisal of the manager's performance.

8 Adjusted market price, i.e. £12 - £2.50 = £9.50 (assuming A will not incur the P&P costs on internal transfers).

REPORTING TO EXTERNAL AGENCIES

INTRODUCTION

Element 7.2 of Unit 7 Preparing Reports and Returns covers the preparation of reports and returns for external agencies. The main types of external party for whom you may need to complete reports or returns are covered in this chapter. Most of the returns that you will need to complete in an assessment will be on pre-printed standard forms. Once the forms have been completed, it is important that they are authorised by relevant personnel before being dispatched to external agencies.

KNOWLEDGE AND UNDERSTANDING

- Main types of outside organisations requiring reports and returns: regulatory; grant awarding; information collecting; trade associations (Element 7.2)
- Main types of performance indicators: productivity; cost per unit; resource utilisation; profitability (Elements 7.1, 7.2)
- Ratios: gross profit margin; net profit margin; return on capital employed (Elements 7.1, 7.2)
- Background understanding that a variety of outside agencies may require reports and returns from organisations and that these requirements must be built into administrative and accounting systems and procedures (Elements 7.2, 7.3)

CONTENTS

PERFORMANCE CRITERIA

- Identify, collate and present relevant information in accordance with the conventions and definitions used by outside agencies (Element 7.2)
- Ensure calculations of ratios and performance indicators are accurate (Element 7.2)
- Obtain authorisation for the despatch of completed reports and returns from the appropriate person (Element 7.2)
- Present reports and returns in accordance with outside agencies' requirements and deadlines (Element 7.2)

1 External agencies requiring reports and returns

1.1 Introduction

Assessments may include a requirement to complete a form or report to an external agency. This will often require calculation of the types of performance indicators considered in the previous chapter and will normally consist of filling in a form with the relevant details.

1.2 Regulatory organisations

There are a number of regulatory organisations which will require regular and non-regular reports and returns. These include:

- HM Revenue & Customs – on a regular basis, organisations must send details of their employees' payroll details to HM Revenue & Customs detailing the Income Tax (PAYE) and National Insurance Contributions deducted from employees' gross pay
  Companies must also provide annual corporation tax returns and VAT returns (covered in detail in a later chapter).
- Department of Trade and Industry – companies must produce annual financial statements
- Health and Safety Executive, Training Commission, Local Authorities' Planning Departments – these government agencies often require non-financial information regarding the operations, employment policies and plans of the business
- Sector regulatory bodies – for example financial services organisations, banks and listed companies are required to submit regular returns concerning their operations and financial position to the appropriate regulatory body such as the FSA, The Bank of England and the Stock Exchange.

1.3 Grant awarding organisations

There are a variety of both government and privately funded schemes which make various awards and grants available to businesses. An example is the Enterprise Initiative Scheme run by the DTI to offer grants, information and advisory services to businesses.

In order to support any application for a grant the business will need to provide a range of both financial and non-financial information, including details of recent performance and profitability, details of the purpose to which the grant will be put, current and future employee details i.e. is the grant award due to provide opportunities for additional employment?

1.4 Information-collecting organisations

There are a number of agencies which collect information from businesses for analysis for their own purposes and for use by other interested parties, often including the organisations supplying the information.

Examples include:

- Office for National Statistics collects information for the compilation of reports and statistics on business performance, consumer expenditure patterns and social trends.
- General market survey organisations – the information required from such organisations is of course voluntary and you should ensure that you only ever provide such information if it is the policy of your organisation to do so.

1.5 Trade associations

☐ DEFINITION

Trade associations are bodies that represent and look after the interests of organisations in the same line of business such as the Publishers' Association or the Association of British Travel Agents (ABTA).

Trade associations conduct voluntary surveys of member businesses concerning such things as wage rates, employment practices, debtor levels, stock holding patterns, fixed asset utilisation and many others. This information is collated and is often put together in the form of an inter-firm comparison for this type of business. This inter-firm comparison is then provided to members in order that they can assess their own stock levels, debtor levels etc against the average, highest and lowest in their sector.

When providing information to trade associations it is likely that this will be required in the form of key ratios such as gross profit and net profit margins and return on capital employed. The trade association may also require information on cost per unit, productivity and resource utilisation. As well as this financial information the trade association may also require non-financial information regarding employment policies, customer profiles etc.

1.6 Nature of information required for external reports

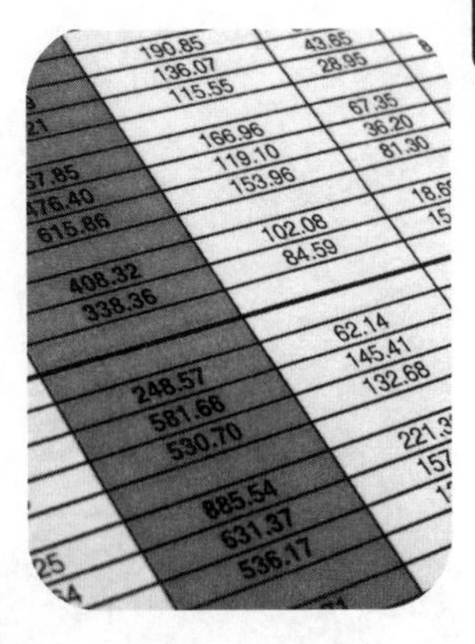

Most of the information required for external reports and returns will be in the form of performance indicators as covered in the previous chapter. There may also be some absolute figures required such as the year end debtor or creditor totals which can be found from the year end financial statements.

1.7 Problems of reporting for external agencies

As we have seen much of the information required for external reports and returns will be available from the normal accounting and administrative systems of the organisation, such as VAT, PAYE and NIC details. However some of the information required is specialised, such as financial statistics and non-financial data which may or may not be part of the organisation's own management accounting requirements.

Therefore there may be a need to set up special data collecting exercises or routines in order to pick up the relevant data and sort it as required for the particular report or return.

2 Standard forms

2.1 Introduction

Most of the returns that you will have to fill out for external agencies will be on pre-printed standard forms. This will make it more likely that the external agency will get the precise information that it requires in the correct format and that information provided by different organisations will be directly comparable.

2.2 Why use forms?

Forms can be a very efficient means by which routine data can be collected or information conveyed. Properly constructed forms will ensure that the **relevant** information at the **right level of detail** in the **required format** is given to the user.

They will generally be relatively **quick and easy to complete,** and are more likely to encourage prompt submission of the required information than if a fully written report were requested.

2.3 Principles of good form design

The qualities of a well-constructed form are outlined below. If you are aware of these it will help you when completing pre-printed forms.

2.4 Requirements

Requirements must be clearly explained and unambiguous

- Terminology must be **standardised** and explained on the back of the form if necessary.

- The **order of completion** of the form (if it matters) should be logical and clear.

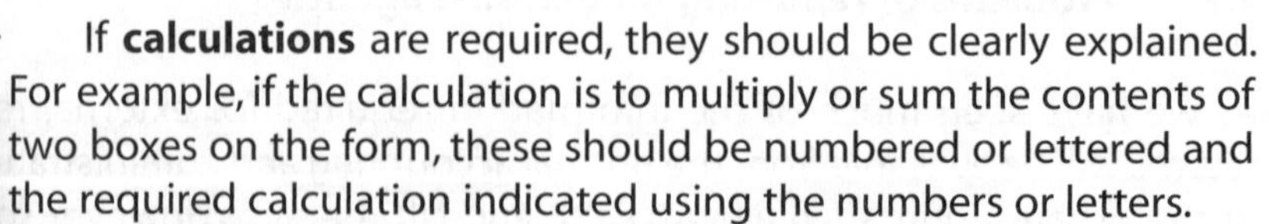

- If **calculations** are required, they should be clearly explained. For example, if the calculation is to multiply or sum the contents of two boxes on the form, these should be numbered or lettered and the required calculation indicated using the numbers or letters.

- If figures are to be given to a **particular level of accuracy** (say to the nearest £), this should be clearly indicated.

2.5 Contents

The amount of writing required should be minimised

- As much information as possible should be **pre-printed.**
- The use of **boxes to tick** or a choice of possible answers offered will cut down on the writing.

2.6 Destination

The destination of the completed form(s) should be clearly indicated

- A section indicating the **name and department or address** of the department or person to whom the form should be returned should be included on the form rather than on a separate accompanying letter or in a manual.
- If the form is multi-part, the **destination of each part** should be clearly shown.

2.7 Form-filling

When **completing a form,** either as part of your assessment, or in practice, you should remember the following points:

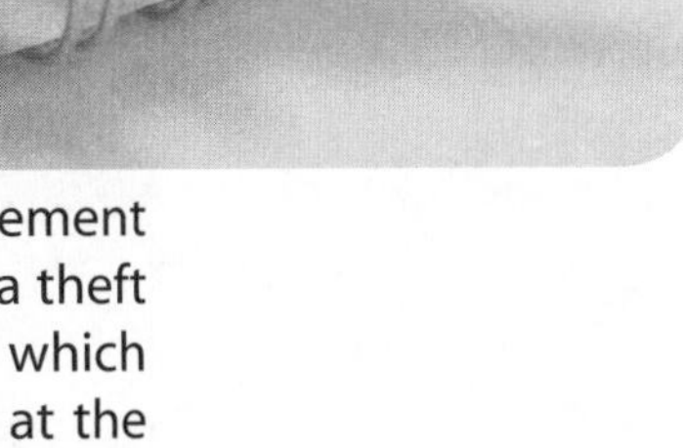

- Have a **quick look through the whole form first,** to ascertain what information will be required for its completion. It will also help to avoid information being given in the wrong place on the form.
- Ensure you **follow general instructions** regarding the method of completion (e.g. in pen, block capitals, figures to two decimal places, option numbers to be crossed through or circled etc).
- Keep **written responses as concise as possible,** preferably within the space provided. However, you should re-read the requirement to ensure you have answered all parts. For example, on a form for a theft insurance claim, you may be asked to explain the circumstances in which the theft took place 'including the exact location of the property at the time, the estimated time of theft, the mode of access and the nature of any security measures taken'.
- Ensure you have **completed all parts of the form.**

As part of an assessment you are likely to have to complete a form for an external agency. This is largely a matter of common sense and following instructions.

▷ ACTIVITY 1

NTL plc

The Toy Manufacturer's Trade Association was established several years ago to assist its member companies with legal/administrative matters and to provide an advisory service. You are employed by the Trade Association and are mainly involved with the advisory service. One of the services offered is an inter-firm comparison which involves collecting quarterly information from its member companies. After analysis, the best and average results are supplied to all participating firms but no company names are revealed. It is up to each company to compare their own results with the figures provided and to decide what action needs to be taken. NTL plc, a new company to this service, asks for your help as it does not understand what calculations it needs to do or what conclusions to draw. The most recent figures for NTL plc are as follows:

Trading and profit and loss a/c for quarter to 30 September 20X3

	£	£
Sales		653,000
Materials	361,109	
Labour	80,319	
Production overheads	108,398	
Production cost		549,826
Distribution and marketing		18,937
Administration		44,404
Total cost		613,167
Net profit		39,833

Balance sheet as at 30 September 20X3

	£	£
Fixed assets		185,729
Current assets		
Stock	92,046	
Debtors	56,192	
	148,238	
Current liabilities		
Creditors	48,075	
Overdraft	40,009	
	88,084	
Working capital		60,154
Capital employed		245,883

Assessment tasks

Task 1

Complete the form below by calculating the inter-firm ratios for NTL plc (calculations to one decimal place).

Toy Manufacturer's Trade Association

Inter-firm comparison report, Quarter to 30 September 20X3

	Most profitable	*Average*	*NTL plc*
Direct materials as a percentage of sales	46.9	52.6	
Dlerct labour as a percentage of sales	10.4	10.1	
Production overheads as a percentage of sales	14.0	16.9	
Production cost as a percentage of sales	71.3	79.6	
Distribution and m,arketing as a percentage of sales	4.9	3.8	
Administration as a percentage of sales	5.6	5.7	
Net profit as a percentage of sales	18.2	10.9	
Net profit as a percentage of capital employed	40.4	22.6	
Current ratio (current assets to current liabilities)	2.2 to 1	1.9 to 1	
Quick ratio (debtors to current liabilities)	1.1 to 1	0.9 to 1	

Task 2

Write a report to the managing director of NTL plc explaining the main differences revealed in Task 1. Comment on both the profitability and the financial position of the company, suggesting areas for further investigation and possible corrective action.

Task 3

The managing director is under pressure from the other managers to spend £20,000 on an advertising campaign, which it is believed would increase sales by 10%. An investigation into production overheads has shown that £32,658 was variable and £75,740 was fixed. To test out the proposed advertising campaign you are asked to:

(a) Recalculate the trading and profit and loss account to 30 September 20X3. Assume that material, labour and variable production overheads increase at the same rate as sales (calculations to the nearest £). (A blank form is given below.)

Re-worked trading and profit and loss account for quarter to 30 September 20X3

	£
Sales	
Materials	
Labour	
Variable production overheads	
Fixed production overheads	
Production cost	
Distribution and marketing (fixed)	
Advertising campaign (fixed)	
Administration (fixed)	
Total cost	
Net profit	

(b) Write a brief report to the managing director explaining whether or not the advertising campaign is justified. [Answer on p. 158]

3 Accuracy and authority

3.1 Introduction

When preparing a report to an external agency you will be providing someone outside the organisation with important information about your own organisation. Therefore it is extremely important that all information is accurate and that the report or return is authorised before being sent out.

3.2 Accuracy

When completing a return or report it is essential that the information required is accurate.

· If there are any instructions or formulae given for calculation or performance indicators, ensure that you use precisely the figures that are requested.

· Check that you have picked out the correct figures from your organisation's data, for example if asked for the balance of debtors at 30 June 20X0 you should not be providing the debtors' balance at 31 July 20X0.

· Check and double check all calculations that you have made on the report or return.

3.3 Deadlines

Ensure that the report or return is completed, ready for authorisation well before the stated deadline for the report or return. This is particularly important for returns to regulatory bodies such as HM Revenue and Customs as a late return can result in a fine for the organisation.

3.4 Authorisation

No report or return should ever be sent out without authorisation from the appropriate person within the organisation. You are providing outside parties with details of your organisation and only senior management will be able to judge whether this is appropriate.

4 Test your knowledge

1 What is a trade association, and what sort of information does it require from its members?

2 Give four principles of good form design. [Answer on p. 160]

5 Summary

In this chapter we have considered the general requirements of external agencies which might require a report or a return from your organisation. Normally the return required will be on a pre-printed form with clear instructions as to how to complete the form and the precise information that is required. Most figures will be in the form of either the standard performance indicators considered in the previous chapter or performance indicators that are clearly defined on the form itself.

Answers to chapter activities & 'test your knowledge' questions

△ ACTIVITY 1

NTL plc

Task 1

Toy Manufacturer's Trade Association
Inter-firm comparison report, Quarter to 30 September 20X3

	Most profitable	*Average*	*NTL plc*
Direct materials as a percentage of sales	46.9	52.6	55.3
Direct labour as a percentage of sales	10.4	10.1	12.3
Production overheads as a percentage of sales	14.0	16.9	16.6
Production cost as a percentage of sales	71.3	79.6	84.2
Distribution and marketing as a percentage of sales	4.9	3.8	2.9
Administration as a percentage of sales	5.6	5.7	6.8
Net profit as a percentage of sales	18.2	10.9	6.1
Net profit as a percentage of capital employed	40.4	22.6	16.2
Current ratio (current assets to current liabilities)	2.2 to 1	1.9 to 1	1.7 to 1
Quick ratio (debtors to current liabilities)	1.1 to 1	0.9 to 1	0.6 to 1

Task 2

To: Managing Director, NTL plc

From: Admin. Assistant, Toy Manufacturers' Trade Association

Subject: Inter-firm ratios **Date:** December 20X3

(1) The comparison report for the last quarter has been completed and is attached to this report.

(2) NTL plc has not had a good quarter. Its ROCE is below the average and well below the 'best' company.

(3) Profit to sales is poor and the biggest influence is production cost. Both material and labour costs are high and an examination of the buying policy and grade of labour employed should be undertaken. Scrap rates and labour efficiency should also be studied.

(4) A significant ratio is that of distribution and marketing to sales. This is rather low and could indicate that more effort and resources need to be committed to marketing.

(5) If an increase in sales could be achieved, then the production overheads and administration overheads ratios could both improve. Certain costs in these areas have to be incurred irrespective of activity achieved.

(6) The financial ratios give some cause for concern. The current ratio indicates that it may be difficult to finance working capital in the near future. The quick ratio is worrying because NTL plc is not able to pay its short-term debts at the moment.

(7) If the bank is not prepared to increase the overdraft, then another source of finance needs to be found. There is a need to control stocks and to retain profits within the company. This matter needs immediate attention.

Task 3

Part (a)

Re-worked trading and profit and loss account for quarter to 30 September 20X3

	£	£	£
Sales			718,300
Materials		397,220	
Labour		88,351	
Variable production overheads	35,924		
Fixed production overheads	75,740		
		111,664	
Production cost			597,235
Distribution and marketing (fixed)			18,937
Advertising campaign (fixed)			20,000
Administration (fixed)			44,404
Total cost			680,576
Net profit			37,724

Part (b)

To: Managing Director

From: Admin. Assistant **Ref:**

Subject: Proposed advertising campaign **Date:** 3 December 20X3

(1) The marketing area was mentioned in my previous report as one which should be expanded. The suggestion of an advertising campaign is to be welcomed.

(2) The purpose of the campaign is to increase sales, which it is expected to do, but it is essential that profits also should be increased. The re-worked accounts (Appendix 1) indicate that profits would be reduced.

(3) The proposed campaign is thus not acceptable but it needs to be reconsidered, not necessarily abandoned. Alternative proposals should be discussed with the major aim being to increase profits.

(4) Before commencing any campaign, it is important that funds are available.

Test your knowledge

1 A trade association is an organisation run on behalf of businesses in a particular trade sector, e.g. the construction industry, insurance sector, small retailers, etc. It gathers information on wage levels, resource utilisation, key ratios, etc which is collated into an inter-firm comparison for use by its members.

2 Unambiguous requirements.
Use of boxes to tick.
Destination(s) of form(s) clearly shown.
Level of accuracy required.

SPREADSHEETS

INTRODUCTION

It is a requirement of Unit 7 that you should be able to produce information for reports using spreadsheets. Here we will consider how to set up, run and produce output from a spreadsheet.

For those unfamiliar with spreadsheet packages, this chapter will provide the basic introduction needed to feel confident to 'get into' Microsoft Excel and carry out simple tabulation tasks. This package has been chosen because it is the most popular and therefore the most likely to be used in your college or work environment. The editions and programs that you are using may not be the same as those used in this text. In that case, the screens you produce will not be identical to those shown here. However, all spreadsheet packages will perform the basic functions covered in this chapter and access to a different package will not cause too many problems.

If you are at all unsure, you should read the manual that accompanies your chosen spreadsheet.

KNOWLEDGE AND UNDERSTANDING

- Tabulation of accounting and other quantitative information using spreadsheets (Elements 7.1, 7.2)

CONTENTS

1 The use of spreadsheets

1.1 What is a spreadsheet used for?

Much of the data of a company is likely to be held on a number of spreadsheets. They are a convenient way of setting up all sorts of charts, records and tables, including:

- profit and loss accounts
- sales forecasting
- budgeting charts
- breakeven point analysis
- mortgage payments
- stock valuation
- exchange rate charts.

Spreadsheets can be used for anything with a rows and columns format.

1.2 Spreadsheets

A spreadsheet is used to manipulate data. You could define it as a table of rows and columns that intersect to form cells. Each row is identified by a number and each column by a letter (or letters). Each cell has a unique identifier formed by a letter (or letters) and a number.

The word **spreadsheet** has its origins in the large sheets of paper used by accountants, over which they spread their figures and calculations in neat rows and columns. The little boxes made by the horizontal and vertical lines have their counterpart in the PC's spreadsheet and are called **cells.**

Into these cells may be entered numbers, text or a **formula.** Formulae are not visible when you are entering data but reside in the background. A formula normally involves a mathematical calculation on the content of other cells, the result being inserted in the cell containing the formula.

The size of spreadsheets, in terms of the number of columns and rows, varies greatly between packages. Spreadsheets with millions of cells are possible. Because most business worksheets are quite large, extending beyond the edge of the computer screen, the screen is in effect a 'window' into the worksheet. Some or all of the spreadsheet can be printed out directly or saved on disk for insertion into reports or other documents using a word processing package.

The power of these systems is that the data held in any one cell on the 'paper' can be made dependent on that held in other cells, so changing a value in one cell can set off a chain reaction of changes through other related cells. This means that a model can be built in which the effect of changing key parameters may be observed (so called 'what if?' analysis).

Three-dimensional spreadsheets have the advantage of consolidation that the two dimensional ones do not have. An example to highlight this facility might be sales figures by region, where the top sheet (All products) might be a total of the sales of all the products that the company has (whilst Products 1 to 4 have separate sheets behind).

1.3 Graphics

Spreadsheet packages tend to offer more than just a spreadsheet; in particular, they usually include the option to create **graphics.**

'A picture is worth a thousand words' is especially true when it comes to numbers; a spreadsheet is no exception. Since a column of numbers can be difficult to interpret, a graphical representation can help decipher the information. Spreadsheets give you the ability to choose the part of the worksheet that you want to illustrate, and will graph the figures to your specification or represent them in some other graphical form such as a pie chart.

2 Accessing a spreadsheet

2.1 Excel

In the instructions that follow you will be using the Excel for Windows® (or similar) package to create a worksheet, make calculations, enter formulae and copy data.

The following should be read and attempted in full if you are unfamiliar with the use of spreadsheets. If you are confident using spreadsheets check through the notes and exercises for any areas you may not have covered previously.

If you do not have access to Excel it will be assumed that you can use a similar package and you should refer to your manual for the basic mouse clicks.

As you are introduced to more commands, the worksheet will provide more information and give you a way to make business forecasts, called the 'What if?' analysis. When you have completed your report, you will print out a copy to present to your manager.

2.2 Running the program

The way to gain access to the spreadsheet package depends upon the type of computer system in use. A menu may be available to allow access to the chosen software by entering a single number or letter or by use of a cursor or mouse.

If you are using the spreadsheet at work, you must check first with your supervisor that it is allowed and that you are using the right version of the software.

If you are working in a **Windows** environment, you will access the spreadsheet package using the mouse. Click on the Start button in the bottom left hand corner of the Window. Keeping the mouse button depressed move to highlight

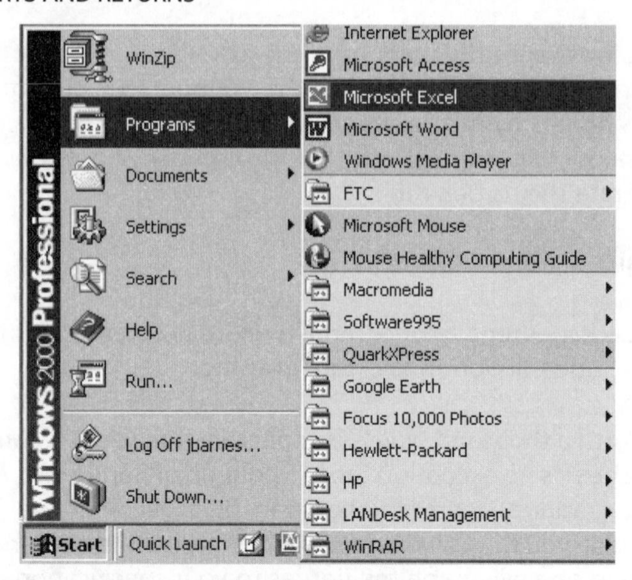

the 'Programs' and then to the package that you want to use. Click on the icon.The opening screen in Microsoft Excel might look like this:

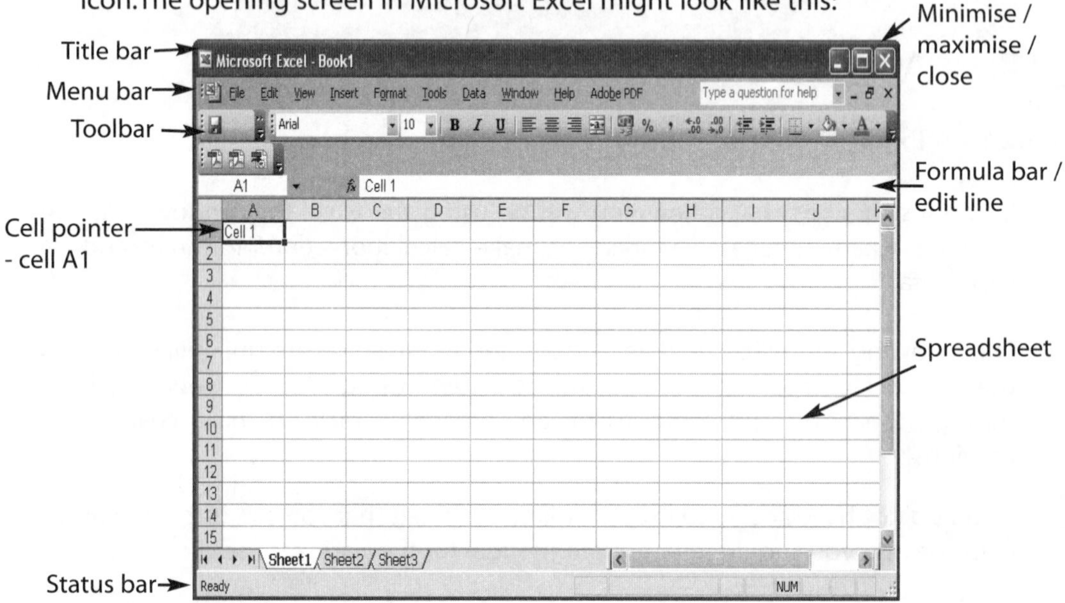

(Yours may be slightly different if you have another version of Excel.)

On the screen you will see the **title bar,** the **menu bar, the function toolbar** and in the top right corner the buttons to **minimise, maximise**/restore and close the worksheet. As with most Windows programs you can change the size and move the Excel Window.

If your screen does not have a formula bar, a formatting bar or a toolbar you can show these by accessing **View** and then Toolbars from the menu at the top of the screen. You can then select (or deselect) what you want to show on the screen. A tick signifies that it is switched on.

The toolbars are below the menu bar. Clicking on any of these buttons provides a shortcut to selecting options from the menu bar. If you pause the pointer over a button a label will appear and, in the **status bar,** Excel will tell you what that button does.

The formula bar is between the spreadsheet and the toolbar. This provides you with information about the contents of the active cell. The co-ordinates of the active cell are displayed on the left-hand side of the format bar.

The status bar is at the bottom of the screen. It gives you information about your spreadsheet, such as when you are opening or saving a file and whether you have CAPS LOCK, NUM LOCK or SCROLL LOCK on.

Scroll bars are used to move your spreadsheet both up and down and left to right. The vertical scroll bar (on the right hand side of the spreadsheet) is used to move up and down. The horizontal scroll bar (below the spreadsheet and above the status bar) is used to move left and right.

2.3 Vocabulary

The spreadsheet is now ready to go to work, but first you will need to know some basic terms and some spreadsheet vocabulary, so that you can give instructions.

- **Worksheet:** a worksheet or spreadsheet (as shown above) is the basis of all the work you do. It could be considered to be the electronic equivalent of an accountant's ledger.
- **Workbook:** is a collection of worksheets. The workbook is simply a folder that binds together your worksheets. When you open a new workbook, it automatically contains 16 worksheets.
- **Cells:** the worksheet is divided into columns and rows. The intersection of a column and a row is known as a 'cell'. To refer to a particular cell, use its column and row location. This is called a 'cell address', for example A1, B22, etc.
- **Columns:** each column is referenced by one or two letters in the column heading. The whole worksheet consists of 256 columns, labelled A through IV.
- **Rows:** each row is referenced by the row number shown in the row heading to the left of a row. There are 65,536 rows in Excel.
- **Sheet tabs:** these are between the worksheet and the status bar and are used to move between worksheets in your workbook.
- **Window:** you can only see part of the worksheet at any time; you could consider the screen to be a window onto the worksheet. You have the facility to move this window, so that you can view any part of the spreadsheet.
- **Cell pointer:** look at the cell that is highlighted; this highlighted area is known as the cell pointer. It indicates the cell in which you are currently working. The current cell location is also displayed on the edit line above the spreadsheet.

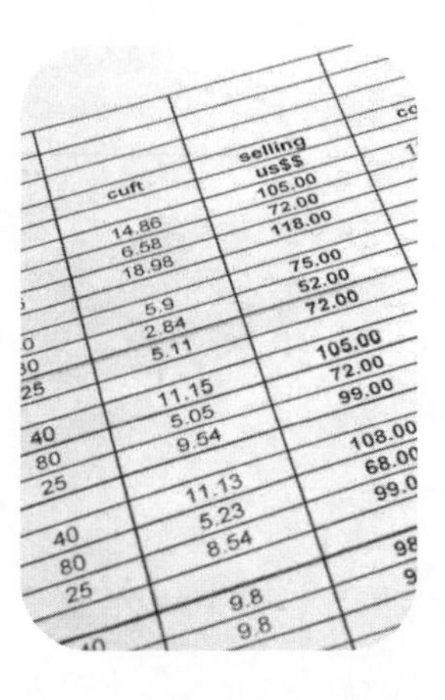

2.4 Creating and saving a new file

When you first open Excel, a blank spreadsheet appears on the screen and you can start typing straight away. At this point you can work on an established

spreadsheet or start on a new one by creating a file as described below.
From the file menu choose the NEW option, and a new Excel workbook will appear on the screen. Once you have created a document, you must save it if you wish to use it in the future. To save a file:

- From the **FILE** menu choose the **SAVE AS** option.
- A dialogue box will appear.
- If necessary, use the DRIVE drop down menu to select the relevant drive.
- In the FILE NAME text box type in the name you wish to use. All spreadsheet packages automatically add a three-digit extension to your filename. In Lotus it will begin with wk and in Excel it will begin with xl.
- Click on the **OK** button.

When you have saved a file once, you do not need to choose the **SAVE AS** option again, but simply choose **SAVE** from the **FILE** menu or click on the icon on the toolbar (picture of a floppy disk).

2.5 Closing a file/Quitting

When you have finished working on a spreadsheet and you have saved it, you will need to close it down. You can do this by either pressing the button at the top right hand side of the worksheet with a cross on it or by choosing the CLOSE or EXIT option from the FILE menu.

If you only want to exit Excel briefly and prefer not to close down the whole package you can switch to another application or back to the Windows Program Manager by pressing <Alt><Tab> repeatedly. This allows you to step through all the opened packages in rotation.

If you have changed the file, Excel will ask if you wish to save the changes you made before closing. Click on the appropriate button.

3 Moving around the spreadsheet

3.1 Cell pointer

The whole worksheet consists of many columns and rows. On opening the spreadsheet, you can only see a small part of it - generally columns A to H and rows 1 to 16. The screen is like a window onto the worksheet and you have the facility to move this window so that you can view any part of the worksheet. The cell pointer highlights the cell you are currently in.

By moving the cell pointer you are able to enter information into any cell of the worksheet. There are a number of ways of moving the cell pointer, but the easiest way is to use the mouse. You can move around the spreadsheet by positioning the **mouse pointer** over the appropriate cell and clicking to select that cell. If the cell address you want is outside the range shown in the current window, it is possible to move down or across the spreadsheet by clicking on the scroll bars to the side or below the Window. Alternatively, you can use the arrow keys on the keyboard.

3.2 Moving directly to a cell: the GOTO command

Sometimes we want to move to a specific address in the spreadsheet that is too far from our present position to warrant using the arrow keys to get there. On the top of the keyboard you can see a row of keys labelled F1 through to F12; these are known as 'function keys'. When these keys are pressed, a special function is invoked. For the moment we will explore the F5 key. This is the **GOTO key** in both Excel and Lotus 123.

Let us assume you wished to go to D19. Press F5 and a dialogue box appears. You are prompted to enter an address or range. Enter D19 and the cell pointer will go directly to cell D19.

Try moving around your worksheet now. You can find where the end is because the spreadsheet will beep whenever you attempt to go beyond the worksheet boundaries.

▷ ACTIVITY 1 

What is the biggest co-ordinate in your worksheet? [Answer on p. 181]

3.3 The help facility

Excel has a comprehensive help facility, which provides both general help and context sensitive help.

To invoke the help command press the 'Help' button on the menu bar, the ? box on the toolbar or, alternatively, the shortcut key F1. To obtain information on any particular subject shown, move the mouse pointer over the required topic and click (or you may be prompted to type in a question).

Context sensitive help is available either when a help button is displayed in a dialogue box or when an error message is flashed onto the screen. Asking for help at this stage by either clicking on the help button, ? box or by pressing F1 will result in the help window appearing at the topic relevant to the problem encountered.

4 Entering data

4.1 Putting data onto the worksheet

Entering data on the worksheet is very easy. You simply type your entry at the keyboard, press return and whatever you typed will be placed in the current cell, i.e. where the cell pointer is.

As you type, each character will be displayed on the edit line at the top of the screen. The entry is not put onto the worksheet until you press the return key.

Move to cell A1. Type ABCDEF <Enter>
Now move to Cell A3. Type 123 <Enter>

When you have finished entering data you can either press the <Enter> key on the keyboard or click on the Enter Box (a green tick) on the formula bar.

If you change your mind about entering the data then either press the <Esc> key on the keyboard or click on the Cancel Box (a red cross) on the formula bar. If you have made a mistake, you can press the 'backspace key' (the key above the ENTER key) to delete what you have done one character at a time. If you have already pressed the ENTER key, you can delete it by highlighting the cell or cells and pressing the Delete key.

There are three types of data that can be entered into your worksheet – text, numbers and formulae.

4.2 Entering text

Text is entered by simply typing into a cell. Typing any letter at the beginning of a cell entry causes it to be accepted as a 'label', rather than a 'value'. If the text you enter is longer than the width of the cell then the text will 'run over' into the next cell. But if the next cell also contains data/information then you will only see part of the text you entered, i.e. the label will be truncated.

There will be times when you want the spreadsheet to treat a number or a formula as text. To do this you must type an apostrophe in front of the number or formula you are entering, e.g. '01707 320903 or '=A4+D5.

4.3 Entering numbers

Numbers can be entered on the spreadsheet by simply typing into a cell. If the space in the cell is insufficient, the number will be shown in an exponential form on the spreadsheet, but the number will still be retained in full in the formula bar. If you want to see the contents of cells in full, the columns can be widened to accommodate the number (or text).

It is not necessary to put the commas in manually when entering large numbers (1,000 or more), because it is easy to format the data to display commas and decimal places to make the data easier to understand.

▷ ACTIVITY 2

You are required to set up a spreadsheet to represent the data shown below. Leave the blank cells blank.

Employees and wages of Bunny & Hutch Ltd – 20X4

	Number of employees			Average weekly wage £	Total annual wage bill £
	1 January	31 December	Average		
Men	2,088	2,124		121.32	
Women	1,871	1,860		87.93	
Total					

[Answer on p. 181]

4.4 Entering formulae

The arithmetic operations and method of writing the basic formulae are very similar in all packages.

The **BODMAS (Brackets, Of, Division, Multiplication, Addition, Subtraction) rule** must be used to evaluate an arithmetic problem:

- Use brackets to clarify the correct order of operation and evaluate expressions within the brackets first.
- Calculate 'of' expressions (e.g. 20% of the total).
- Perform division and multiplication before addition and subtraction.
- Work from left to right if the expression contains only addition and subtraction.

The basic commands for **statistical functions** that calculate lists of values are also very similar throughout the range of spreadsheet packages. Examples of these are:

SUM	The sum of the values in list
AVG	The average of the values in list
COUNT	The number of non-blank entries in list
MAX	The maximum value in list
MIN	The minimum value in list

A formula always starts with an equal sign (=) in Excel. If you start it with an equal sign (=) in Lotus 123, it automatically converts it to a plus (+) sign. Formulae consist of numbers, cell co-ordinates (e.g. A2, F7), operators and functions. Operators perform actions on numbers and co-ordinates. Examples of operators are plus, minus, divide and multiply. Functions perform more advanced actions on numbers and co-ordinates.

To enter a formula:

- Select the cell where you want to enter the formula.
- Press the equal sign (=) on the keyboard or click on the sign in the formula bar, if you have one.
- Key in the formula directly from the keyboard or use the mouse to select the cells you want in the formula. There are no spaces in a formula.
- Press the <Enter> key.

When you have entered a formula, the resulting value appears in that cell. The formula is only visible in the formula bar.

Typical formulae:

=(A6+C10)-E25	Adds A6 with C10 and subtracts E25
=(H19*A7)/3	Multiplies H19 with A7 and divides the total by 3
=SUM(L12:L14)	A quick way of adding L12 + L13 + L14

An even quicker way to add a row or column of numbers is to click the +1 2 3 button in the toolbar for Lotus 1-2-3.

The equivalent button in MS Excel is the Greek symbol sigma Σ .

4.5 What to do if you make a mistake

If you enter data incorrectly and you notice the error before pressing the return key then you can use the backspace key, which deletes characters from the entry, working from right to left. For example, let us assume that you wanted to enter the label 'Costs' into cell C1, but instead typed 'Cists'.

- Move cell pointer to C1
- Type Cists (do not press the return key)
- Press backspace key five times
- Type Costs
- Press the return key and 'Costs' will now appear in C1

Another method you can use if you notice the error before pressing **Enter** is to press the **Esc** key. The program will cancel what you have entered and return you to the Ready mode. You then simply re-key.

If you spot the error after you have pressed the **Enter** key then you could simply retype the entry, press **Enter** and the current contents of the cell will be replaced with this entry. For example, if you wished to change the contents of cell C1 from 'Costs' to read 'Total', simply re-key the entry.

- Ensure the cell pointer is still at C1
- Type Total
- Total will now appear in C1

It would be frustrating if you had completed a long entry, spotted an error, and had to re-key the whole entry again. The spreadsheet comes to your aid with F2 – the **Edit** key.

Move the cell pointer to the cell containing the error, press F2. You will be put into **Edit** mode. The contents of the cell will be displayed on the edit bar with the cursor placed after the last character of the entry. You may then use the following editing features.

- Arrow Left – will move the cursor one character to the left
- Arrow Right – will move the cursor one character to the right
- Home – will move the cursor to the first character of the entry
- End – will move the cursor to the last character of the entry

To Insert/Overwrite/Delete a character:

- **Insert** <Ins> – will allow you to insert a character where the cursor is placed. The characters to the right of the cursor are moved to the right. It is a toggle key; you press once to go into overtype mode and press again to return to **Insert** mode. When in overtype mode, the cursor is replaced by the letter being highlighted.
- **Delete** <Del> – will delete the character under the cursor.

4.6 Selecting a range in Excel

When you select items to cut or copy it is usual to select a large range rather than a specific word or cell. This can be done in the following way.

Keyboard – move to the first cell (usually top left hand corner of selection) and hold down the shift key. Use your other hand to move to the last cell (bottom right) using the arrow keys. You will notice the selection expanding on the screen. Once you have covered the cell intended you can release both keys and proceed.

Mouse – using the mouse pointer move to the first cell in the selection, press the left hand mouse button and hold down. Move the mouse pointer to the last cell and then release the button.

If you are copying a range of cells to a new location then you will be asked to specify their new position. This can be done by clicking in the cell that you wish to be the first cell (i.e. the top left).

4.7 Basic data entry

In Excel, open a new blank worksheet and enter the following data. Leave plenty of space so that the titles are distinct. You will probably be putting the first invoice number in row 6.

Sales Invoices	**August 20X0**		
Invoice	**Firm**	**Items**	**Price**
1001	AB Plastics Ltd	10	0.2
1002	J Cables Ltd	21	0.2
1003	DC Covers Ltd	45	0.2
1004	DC Covers Ltd	42	0.2
1005	J Cables Ltd	500	0.2
1006	AB Plastics Ltd	25	0.2
1007	J Hoggs Ltd	300	0.2
1008	L Quick Ltd	1000	0.2
1009	DC Covers Ltd	50	0.2
1010	AB Plastics Ltd	12	0.2
1011	AB Plastics Ltd	15	0.2
1012	J Hoggs Ltd	350	0.2
1013	L Quick Ltd	1500	0.2
1014	J Hoggs Ltd	400	0.2
1015	L Quick Ltd	1250	0.2
1016	DC Covers Ltd	90	0.2
1017	F Browns Ltd	48	0.2
1018	L Quick Ltd	500	0.2
1019	F Browns Ltd	52	0.2
1020	F Browns Ltd	25	0.2

Adding basic formulae

Excel allows you to build up mathematical formulae to perform many useful functions, e.g. add up data, find average values, produce variances, add or subtract VAT, etc.

It has the capability of producing complex analyses and as your experience grows you can pick up more of these using a manual or the on-screen help function.

We will look at building up some basic formulae, which are commonly used in financial spreadsheets. In this exercise, we are going to calculate the Net price, the VAT and the Gross. You need to add three more columns after Price and label them – NET, VAT and Gross respectively.

(a) **Multiply** – in the 'Net' column we are going to put a formula to multiply the Items by the Price.
- Click on first entry in Net column (E6 probably)
- Type an = in the formula bar
- Click on first entry in the Items column (or type the address in – C6 probably)
- Type a * (to multiply)
- Click on first entry in the Price column (D6 probably)
- Press <Return> or OK

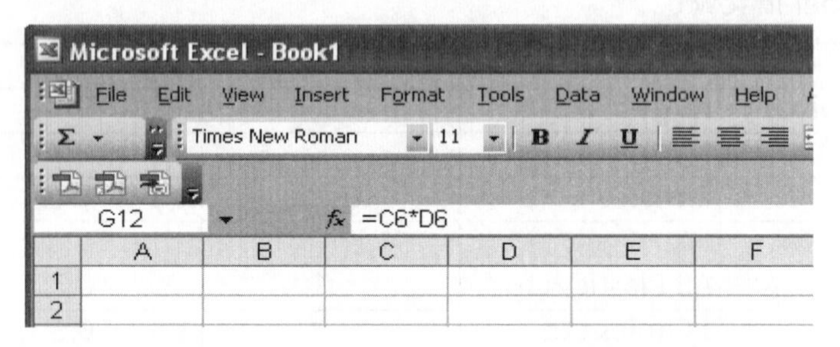

(b) Using the same type of multiply formula in the VAT column (F6 probably), calculate the VAT on the Net figure: this will be =E6*0.175.

(c) **Add** – we want to add the VAT to the Net to give us the Gross figure in G6
- Click on G6
- Type an = in the formula bar (or click on the = sign)
- Click on E6
- Type a +
- Click on F6
- Press <Return> or OK

(d) Another useful function is SUM. This can be used to total a list of values in a row or column without specifying each one individually.
We need to copy these formulae to the rest of the entries in the work-sheet before we can total the columns.

4.8 Copying

Shown below are the Cut, Copy and Paste buttons toolbar at the top of the screen on both Excel (left) and Lotus.

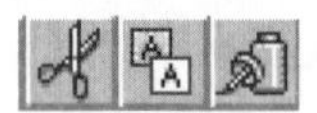

If you can't find all of these on your toolbar, click on the >> button – this will display more buttons.

Cut then **paste** is used to move cells from one area of the spreadsheet to another.

Copy then **paste** is used to copy cells from one area to another.

Copying and pasting or cutting and pasting operations always have two parts:

- define the range you want to copy or cut **from,** then
- define the range that you want to copy or move **to.**

Click on cell D5 and key in '£, press Enter. Go back to D5 and click on the 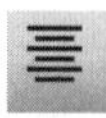 button to place the text in the centre of the cell.

This is the range you want to copy from. (Here the range is a single cell.)

Click the copy button on the toolbar (next to scissors). The border of D5 will start to shimmer.

Position the cursor over cell D5, hold down the mouse button and drag to the right until cells D5 to G5 have been highlighted (D5 will be white, E5 to G5 will be black or blue). This is the range to copy to.

Click on the paste button on the toolbar. The '£' sign has been copied from D5 and should now appear in E5 to G5.

You can copy formulae to different cells by the same method. Try to copy the formula from E6 to E25. Then from F6 to F25 and G6 to G25.

Note that the cell references change automatically when formulae are copied.

5 Improving the spreadsheet's appearance

5.1 Finishing the spreadsheet

We are going to tidy up the spreadsheet and finish with the totals in row 27 and the averages in row 29.

- In E27 we are going to total the column of values in cells E6 to E25.
- In E27 type =SUM(
- Click in E6 and look in the cell value bar. It should now read =SUM(E6
- Type : to indicate a range, then click on cell E25 and type)
- Press <Return> or OK

The answer to the sum of the cell values should appear in cell E27. Label this row.

All formulae can be entered by a combination of typing and using the pointer.

- **Note.** A shortcut to summary values is to use the Σ symbol from the toolbar.
- Try this in columns F and G. In F27 click on Σ and press enter. Excel will automatically total the numbers in the cells above.

- Another useful function is =AVERAGE. This will average cell values in a range specified using the pointer as for =SUM.

- Try this in E29, F29 and G29.

5.2 Formatting numbers

To make your monetary data look clearer, we need to format it to currency amounts. To do this for each column with a '£' at the top (probably D, E, F and G):

- Highlight the column of figures to be formatted (e.g. E6 to E27).
- Click on 'Format' in the menu bar and pick option 'cells'.
- On the 'Category' list choose 'Currency' – you will probably see it automatically assigning a '£' and 2 decimal places. Choose 'OK'.
- Each monetary amount should now appear as '£2.00', etc.

5.3 Formatting text

Making the spreadsheet look good is more than just a cosmetic exercise. Proper formatting, underlining and emboldening can make the spreadsheet easier to follow, draw attention to important figures and reduce the chance of errors.

To format the data you have entered and improve the appearance of the spreadsheet, we are going to do a number of things:

- Change the font to Times New Roman throughout. To do this click on the first cell with an entry in it and drag the mouse to the last cell with an entry in it. The area covered should go coloured. Then go to the Format menu and select Cells. Select Font and then the chosen style.

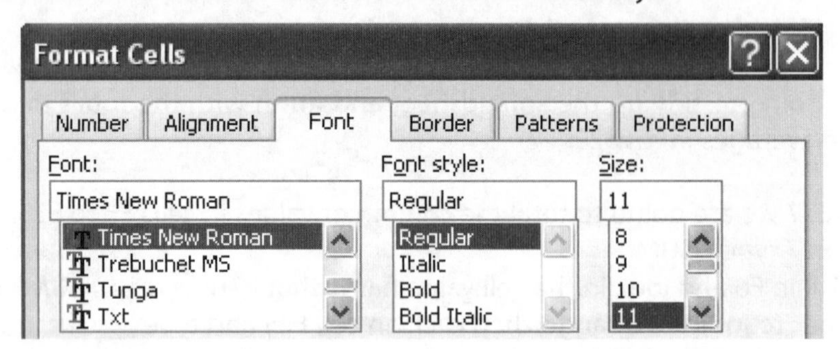

- The style format should be Times New Roman throughout with a font size of 14 for the titles and 11 for the main body of the text.
- Put the titles in bold. One way of doing this would be to activate the cells by clicking and dragging the cursor over them, then clicking on the **B** button (Bold) on the toolbar. Alternatively, all entries in a row or column can be selected by clicking on the letter at the head of the column or the number at the very left of the row.
- The Invoice column A and the Firm column B will not be wide enough initially to enter the full details. Change the column width of B to 15 characters by placing the mouse pointer in the column heading at the

intersection between column B and C. A two headed arrow should appear. Drag this to the right until the column is wide enough. Adjust the width of the other columns to accommodate the entries comfortably.

- Align the column headings. If you look at your spreadsheet so far you will see that all the text is left justified in the cells (moved as far as possible to the left) and the numbers are all right justified (moved to the right in each cell). To adjust this use the align buttons on the formatting toolbar (to the right of the underline U).

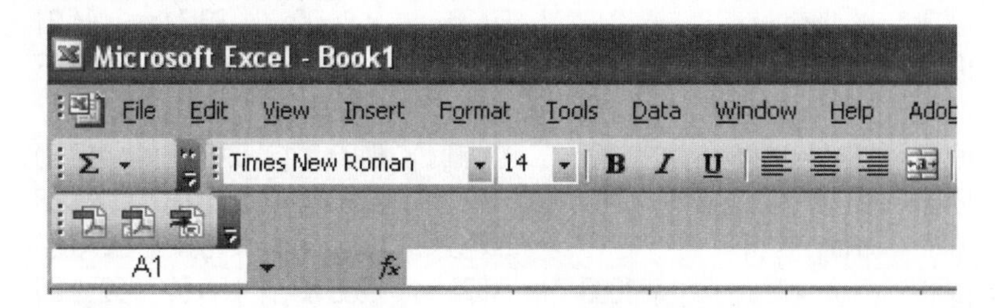

- Underline the totals by outlining the cells containing the totals. Highlight these cells, then move the mouse pointer to Format on the menu bar right at the top of the spreadsheet. Click the mouse button, and a menu will appear. Click on 'Cells' then 'Border' and a window similar to the following will appear.

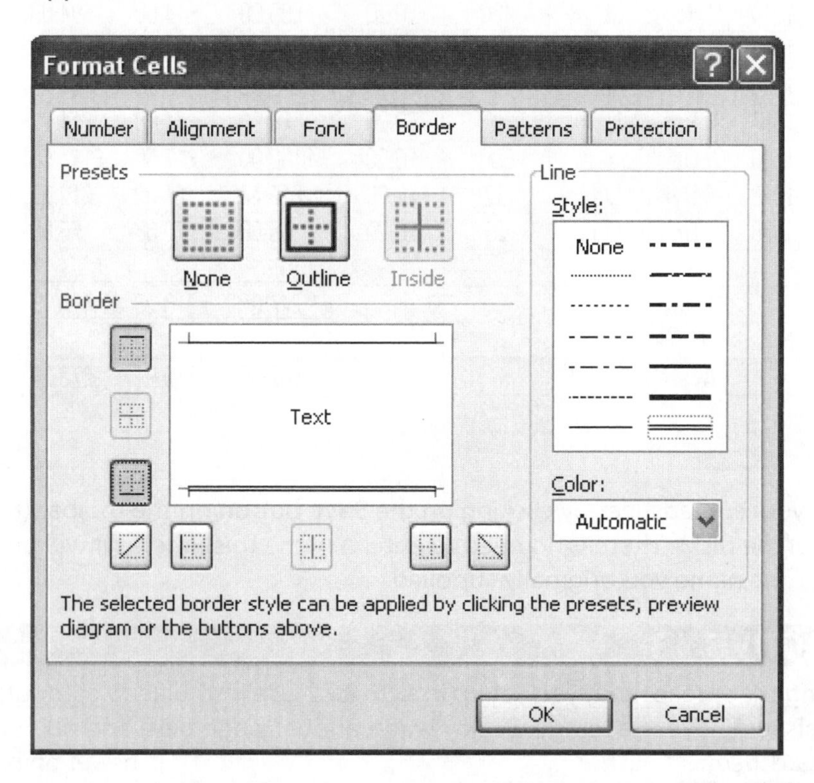

The box on the left shows the edges of the cell or selection of cells, which will have a border. The box on the right shows the types of lines that are available. Click on the top line on the left-hand list and then on the single, non-bold line (probably already selected) in the right hand options. The top of the 'totals' cells should now have a single underlining. Now click on the bottom line and then on the double under-lining style. Click on OK.

The finished spreadsheet should appear as follows:

	A	B	C	D	E	F	G	H
1								
2	**Sales Invoices**		**August 20X0**					
3								
4	**Invoice**	**Firm**	**Items**	**Price**	**Net**	**VAT**	**Gross**	
5				£	£	£	£	
6	1001	AB Plastics Ltd	10	£0.20	£2.00	£0.35	£2.35	
7	1002	J Cables Ltd	21	£0.20	£4.20	£0.74	£4.94	
8	1003	DC Covers Ltd	45	£0.20	£9.00	£1.58	£10.58	
9	1004	DC Covers Ltd	42	£0.20	£8.40	£1.47	£9.87	
10	1005	J Cables Ltd	500	£0.20	£100.00	£17.50	£117.50	
11	1006	AB Plastics Ltd	25	£0.20	£5.00	£0.88	£5.88	
12	1007	J Hoggs Ltd	300	£0.20	£60.00	£10.50	£70.50	
13	1008	L Quick Ltd	1000	£0.20	£200.00	£35.00	£235.00	
14	1009	DC Covers Ltd	50	£0.20	£10.00	£1.75	£11.75	
15	1010	AB Plastics Ltd	12	£0.20	£2.40	£0.42	£2.82	
16	1011	AB Plastics Ltd	15	£0.20	£3.00	£0.53	£3.53	
17	1012	J Hoggs Ltd	350	£0.20	£70.00	£12.25	£82.25	
18	1013	L Quick Ltd	1500	£0.20	£300.00	£52.50	£352.50	
19	1014	J Hoggs Ltd	400	£0.20	£80.00	£14.00	£94.00	
20	1015	L Quick Ltd	1250	£0.20	£250.00	£43.75	£293.75	
21	1016	DC Covers Ltd	90	£0.20	£18.00	£3.15	£21.15	
22	1017	F Browns Ltd	48	£0.20	£9.60	£1.68	£11.28	
23	1018	L Quick Ltd	500	£0.20	£100.00	£17.50	£117.50	
24	1019	F Browns Ltd	52	£0.20	£10.40	£1.82	£12.22	
25	1020	F Browns Ltd	25	£0.20	£5.00	£0.88	£5.88	
26								
27		**Total**			£1,247.00	£218.23	£1,465.23	
28								
29		**Average**			£62.35	£10.91	£73.26	
30								
31								

Save your spreadsheet by clicking on the **Save** button on the toolbar (the picture of the disk). There is no need to enter a name this time, as it will be saved under the name you originally supplied.

▷ ACTIVITY 3 

Using the spreadsheet you set up in Activity 2, use formulae to compute the totals (employees, average weekly wage, annual wage bills) and tidy up the spreadsheet. [Answer on p. 181]

6 Producing reports

6.1 Assumptions

Although the spreadsheet that you have completed is very simple, you still have the basis of a powerful planning and analysis tool. Assumptions and figures can be changed and the spreadsheet will automatically recalculate the results. The main benefit of the spreadsheet is the ability to do 'What if?' experiments.

This allows you to see what happens if, for example, the prices are raised with a subsequent reduction in sales. It can also be used to calculate the overdraft facility if different variables are changed in a cash flow calculation.

Another facility is 'goal seeking'. This is different from seeing what results you get from changing the variables. It gives you the opportunity to state the result you want and make changes until you get that result.

6.2 Changing the variables

In your spreadsheet, you are going to change some of the entries.

▷ ACTIVITY 4 

The price to all customers is going to be raised by 10%, but the organisation assumes that AB Plastics Ltd will use another supplier, so they will lose this business. Would the 10% rise be beneficial to the organisation?

[Answer on p. 182]

6.3 Charts and graphs

Most spreadsheet packages make it easy to draw charts and graphs from the data in your worksheet. In Excel, the Chart Wizard is the icon that looks like a chart.

O EXAMPLE 

After the Activity 4 changes the remaining customers' total invoice values can be computed as:

DC Covers Ltd	£58.68
F Browns Ltd	£32.31
J Cables Ltd	£134.68
J Hoggs Ltd	£271.43
L Quick Ltd	£1,098.63

Set up a worksheet with two columns. This will form the basis of your chart.

With the two columns selected, click on the Chart Wizard. Select the type of chart or graph that you prefer and experiment with changing the data labels and percentages. Two examples are shown below.

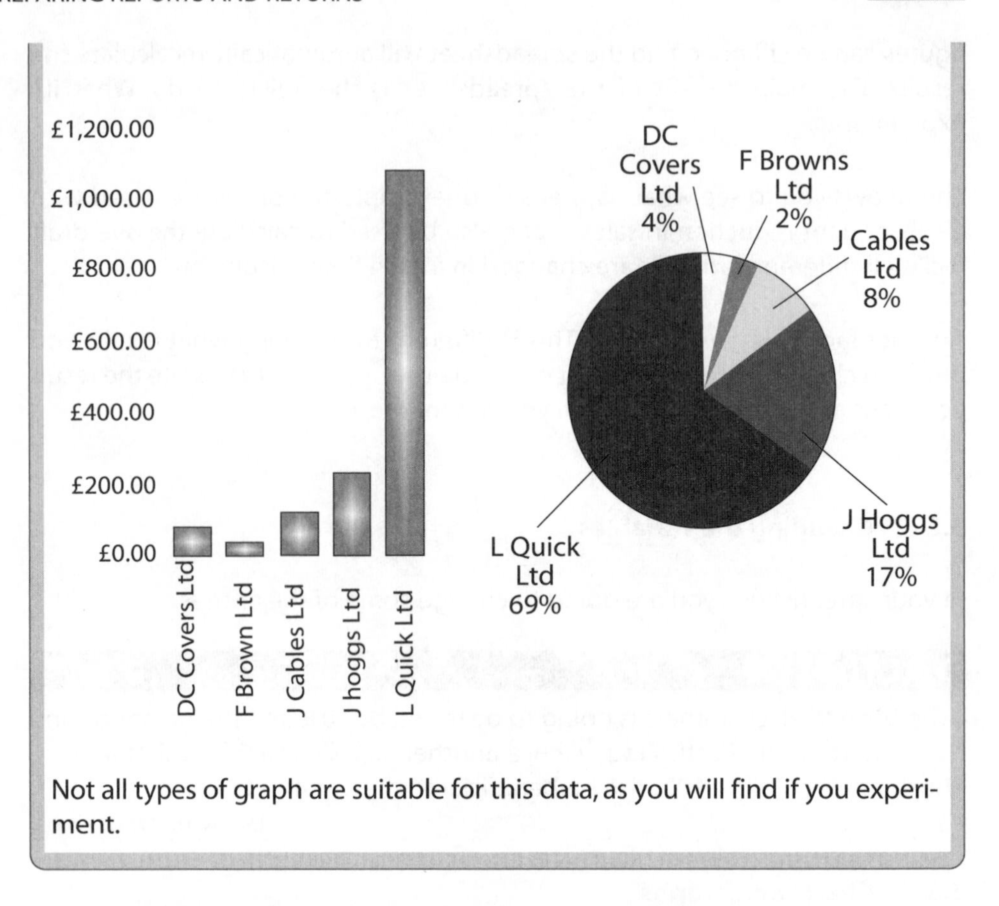

Not all types of graph are suitable for this data, as you will find if you experiment.

6.4 Transferring to another document

Under Windows, you can transfer (or copy) a chart or other diagrams from your worksheet to another document, such as a word processing package. You do this by using the copy and paste facilities.

It is easier if you have both files open at the same time so that you can switch from one to the other using the task bar at the bottom of the screen showing the windows that are currently open. For example, if you are switching from Excel to Word, you just click on the icon with the W on it. Vice versa, it has an X on it.

To copy a chart from Excel to a file in Word:

- Access the correct area of your worksheet
- Highlight the area you want to transfer or copy to another document
- Click on Copy
- Switch to the other document by clicking onto it on the task bar
- Position the cursor where you want the chart to be and click on Paste. You can alter this position by grabbing the picture and dragging it to its position.

▷ ACTIVITY 5

Set up a worksheet with the following headings and values:

Sales £m	*20X0*	*20X4*
Cat food	80	120
Dog food	80	100
Bird seed	25	20

Use your spreadsheet to draw two pie charts showing the percentage make up of the sales for both of the years. Copy both of them to a Word file.

[Answer on p. 182]

6.5 Report design

The appearance of reports is very important and the design should incorporate the following:

- A clear **heading** to indicate what the report is about.
- A **date** that the report relates to.
- A **date** that the report was **printed** (in case it is amended and printed again).
- **Page numbers** to help control large reports over several pages (possibly also the total number of pages).
- **Column headings** to explain what each column contains.
- **Units** for data to ensure that monetary amounts are clearly stated as being in £, £'000 or £m.

6.6 Printing a report

When you are required to produce a report, you should try to concentrate on important information, starting and stopping at relevant points. However, this need to limit the scope of a report should not be at the expense of accuracy, and items that are necessary should not be omitted.

The performance criteria for this course are that you ensure that the required range and report are correctly specified. You also need to demonstrate that printed information is correct and complete and that hard copy is clean, clearly printed and aligned correctly.

To print from your computer make sure that it is connected to a printer and that it is switched on and loaded with the correct paper.

The quickest way to print anything in a Windows environment is to press the Print icon on the toolbar. If you want to print more than one copy, specific pages or a highlighted area you must select the Print option from the File menu. If necessary, change the number of copies required or change the page range to specify which pages to print.

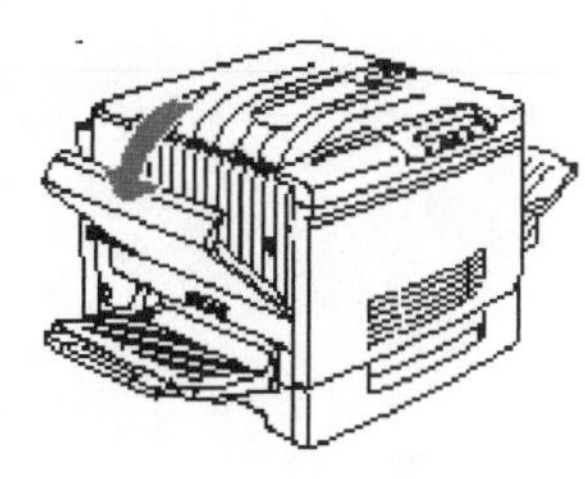

To print an area from your worksheet, highlight the area that you want to print. Select Print Area then Print Preview. This shows you what your print will look like on the page.

The worksheet might be compressed if the page is set up in Portrait. To change to Landscape, click on Page Set Up and change the orientation.

When you are ready to print, click the OK button.

7 Test your knowledge

1 Give three methods of adding up a column of numbers on an Excel spreadsheet.
2 Describe what these spreadsheet formulae will do:
(i) =(A6+B6)*17.5/100
(ii) =F7*F10/SUM(E1:E6)
3 How would you display cell contents of 1234.678 as 1,234.7?

[Answers on p. 183]

8 Summary

You started by learning how to enter and exit the software package. Accessing any new software can be a daunting process for the novice, but with practice you will become very proficient in a short time. The main reason for accessing the package is to enter some data and process it somehow to produce the information required. This information should be produced in a format that is acceptable to the person who is to receive it.

You now understand how to improve the appearance of your spreadsheet by formatting individual cells. The examples given are only a few of the many ways in which the appearance of cells can be changed. You should experiment with others on a separate spreadsheet.

Answers to chapter activities & 'test your knowledge' questions

ACTIVITY 1

In the Excel worksheet that is used in this chapter it is IV65536.

ACTIVITY 2

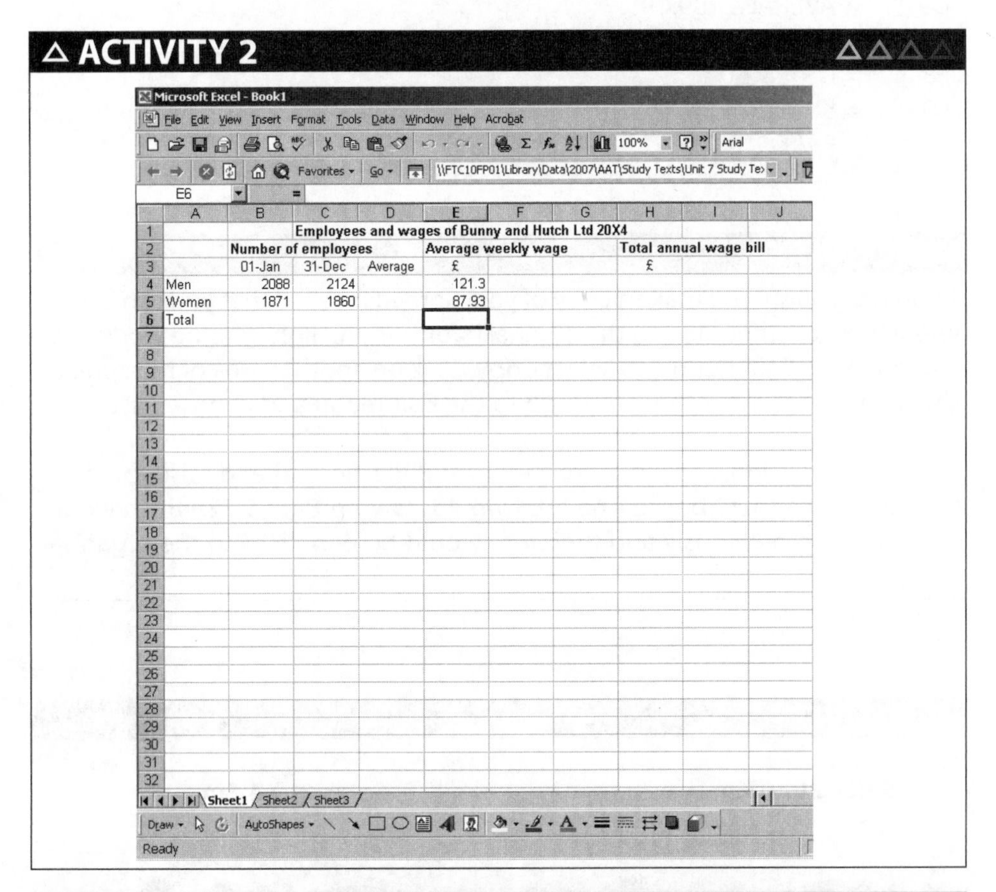

	A	B	C	D	E	F	G	H
1			Employees and wages of Bunny and Hutch Ltd 20X4					
2		Number of employees			Average weekly wage			Total annual wage bill
3		01-Jan	31-Dec	Average	£			£
4	Men	2088	2124		121.3			
5	Women	1871	1860		87.93			
6	Total							

ACTIVITY 3

	A	B	C	D	E	F
1	**Employees and wages of Bunny and Hutch Ltd 20X4**					
2						
3					Average weekly	Total annual
4		Number of employees			wage bill	wage bill
5		01 Jan	31 Dec	Average	£	£
6						
7	Men	2,088	2,124	2,106	£121.32	£12,774,996
8	Women	1,871	1,860	1,865.5	£87.93	£8,201,671
9	Total	3,959	3,984	3,971.5	£105.64	£20,976,667

Notes:

In cell	Formula used
B9	= SUM (B7:B8)
C9	= SUM (C7:C8)
D9	= AVERAGE (B9:C9)
F7	= D7*E7*50
F8	= D8*E8*50
F9	= SUM (F7:F8)
E9	= F9/(D9*50)

△ ACTIVITY 4

To do this you should make a copy of your spreadsheet so that you can experiment with it without losing the original information. Highlight the worksheet and go to the Edit menu and select Copy. Click on another area of the spreadsheet and press the return key or go to the Edit menu and choose Paste.

In the copy version, remove all entries for AB Plastics Ltd and raise the price from 20 pence to 22 pence. The total would now be £1,595.72, which would be more than previously and therefore would be beneficial to the organisation.

△ ACTIVITY 5

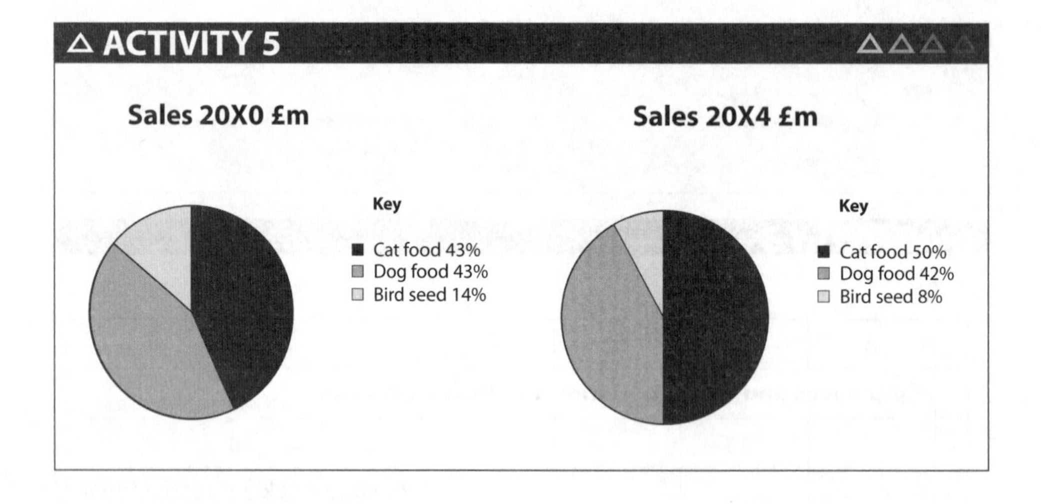

Test your knowledge

1 (i) SUM(x:y) where x and y are the start and end cells of the column.
 (ii) Put the cell pointer on the cell below the column and click on Σ button in the toolbar.
 (iii) A1+A2+A3+ ...

2 (i) Add contents of A6 to that of B6, then multiply the result by 17.5%.
 (ii) Multiply the content of cell F7 by that of F10 and divide the result by the sum of the column cells E1 to E6.

3 On the menu bar, click on Format then on the Number tab, then on Number in the Category list, then select one decimal place and tick the 'Use 1000 separator' box. Click on OK.

VAT – REGISTRATION AND ADMINISTRATION

INTRODUCTION

Element 7.3 covers the preparation of VAT returns. This is the first of three chapters covering VAT, and in this chapter we are going to be looking at the registration and administration of VAT.

VAT (Value Added Tax) is a European tax which applies throughout the European Community (EC). We are going to look at VAT within the United Kingdom only (this includes England, Wales, Northern Ireland and Scotland, and excludes the Channel Islands).

As well as being able to complete a VAT return you also need to understand how the VAT system works and how VAT is administered – we shall be covering all of these things in this chapter.

KNOWLEDGE AND UNDERSTANDING

- Basic law and practice relating to all issues covered in the range statement and referred to in the performance criteria. Specific issues include: the classification of types of supply; registration requirements; the form of VAT invoices; tax points (Element 7.3)
- Sources of information on VAT: HM Revenue and Customs Guide (Element 7.3)
- The processes and systems required to complete and submit VAT returns in accordance with current legislation (Element 7.3)
- Special schemes: annual accounting; cash accounting; bad debt relief (Element 7.3)
- The basis of the relationship between the organisation and the VAT office (Element 7.3)

CONTENTS

PERFORMANCE CRITERIA

- Correctly identify and calculate relevant inputs and outputs (Element 7.3)
- Ensure guidance is sought from the VAT office when required, in a professional manner (Element 7.3)

1 Value Added Tax (VAT) – how it works

1.1 How does VAT work?

VAT is a tax paid by consumers but it is collected by businesses on behalf of HM Revenue and Customs.

- Businesses who make **taxable supplies** collect the tax from their customers. (The definition of **taxable supplies** is wider than just sales. It includes goods taken from the business for personal use.)

□ DEFINITION 

The VAT charged on sales or taxable supplies is known as **output VAT.**

- Those businesses **(taxable persons)** have to assess the amount of tax payable on goods and services provided **(output tax).** They pay it over on a regular basis to HM Revenue and Customs.
- When a business makes purchases or pays expenses it will also be paying the VAT on those purchases/expenses.

□ DEFINITION 

VAT on purchases or expenses is known as **input VAT.**

- As the businesses themselves are not being taxed, they are allowed to reclaim tax on their own expenditure **(input VAT).**
- The input VAT is deducted from the output VAT and the net amount is paid each quarter to HM Revenue and Customs, or recovered from them.

○ EXAMPLE

A business makes sales of £10,000 plus £1,750 of VAT. Its expenditure totals £7,000 plus £1,225 of VAT. How much VAT is due to Revenue and Customs?

Solution

	£
Output VAT	1,750
Less: Input VAT	1,225
VAT due	525

1.2 VAT place of supply

A supply must take place within the United Kingdom to be a **taxable supply** under United Kingdom VAT law.

Generally, if a business makes a **supply of goods from stocks held in the United Kingdom,** then the supply takes place in the United Kingdom. If the business must install the goods at the customer's premises, then the supply takes place at those premises.

When supplying services, the **place of supply is the place where the supplier belongs,** e.g. where a supplier has fixed business premises.

1.3 Time of supply

Most businesses account for input and output VAT according to the **dates that they issue and receive invoices.** The time of supply is known as the **tax point** and this is covered in more detail in the next chapter.

1.4 VAT Guide

HM Revenue and Customs issue a booklet called the VAT Guide which is a guide to the main VAT rules and procedures. If you are dealing with accounting for VAT and VAT returns in practice then you should become familiar with the contents of the VAT Guide in order to be able to refer to it when necessary.

2 Registration for VAT

2.1 Compulsory registration for VAT

Anyone in business whose **taxable supplies exceed a certain annual limit** must register. This includes sole traders, partnerships and limited companies. Penalties for failing to register can be severe.

A business must register if:

- at the end of any month the value of taxable supplies in the past year has exceeded the annual limit of £67,000, or
- at any time there are reasonable grounds for believing that the value of taxable supplies to be made in the next 30 days will exceed the annual limit of £67,000, or
- their acquisitions from other EC member states are more than £67,000 in the calendar year.

2.2 Voluntary registration for VAT

A business may **volunteer to register for VAT.** HM Revenue and Customs may refuse registration if the applicant is unable to show that supplies are being made in the course of business. The reason why someone might wish to voluntarily register for VAT will be considered later in the chapter.

2.3 More than one business

It is the **person not the business** which is required to register. So, if a person is carrying on several businesses, only a single registration is required and the turnovers of all businesses carried on by that person must be considered together when considering registration limits.

EXAMPLE

Robert Parker is a sole trader with three businesses: a hairdressing business (taxable turnover £29,000 per annum), a printing business (taxable turnover £15,000 per annum) and he also deals in second-hand cars (taxable turnover £30,000 per annum). Does he have to register for VAT?

Solution

The VAT registration limit applies to the total taxable turnover of all the business interests of a taxable person. In this case each business venture is below the limit, but in total they exceed the limit. Robert Parker would have to register for VAT.

Let us now assume that the hairdressing business is a partnership with Peter Green. The partnership would be treated as a different taxable person from Robert Parker trading alone. Both taxable persons (Robert Parker and the partnership) would avoid registration

2.4 Deregistration for VAT

A taxable person may **deregister** if the value of his taxable supplies (net of VAT) is expected to be less than £65,000 in the following 12 months. If the taxable person changes – for example, when a sole trader incorporates – then the registration of the sole trader will be cancelled.

If a person reaches the registration limit for VAT then they must register immediately. If not it is entirely possible that they will have to pay the VAT that should have been charged out of their own pockets.

3 Types of supply

3.1 Rates of VAT

There are three types of supply: **standard-rated** (with a reduced rate for domestic fuel and power), **zero-rated** and **exempt.** These are examples of zero-rated and exempt items.

Zero-rated	Exempt
· Water and most types of food	· Land (including rent on property)
· Books and newspapers	· Insurance
· Drugs and medicines	· Postal services
· Public transport	· Betting, gaming and lorries
· Children's clothing and footwear	· Finance (e.g. making loans)
· Sewerage + water services	· Non profit-making education
· New house building	· Health services provided by doctors and dentists

All supplies that are not zero-rated or exempt are standard-rated at 17.5%. The exception is the supply of domestic fuel and power which is at a rate of 5%.

The turnover limits for registration mentioned above include both zero-rated and standard-rated supplies. They do not include exempt supplies.

3.2 Zero-rated and exempt supplies

The distinction between zero-rated supplies and exempt supplies is important. If a person makes zero-rated supplies then input VAT can be reclaimed from HM Revenue and Customs. However if a person makes exempt supplies he cannot register for VAT and therefore cannot reclaim any input tax from HM Revenue and Customs.

3.3 Voluntary registration for VAT

The reason a person may voluntarily register for VAT is if they have zero-rated supplies and wish to register in order to reclaim their input tax.

3.4 Partial exemption for VAT

A taxable person who makes both taxable supplies (standard and zero–rated) and exempt supplies is referred to as **'partially exempt'**. For this purpose, zero-rated supplies are treated as taxable. The problem which arises from partial exemption is that taxable supplies entitle the supplier to a credit for input tax, whereas exempt supplies do not. It is therefore necessary to apportion input tax between taxable and exempt supplies, using a method set out by HM Revenue and Customs.

VAT can only be reclaimed if it is incurred in making taxable supplies.

3.5 Non-reclaimable input tax

There are some items of expense upon which VAT is charged but the VAT cannot be reclaimed from HM Revenue and Customs. These include:

- business entertainment expenses
- purchase of a car for use within the business
- goods and services purchased but not used within the business i.e. used by the owner instead.

▷ ACTIVITY 1

In the most recent quarter a business has made standard-rated supplies of £22,400 (net of VAT) and zero-rated supplies of £5,500. The total of purchases and expenses on which VAT has been charged for the quarter are £16,300 (net of VAT).

How much VAT is due to or from HM Revenue and Customs?

[Answer on p. 194]

4 Administration of VAT

4.1 Introduction

The main source of law on VAT is the **VAT Act 1994,** the annual **Finance Acts** and other regulations issued by the government.

HM Revenue and Customs is the government department that is responsible for administering VAT in the United Kingdom. VAT offices across the country are responsible for the local administration of VAT within a particular geographical area.

Officers from the **local VAT office** deal with registration, visit taxpayers to check returns and deal with routine enquiries. They are also responsible for enforcing the tax.

Taxpayers send their returns and payments to the **VAT Central Unit** at Southend-on-Sea that keeps central records.

4.2 HM Revenue and Customs power

HM Revenue and Customs has certain powers that helps it administer the tax. It has the power to examine records, inspect premises, make assessments for underpaid tax and raise penalties for breaches of VAT law. Penalties may be made for (amongst other things) failing to register for VAT, failing to make returns or failing to make payments on time. They also decide whether or not supplies are liable to VAT.

The decisions of HM Revenue and Customs are **not legally binding.**

There are inevitably **disputes between the taxpayer and HM Revenue and Customs.** HM Revenue and Customs has its own administrative procedures to deal with disputes. In certain cases the taxpayer may appeal to a VAT tribunal. The taxpayer may appeal against the decision of a VAT tribunal to the High Court (on a point of law only). Beyond that appeals may go to the Court of Appeal and then to the House of Lords. The ultimate legal authority on VAT is the European Court of Justice.

4.3 VAT records

The form of records must allow HM Revenue and Customs to check VAT returns adequately. Generally, the business must keep records of:

- all taxable and exempt **supplies made** in the course of business
- all taxable **supplies received** in the course of business
- a summary of the total output tax and input tax for each tax period – the **VAT account** (see later chapter).

4.4 Details to be kept

The business must keep records to prove the figures shown on the VAT returns for **the previous six years.** These records might include the following:

- orders and delivery notes
- relevant business correspondence
- appointment and job books
- purchases and sales books
- cash books and other account books
- bank statements, paying-in slips and cheque stubs
- purchase invoices and copy sales invoices
- recordings of daily takings, including till rolls
- annual accounts
- import and export documents
- VAT accounts
- any credit notes issued or received.

Registered businesses may be visited by a VAT officer on occasion to ensure that their records are being correctly maintained.

A business can keep its records on **microfilm.** The business must tell HM Revenue and Customs. It must be possible to inspect the records.

Any business that maintains its records on **computer** must tell HM Revenue and Customs. The system must comply with VAT regulations.

Some businesses send or receive invoices by **electronic means.** Again they must tell HM Revenue and Customs and check that they are complying with regulations.

You must be able to list the records that must be kept for VAT purposes.

4.5 Special schemes

Normally a **VAT return** is completed by a registered person every three months and any amounts of VAT due paid over to HM Revenue and Customs with the return or a claim made for VAT to be reimbursed.

However, there are some special schemes that are different – the two that you are required to be aware of for Unit 7 are the annual accounting scheme and the cash accounting scheme. We also include brief details of the flat rate accounting scheme.

4.6 VAT: Annual accounting scheme

Under this scheme a VAT return is only made once a year rather than quarterly.

In order to qualify for this scheme the registered person must have annual taxable supplies of no more than £1,350,000. An estimate is made of the likely annual VAT due. This agreed figure is paid by making either three (quarterly) or nine (monthly) instalments (usually by direct debit) towards the end of year VAT liability.

The balance is then due with the annual VAT return.

The benefit of this scheme to a sole trader is that he does not have to spend valuable time every quarter completing a VAT return. However it does mean that his VAT records must be kept accurately as the VAT return is only completed once a year.

4.7 VAT: cash accounting scheme

Normally VAT is due from the date invoices are sent out and can be reclaimed from the date a supplier's invoice is received (details in the next chapter). However under the cash accounting scheme a business accounts for VAT due on the basis of the time when the payment is actually received from customers or made to suppliers.

In order to qualify for this scheme the registered person must have expected annual taxable supplies of £1,350,000 or less and have a clean VAT record. The trader must leave the scheme if turnover exceeds £1,600,000.

If registered under this scheme invoices will still be sent out to customers and received from suppliers but the key record that must be kept is a cash book summarising all payments made and received and their date with a **separate column for VAT.**

The benefit of this scheme is in terms of cash flow for a trader who must pay his suppliers promptly but has to wait a considerable time before being paid by his customers. It also means that there is automatic relief for VAT on bad debts because, if the customer does not pay, then the VAT is not due (bad debt relief in normal circumstances is considered in a later chapter).

4.8 VAT: flat rate accounting scheme

This is intended to simplify the way small businesses account for VAT. Under this scheme, businesses with a taxable turnover up to £150,000 do not have to keep records of the VAT charged on each individual purchase and sales invoice. Instead, their net VAT liability is calculated by applying a flat rate percentage to the business's total turnover. The actual percentage used depends upon the particular industry sector in which the business operates.

This cuts down on the paperwork involved in accounting for VAT, thereby offering administrative cost savings. However, VAT invoices will still need to be issued to VAT registered customers for their own VAT requirements.

5 Test your knowledge

1 Who ultimately (i) bears the cost of; (ii) gains benefit from VAT?
2 Why might a business voluntarily register for VAT even if not required to?
3 Give two examples each of (i) zero-rated and (ii) exempt supplies.
4 What records must a business keep for VAT purposes and for how long?
5 How do the special VAT schemes help the small business?

[Answers on p. 194]

6 Summary

This chapter has served as an introduction to the VAT system. You should now understand how VAT is collected by businesses but is a tax paid by the final consumer.

You must know when a person should register for VAT and deregister if relevant. You should also be clear as to the different types of supply and the difference to a trader between making zero-rated supplies and exempt supplies.

We also considered how VAT is administered by local VAT officers and the documents and records that must be kept for six years in order to ensure that the correct amount of VAT has been paid.

Finally we considered two special schemes for VAT payment – the annual accounting scheme and the cash accounting scheme.

Answers to chapter activities & 'test your knowledge' questions

△ ACTIVITY 1

	£
Output VAT	
Standard-rated (22,400 x 17.5%)	3,920.00
Zero-rated	–
	3,920.00
Less: input VAT (16,300 x 17.5%)	2,852.50
VAT due to HM Revenue and Customs	1,067.50

Test your knowledge

1 (i) The final consumer (customer) who buys goods/services from a VAT registered supplier.

(ii) The government – businesses simply act as collection agencies between the two.

2 Registering for VAT means that the business will have to add VAT onto its sales invoices (unless they are exempt supplies), but they can also reclaim VAT on their purchases and expenses. Provided it is felt that the addition to VAT on sales prices will not result in a significant loss of demand (e.g. if their customers are mainly registered themselves to whom VAT is not a cost) the benefits may well outweigh the costs – particularly if the business makes largely exempt supplies.

3 (i) **Zero-rated:** water/most types of food; books/newspapers; drugs; public transport; children's clothes; sewerage and water services; new house building.

(ii) **Exempt:** land; insurance; postal services; education; health services; finance; betting.

4 The records must be sufficient to show details of all taxable and exempt supplies made and all supplies received in the course of business (invoices, cash books, day books, etc), along with a summary of total input and output tax for each period (in a VAT account). They must be kept for six years.

5 The annual accounting scheme, cash accounting scheme and flat rate scheme are all designed to 'ease the impact of VAT on small businesses' – the annual accounting scheme by removing the need for a VAT return to be prepared each quarter, the cash accounting scheme by helping cash flow in that VAT is only paid/recovered once the cash from the related transactions has actually been received/paid, and the flat rate scheme by removing the need to account for VAT on each individual sale and purchase.

VAT – INVOICES AND TAX POINTS

INTRODUCTION

In this second chapter covering the preparation of VAT returns we are going to look at how VAT is collected via a VAT invoice and all of the details that are required to be shown on such an invoice. We will also be looking at the rules regarding tax points (i.e. the time period in which VAT is to be accounted for) and therefore the figures that will eventually appear on the VAT return. There are lots of important rules concerning VAT covered in this chapter and it is important that you remember them when performing VAT calculations in an assessment.

KNOWLEDGE AND UNDERSTANDING

- Basic law and practice relating to all issues covered in the range statement and referred to in the performance criteria. Specific issues include: the classification of types of supply; registration requirements; the form of VAT invoices; tax points (Element 7.3)

CONTENTS

PERFORMANCE CRITERIA

- Correctly identify and calculate relevant inputs and outputs (Element 7.3)

1 VAT invoices

1.1 Introduction

All businesses that are registered for VAT must collect tax on taxable supplies. In order to do this the supplier must give or send to the purchaser a VAT invoice within 30 days of the supply.

1.2 Form of a VAT invoice

There is **no standard format for invoices.** The exact design is the choice of the business, but **it must show the following details** (unless the invoice is a **less detailed tax invoice** that you will see later):

- identifying number
- date of supply (or tax point – see below) and the date of issue of the invoice
- supplier's name and address and registration number
- name and address of customer, i.e. the person to whom the goods or services are supplied
- type of supply
  - sale
  - hire purchase, credit sale, conditional sale or similar transaction
  - loan
  - exchange
  - hire, lease or rental
  - process (making goods using the customer's own materials)
  - sale on commission (e.g. by an estate agent)
  - supply on sale or return
- description of the goods or services
- quantity of goods or extent of services.
- rate of tax and amount payable (in sterling) excluding VAT for each separate description
- total amount payable (excluding VAT) in sterling
- rate of any cash discount offered (these are also called settlement discounts)
- separate rate and amount of VAT charged for each rate of VAT
- total amount of VAT chargeable.

A VAT invoice is not strictly required where the purchaser is not registered for VAT, however as the seller will not know whether a purchaser is registered, one will be sent.

1.3 VAT and discounts

If a trade discount is given then this is deducted before the VAT is calculated. If a settlement discount is offered then the VAT is always calculated on the **lowest amount that the customer may pay.** You must assume that the customer will take the discount.

1.4 What a VAT invoice looks like

Here is an example of a tax invoice.

MICRO TRAINING GROUP LTD Unit 34 Castlewell Trading Estate Manchester M12 5RHF				
To: JF Jenkins & Co 65 Green Street Manchester M12 4ED		Sales invoice nummber: 35 VAT registered number: 234 5566 87 Tax point: 12 September 20X2		
Sales:				
Quantity	**Description and price**	**Amount ex VAT**	**VAT rate**	**VAT**
6	Programmable calculators			
	FR34 at £24.76	148.56	17.5%	
12	Programmable calculators			
	GT60 at £36.80	441.60	17.5%	
		590.16		101.21
	Delivery	23.45	17.5%	4.02
Terms: Cash discount of 2% if paid within 10 days		613.61		105.23
VAT		105.23		
TOTAL		718.84		

▷ ACTIVITY 1

An invoice is issued for standard-rated goods with a list price of £380.00 (excluding VAT). A 10% trade discount is given and a 4% settlement or cash discount is offered.

How much VAT should be included on the invoice? [Answer on p. 203]

1.5 Rounding VAT

Usually, the amount of VAT calculated will not be a whole number of pounds and pence. You will therefore need a rounding adjustment. The rules governing this adjustment are quite tricky, and permit more than one method. For simplicity, the following approach is recommended.

- On an invoice containing several lines, where the VAT is shown separately for each line, calculate the amount of VAT for each line by rounding to the nearest 1p. For example, 87.7p would be rounded up to 88p. Then simply add up the VAT for each line to arrive at the total VAT.
- On an invoice containing just one (total) figure for VAT, calculate the amount of VAT by rounding down to the nearest 1p. For example £20.877 would be rounded down to £20.87.

▷ ACTIVITY 2

(a) Given below is an extract from a VAT invoice:

Quantity	Description and price	Net of VAT	VAT rate	VAT
16	6 metre hosepipes @ £3.23	51.68	17.5%	
24	12 metres hosepipes @ £5.78	138.72	17.5%	

Calculate the VAT for each line of the invoice and the total VAT charged.

(b) An invoice includes a net total for goods of £1,084.50. How much VAT should be charged for these goods? [Answer on p. 203]

1.6 Less detailed VAT invoices

Retailers do not have to issue a detailed VAT invoice every time they make a sale. This would make trading impossible. If the total amount of the supply (including VAT) by the retailer does not exceed £100.00, a retailer may issue a **less detailed tax invoice.** However, if requested by a customer a full VAT invoice must be issued. The supplier only needs to show the following details on the invoice:

- supplier's name and address
- supplier's VAT registration number
- date of supply
- description sufficient to identify the goods or services
- amount payable (including VAT) for each rate (standard and zero)
- each rate of VAT.

The main differences here are that the customer's name and address can be omitted, and the total on the invoice includes the VAT without the VAT itself being shown separately.

Although this invoice shows less detail, it is still a valid **tax invoice.**

All retailers must keep a record of their **daily gross takings** so that VAT can be calculated on the total of cash takings, not individual invoices. This means that the retailer will need to keep a careful note of any money taken for own use.

1.7 Calculating the VAT

When a less detailed VAT invoice is issued or received it will be necessary to calculate the amount of the VAT that is included in the invoice total in order to record the sale or purchase in the accounting records.

The VAT element is calculated by multiplying the invoice total (for standard-rated goods) by the fraction 17.5/117.5 or 7/47.

O EXAMPLE

If the VAT inclusive amount is £48.66 what is the VAT element?

Solution

$$\text{VAT} = 48.66 \times \frac{17.5}{117.5} = £7.24$$

or

$$\text{VAT} = 48.66 \times \frac{7}{47} = £7.24$$

Remember that the VAT is rounded down to the nearest penny.

▷ ACTIVITY 3 

The total of a less detailed invoice for standard-rated goods is £68.90. How much VAT is included in this amount? [Answer on p. 203]

1.8 Modified invoices

For a sale of any amount, if the buyer agrees, then a modified invoice can be issued. This shows the VAT inclusive amount for each item sold and then at the bottom of the invoice the following amounts must be shown:

- the overall VAT inclusive total
- the total amount of VAT included in the total
- the total value of the supplies net of VAT
- the total value of any zero-rated and exempt supplies.

1.9 Proforma invoices

When a business issues a sales invoice that includes VAT, the VAT becomes payable to HM Revenue and Customs next time the business submits a return.

This can cause cashflow problems if the customer has not yet paid the invoice, because the business then has to pay the VAT before collecting it from the customer.

To avoid this, a business may issue a **proforma invoice,** which essentially is a demand for payment. Once payment is received, the business will then issue a 'live' invoice to replace the proforma.

Because a proforma invoice **does not rank as a VAT invoice** the supplier is **not** required to pay VAT to HM Revenue and Customs until the 'live' invoice is issued. By the same token, the customer cannot reclaim the VAT on a proforma invoice, but must instead wait until the valid tax invoice is received.

Pro-forma invoices should be clearly marked 'THIS IS NOT A VAT INVOICE'.

1.10 Credit notes and VAT

A credit note involving a taxable supply must show:

- the identifying number and date of issue
- the supplier's name, address and registration number
- the customer's name and address
- the reason for the credit (e.g. goods returned)
- a description of the goods or services for which the credit is being allowed
- the quantity and amount credited for each description
- the total amount credited, excluding VAT
- the rate and amount of VAT credited.

The number and date of the original tax invoice should also appear on the credit note.

If the supplier issues the credit note without making a VAT adjustment the credit note must say: **'This is not a credit note for VAT'.**

A supplier is **not allowed to issue a credit note to recover VAT on bad debts.** See the section in Chapter 10 on bad debts for the detailed procedures.

2 Tax points

2.1 Introduction

☐ DEFINITION

The **tax point** is the date on which the liability for output tax arises – it is the date on which it is recorded as taking place for the purposes of the tax return.

Most taxable persons make a VAT return each quarter. The return must include all supplies whose tax points fall within that quarter.

2.2 The basic tax point

The **'basic tax point'** is the date of delivery of goods or the date the customer takes the goods away or the date of completion/performance of services.

2.3 Actual tax point

Where an invoice is issued or payment received before the basic tax point, **this earlier date becomes the 'actual tax point'.**

If a supplier issues an invoice within 14 days after the basic tax point, the invoice date becomes the actual tax point and is used as the tax point for the tax return, unless payment has been received earlier, in which case the payment date is the actual tax point.

Provided that written approval is received from the local VAT office the 14-day rule can be varied, for example to accommodate a supplier who issues all of his invoices each month on the last day of the month.

2.4 Deposits received in advance

Any **deposits received in advance** create a basic tax point. The business must account for the VAT element. The VAT included in the deposit must be calculated and entered in the accounting records.

EXAMPLE

A £50.00 deposit is received in advance of the goods being delivered. What is the VAT on this amount?

Solution

The amount of VAT included in the deposit = £50.00 x $\frac{7}{47}$ = £7.44.

ACTIVITY 4

In each of the following cases state the date of the tax point and whether it is a basic tax point or actual tax point:

(i) Goods delivered to a customer on 10 July, invoice sent out on 15 July and payment received on 30 July.

(ii) Invoice sent out to a customer on 12 August, goods delivered to the customer on 16 August, payment received 20 September.

(iii) Payment received from customer on 4 September, goods sent to customer on 5 September together with the invoice.

(iv) Goods delivered to a customer on 13 September, invoice sent out on 30 September and payment received on 31 October. [Answer on p. 203]

3 Test your knowledge

1 How are trade/settlement discounts dealt with when computing VAT on an invoice?
2 What is the advantage of issuing a proforma invoice?
3 In what circumstances will a business become liable for output tax prior to goods being delivered to the customer? [Answers on p. 204]

4 Summary

This chapter has covered two important areas for VAT – invoicing and tax points. VAT invoices must include certain details and in normal circumstances must be given or sent to a VAT registered purchaser. In practice this means that all purchasers will be provided with a VAT invoice whether they are registered or not. However, retailers are allowed to issue less detailed or modified invoices if the customer is happy with this, showing only the total amount due without any breakdown of the VAT included. Any credit notes sent out by a business must include the same details as the invoices.

The tax point for a supply of goods is important as this determines the date on which the VAT becomes accountable therefore determining which VAT return the VAT for that supply of goods appears on. You must know the rules for the basic tax point and for actual tax points.

Answers to chapter activities & 'test your knowledge' questions

ACTIVITY 1

	£
List price	380.00
Less: trade discount 10%	38.00
	342.00

VAT = £342.00 x 96% x 17.5%
= £57.45

ACTIVITY 2

Part (a)

Quantity	Description and price	Net of VAT	VAT rate	VAT
16	6 metre hosepipes @ £3.23	51.68	17.5%	9.04
24	12 metre hosepipes @ £5.78	138.72	17.5%	24.28

Part (a)

VAT = £1,084.50 x 17.5%
= £189.78

ACTIVITY 3

VAT = £68.90 x 17.5/117.5
= £10.26

ACTIVITY 4

(i) 15 July actual tax point
(ii) 12 August actual tax point
(iii) 4 September actual tax point
(iv) 13 September basic tax point

Test your knowledge

1 In both cases the maximum discount the customer might take is deducted from the gross invoice total before VAT is calculated.

2 A proforma invoice is not a VAT invoice (and should be marked accordingly) but a demand for payment. Once payment is made, a VAT invoice is issued. It allows the supplier to collect the VAT in from the customer before it has to be paid over to the HMRC.

3 Where an invoice is issued or payment received before the date of delivery, the date of issue/receipt becomes the actual tax point, when output tax liability arises.

VAT RETURNS

INTRODUCTION

In the final chapter of this study text we are going to conclude our VAT studies by looking at how to complete a VAT return correctly and on time. Businesses must complete a VAT return (a VAT 100 form) at the end of each quarter. The purpose of a VAT return is to summarise the transactions of a business for a period. In an assessment you are likely to be required to complete an organisation's VAT return so that it is ready for authorisation and despatch.

We shall also be looking at situations that may give rise to VAT penalties and how to avoid them.

KNOWLEDGE AND UNDERSTANDING

- Special schemes: annual accounting; cash accounting; bad debt relief (Element 7.3)
- The basis of the relationship between the organisation and the VAT office (Element 7.3)

CONTENTS

PERFORMANCE CRITERIA

- Complete and submit VAT returns correctly, using data from the appropriate recording systems, within the statutory time limits (Performance Criteria Element 7.3)
- Ensure submissions are made in accordance with current legislation (Element 7.3)
- Ensure guidance is sought from the VAT office when required, in a professional manner (Element 7.3)

1 The VAT return

1.1 Introduction

The tax period for VAT is **three months,** or one month for taxpayers who choose to make monthly returns (normally taxpayers who receive regular refunds).

The taxpayer must complete a **VAT return (a VAT 100 form) at the end of each quarter.** The return summarises all the transactions for the period.

1.2 Timing of the VAT return

The taxpayer must make the return within one month of the end of the tax period. The taxable person must send the amount due at the same time (i.e. output tax collected less input tax deducted). Payment may be by cheque (made payable to 'HM Revenue and Customs only') or by credit transfer.

If VAT is due from HM Revenue and Customs the VAT return must still be completed and submitted within one month of the end of the quarter in order to be able to reclaim the amount due.

1.3 What a VAT return looks like

Given below is an example of a VAT return:

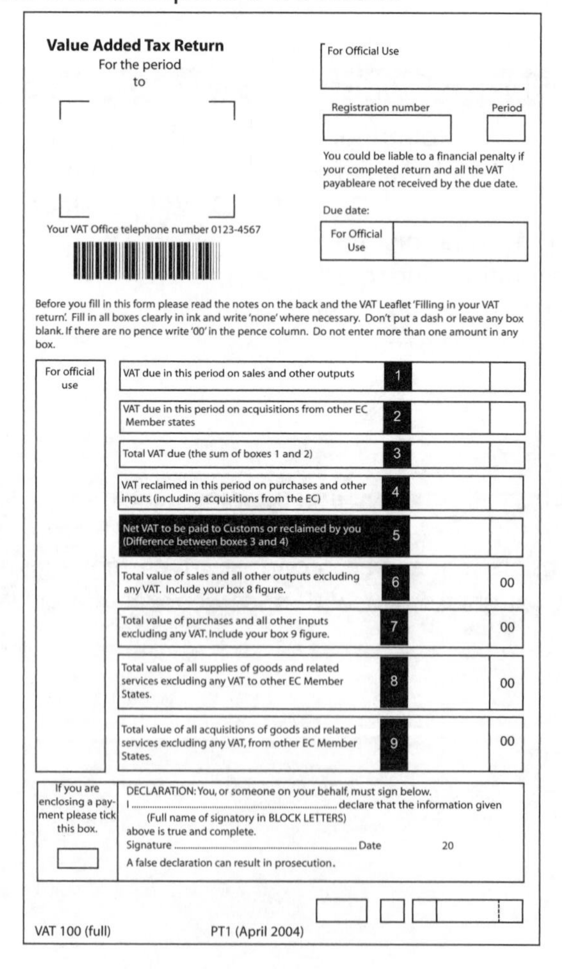

Value Added Tax Return
For the period
to

For Official Use

Registration number | Period

You could be liable to a financial penalty if your completed return and all the VAT payableare not received by the due date.

Due date:

For Official Use

Your VAT Office telephone number 0123-4567

Before you fill in this form please read the notes on the back and the VAT Leaflet 'Filling in your VAT return'. Fill in all boxes clearly in ink and write 'none' where necessary. Don't put a dash or leave any box blank. If there are no pence write '00' in the pence column. Do not enter more than one amount in any box.

For official use		Box	£	p
	VAT due in this period on sales and other outputs	1		
	VAT due in this period on acquisitions from other EC Member states	2		
	Total VAT due (the sum of boxes 1 and 2)	3		
	VAT reclaimed in this period on purchases and other inputs (including acquisitions from the EC)	4		
	Net VAT to be paid to Customs or reclaimed by you (Difference between boxes 3 and 4)	5		
	Total value of sales and all other outputs excluding any VAT. Include your box 8 figure.	6		00
	Total value of purchases and all other inputs excluding any VAT. Include your box 9 figure.	7		00
	Total value of all supplies of goods and related services excluding any VAT to other EC Member States.	8		00
	Total value of all acquisitions of goods and related services excluding any VAT, from other EC Member States.	9		00

If you are enclosing a payment please tick this box.

DECLARATION: You, or someone on your behalf, must sign below.
I .... declare that the information given
(Full name of signatory in BLOCK LETTERS)
above is true and complete.
Signature .... Date 20
A false declaration can result in prosecution.

VAT 100 (full) PT1 (April 2004)

As you will see there are nine boxes to complete with the relevant figures. Boxes 2, 8 and 9 are to do with supplies of goods and services to other European Community (EC) Member States and acquisitions from EC Member States. Therefore we will now consider how VAT is affected by exports and imports.

1.4 VAT: Exports and imports to or from non-EC members

(a) Generally, goods **exported** from the United Kingdom to a non-EC country are normally **zero-rated** (i.e. there is no tax charged on them, even if there normally would be) provided there is documentary evidence of the export.

(b) Goods that are **imported** from outside the EC have to have customs duty paid on them when they enter the country (these are outside the scope of Unit 7 and we will not consider them further). However, goods that would be taxed at the standard rate of VAT if supplied in the United Kingdom are also subject to VAT. The amount payable is based on their value including customs duty. This applies to all goods whether or not they are for business use. The aim of the charge is to treat foreign goods in the same way as home-produced goods. The VAT is paid at the port of entry and the goods will typically not be released until it is paid. If the imported goods are for business use and the business uses them to make taxable supplies, it can reclaim the VAT paid in the usual way as input tax on the VAT return (Box 4).

1.5 Exports and imports to and from countries within the EC

When both the exporting and importing country are EC members the situation is rather complicated and we shall look at it carefully.

Movements of goods between EC Member States are no longer known as imports and exports but as acquisitions.

In what follows we refer to HM Revenue and Customs as the collecting authority, even though in different countries it will have a different name.

(a) **Sale to a VAT registered business**

When an EC member sells goods to a VAT registered business in another EC country, it is the **buyer** who pays over the VAT to HM Revenue and Customs (or the equivalent in the buyer's country). Provided the seller has the buyer's VAT number, the seller sells the goods zero-rated to the buyer. The buyer will then pay VAT to HM Revenue and Customs at the appropriate rate. The buyer can also reclaim the VAT from HM Revenue and Customs.

We can summarise this as follows:

The seller

The seller will supply the goods zero-rated.

The seller makes no entries in Boxes 1 to 4 of the VAT return.

The seller will enter the value of the sale in Box 8.

The buyer

The VAT registered buyer will pay the seller the sale price of the goods (excluding any VAT) .

The buyer will enter the VAT output tax in Box 2 of the return and the VAT input tax in Box 4 of the return. Thus, the net amount of VAT the buyer pays to HM Revenue and Customs is nil.

The buyer will also enter the VAT exclusive price of the goods in Box 9.

(b) **Sale to a non-VAT registered buyer**

When a sale is made to a non-VAT registered buyer, the seller has to charge VAT at the standard rate. The buyer will pay the VAT inclusive price to the seller.

We can summarise this as follows:

The seller

The seller supplies the goods and charges VAT.

The seller enters the VAT in Box 2.

The seller enters the VAT exclusive price in Box 8.

The buyer
The non-VAT registered buyer pays the VAT inclusive price to the seller and of course makes no entries in a VAT return because he is not registered.

2 Completing the VAT return

2.1 The VAT account

The main source of information for the VAT return is the VAT account which must be maintained to show the amount that is due to or from HM Revenue and Customs at the end of each quarter.

2.2 How the VAT account should look

Given below is a pro-forma of a VAT account as suggested by the VAT Guide.

1 April 20X5 to 30 June 20X5

VAT deductible – input tax		**VAT payable – output tax**	
VAT on purchases		VAT on sales	
April	X	April	X
May	X	May	X
June	X	June	X
VAT on imports	X		
VAT on acquisition from EC	X	VAT on acquisiton from EC	X
Adjustments of previous errors (if £2,000 or less)			
Net underclaim	X	Net overclaim	X
Bad debt relief	X		
Less: Credit notes received	(X)	Less: Credit notes issued	(X)
Total tax deductible	X	Total tax payable	X
		Less: total tax deductible	(X)
		Payable to HM Revenue and Customs	X

You will note that the VAT shown is not strictly a double entry account as the VAT on credit notes received is deducted from input tax and the VAT on credit notes issued is deducted from output tax instead of being credited and debited respectively.

2.3 Information required for the VAT return

Boxes 1 to 4 of the VAT return can be fairly easily completed from the information in the VAT account. However, Boxes 6 and 7 require figures for total sales and purchases excluding VAT. This information will need to be extracted from the totals of the accounting records such as sales day book and purchases day book totals.

Boxes 8 and 9 require figures, excluding VAT, for the value of supplies to other EC Member States and acquisitions from other EC Member States. Therefore the accounting records should be designed in such a way that these figures can also be easily identified.

▷ ACTIVITY 1

Panther

You are preparing the VAT return for Panther Alarms Ltd and you must first identify the sources of information for the VAT account.

Suggest the best sources of information for the following figures:

(a) sales
(b) credit notes issued
(c) purchases
(d) credit notes received
(e) capital goods sold
(f) capital goods purchased
(g) goods taken from business for own use
(h) bad debt relief. [Answer on p. 221]

EXAMPLE

Given below is a VAT account for Thompson Brothers for the second VAT quarter of 20X5.

Thompson Brothers Ltd

1 April 20X5 to 30 June 20X5

VAT deductible – input tax		**VAT payable – output tax**	
VAT on purchases	£	VAT on sales	£
April	525.00	April	875.00
May	350.00	May	1,750.00
June	350.00	June	700.00
	1,225.00		3,325.00
EC acquisitions	210.00		210.00
Other adjustments			
Less: Credit notes received	(17.50)	Less: Credit notes issued	(105.00)
Total tax deductible	1,417.50	Total tax payable	3,430.00
		Less: total tax deductible	(1,417.50)
		Payable to HM Revenue and Customs	2,012.50

You are also given the summarised totals from the day books for the three-month period:

Sales Day Book

	Net	*VAT*	*Total*
	£	£	£
Standard-rate	19,000.00	3,325.00	22,325.00
Zero-rated	800.00	–	800.00
EC Member States	1,500.00	–	1,500.00

Sales Returns Day Book

	Net	*VAT*	*Total*
	£	£	£
Standard-rate	600.00	105.00	705.00
Zero-rated	40.00	–	40.00
EC Member States	–	–	–

Purchase Day Book

	Net	*VAT*	*Total*
	£	£	£
Standard-rate	7,000.00	1,225.00	8,225.00
Zero-rated	2,000.00	–	2,000.00
EC Member States	1,200.00	210.00	1,410.00

Purchases Returns Day Book

	Net	*VAT*	*Total*
	£	£	£
Standard-rate	100.00	17.50	117.50
Zero-rated	–	–	–
EC Member States	–	–	–

We also need the address and VAT registration number of the business:

Thompson Brothers Ltd
Arnold House
Parkway
Keele
KE4 8US

VAT registration number 165 4385 32.

We are now in a position to complete the VAT return.

Solution

Step 1

Fill in the VAT registration number, VAT period, name and address of the business and the due date of the return which is one month after the end of the quarter.

Step 2

Fill in Box 1 with the VAT on sales less the VAT on credit notes issued – this can be taken either from the VAT account or from the day book summaries: £3,325 - £105 = £3,220.00.

Note that the instructions at the top of VAT return require '00' to be shown if there are no pence in the total.

Step 3

Fill in Box 2 with the VAT payable on acquisitions from other EC Member States – this figure of £210.00 can be taken either from the VAT account or from the Purchases Day Book.

Note that this figure will be included here on the VAT return as output tax payable to HM Revenue and Customs and also in Box 4 as input tax reclaimable.

Step 4

Complete Box 3 with the total of Boxes 1 and 2.

Step 5

Fill in Box 4 with the total of VAT on all purchases (including acquisitions from EC Member States) less the total VAT on any credit notes received. These figures can either be taken from the VAT account or from the day book totals: £1,225.00 + £210.00 – £17.50 = £1,417.50.

Step 6

Complete Box 5 by deducting the figure in Box 4 from the total in Box 3. This is the amount due to HM Revenue and Customs and should equal the balance on the VAT account.

If the Box 4 figure is larger than the Box 3 total then there is more input tax reclaimable than output tax to pay – this means that this is the amount being reclaimed from HM Revenue and Customs.

Step 7

Fill in Box 6 with the VAT exclusive figure of all sales less credit notes issued – this information will come from the day books - this figure includes sales to EC Member States: £19,000 + £800.00 + £1,500.00 – £600.00 – £40.00 = £20,660.

Note that this figure includes zero-rated supplies and any exempt supplies that are made.

Step 8

Fill in Box 7 with the VAT exclusive total of all purchases less credit notes received - again this will be taken from the day books: £7,000 + £2,000 + £1,200.00 – £100.00 = £10,100.00.

Step 9

Fill in Box 8 with the VAT exclusive total of all supplies made to EC Member States (less any credit notes) – this figure is taken from the Sales Day Book: £1,500.00.

Step 10

Fill in Box 9 with the VAT exclusive total of all acquisitions from other EC Member States (less any credit notes) – this figure is taken from the Purchases Day Book: £1,200.00.

Note that no pence are required for the final four boxes. Also note the instruction that if there is no entry for any box then 'none' should be written in the box.

Step 11

Write in the name of the person within the organisation (senior management or owner) who will be authorising the VAT return with their signature.

Step 12

If VAT is due to HM Revenue and Customs a cheque must be sent with the VAT return and the box at the bottom of the return must be ticked.

Value Added Tax Return
For the period
1/4/X5 to 30/6/X5

For Official Use

Thompson Brother Ltd
Arnold House
Parkway
Keele
KE4 8US

Registration number	Period
165 4385 32	20X5

You could be liable to a financial penalty if your completed return and all the VAT payable are not received by the due date.

Due date: 31 July 20X5

Your VAT Office telephone number 0123-4567

For Official Use

Before you fill in this form please read the notes on the back and the VAT Leaflet 'Filling in your VAT return'. Fill in all boxes clearly in ink and write 'none' where necessary. Don't put a dash or leave any box blank. If there are no pence write '00' in the pence column. Do not enter more than one amount in any box.

For official use

	Box	£	p
VAT due in this period on sales and other outputs	1	3,220	00
VAT due in this period on acquisitions from other EC Member States	2	210	00
Total VAT due (the sum of boxes 1 and 2)	3	3,430	00
VAT reclaimed in this period on purchases and other inputs (including acquisitions from the EC)	4	1,417	50
Net VAT to be paid to Customs or reclaimed by you (Difference between boxes 3 and 4)	5	2,012	50
Total value of sales and all other outputs excluding any VAT. Include your box 8 figure.	6	20,660	00
Total value of purchases and all other inputs excluding any VAT. Include your box 9 figure.	7	10,100	00
Total value of all supplies of goods and related services excluding any VAT to other EC Member States.	8	1,500	00
Total value of all acquisitions of goods and related services excluding any VAT, from other EC Member States.	9	1,200	00

If you are enclosing a payment please tick this box. ✓

DECLARATION: You, or someone on your behalf, must sign below.
I ....A Thompson............................ declare that the information given
(Full name of signatory in BLOCK LETTERS)
above is true and complete.
Signature .... Date 20
A false declaration can result in prosecution.

VAT 100 (full) PT1 (April 2004)

If the business makes sales or purchases for cash then the relevant net and VAT figures from the cash receipts and payments books should also be included on the VAT return.

▷ ACTIVITY 2

Given below is a summary of the day books of a business for the three months ended 31 March 20X1. The business is called Long Supplies Ltd and trades from Vale House, Lilly Road, Trent, TR5 2KL. The VAT registration number of the business is 285 3745 12.

Sales Day Book

	Net	*VAT*	*Total*
	£	£	£
Standard-rate	15,485.60	2,709.98	18,195.58
Zero-rated	1,497.56	–	1,497.56

Sales Returns Day Book

	Net	*VAT*	*Total*
	£	£	£
Standard-rate	1,625.77	284.50	1,910.27
Zero-rated	106.59	–	106.59

Purchase Day Book

	Net	*VAT*	*Total*
	£	£	£
Standard-rate	8,127.45	1,422.30	9,549.75
Zero-rated	980.57	–	980.57
EC Member States	669.04	117.08	786.12

Purchases Returns Day Book

	Net	*VAT*	*Total*
	£	£	£
Standard-rate	935.47	163.70	1,099.17
Zero-rated	80.40	–	80.40
EC Member States	–	–	–

Required

(a) Write up the VAT account to reflect these figures.

(b) Complete the VAT return given. [Answer on p. 221]

Value Added Tax Return
For the period
to

For Official Use

Registration number | Period

You could be liable to a financial penalty if your completed return and all the VAT payable are not received by the due date.

Due date:

For Official Use

Your VAT Office telephone number 0123-4567

Before you fill in this form please read the notes on the back and the VAT Leaflet 'Filling in your VAT return'. Fill in all boxes clearly in ink and write 'none' where necessary. Don't put a dash or leave any box blank. If there are no pence write '00' in the pence column. Do not enter more than one amount in any box.

For official use		Box	£	p
	VAT due in this period on sales and other outputs	1		
	VAT due in this period on acquisitions from other EC Member States	2		
	Total VAT due (the sum of boxes 1 and 2)	3		
	VAT reclaimed in this period on purchases and other inputs (including acquisitions from the EC)	4		
	Net VAT to be paid to Customs or reclaimed by you (Difference between boxes 3 and 4)	5		
	Total value of sales and all other outputs excluding any VAT. Include your box 8 figure.	6		00
	Total value of purchases and all other inputs excluding any VAT. Include your box 9 figure.	7		00
	Total value of all supplies of goods and related services excluding any VAT to other EC Member States.	8		00
	Total value of all acquisitions of goods and related services excluding any VAT, from other EC Member States.	9		00

If you are enclosing a payment please tick this box.	DECLARATION: You, or someone on your behalf, must sign below. I .... declare that the information given (Full name of signatory in BLOCK LETTERS) above is true and complete. Signature .... Date 20 A false declaration can result in prosecution.

VAT 100 (full) PT1 (April 2004)

2.4 VAT: Adjustment of previous errors

You will notice in the pro-forma VAT account that there are entries for net underclaims and net overclaims. Net errors made in previous VAT returns of £2,000 or less can be adjusted for on the VAT return through the VAT account.

DEFINITION

Net error means the difference between any earlier errors in output tax and any earlier errors in input tax.

The one single figure for net errors will then be entered as additional input tax if there has been an earlier net underclaim of VAT and as additional output tax if the net error was a net overclaim in a previous return.

2.5 Errors of more than £2,000

If the net error from a previous return totals more than £2,000 then the VAT office should be informed immediately either by a letter or on Form VAT 652. This is known as voluntary disclosure. The information provided to the VAT office should be:

- the amount of the error
- the VAT period in which it occurred
- whether the error was involving input or output tax
- whether the error is in favour of the business or HM Revenue and Customs.

2.6 VAT: Bad debt relief

You will notice that there is an entry in the pro-forma VAT account for bad debt relief as additional input tax.

When a supplier invoices a customer for an amount including VAT, the supplier must pay the VAT to HM Revenue and Customs. If the customer then fails to pay the debt, the supplier's position is that he has paid output VAT which he has never collected. This is obviously unfair, and the system allows him to recover such amounts.

We saw in Chapter 9 that **suppliers cannot issue credit notes to recover VAT on bad debts.**

Instead, the business must make an **adjustment through the VAT return.**
The business can reclaim VAT already paid over if:

- output tax was paid on the original supply
- six months have elapsed between the date of supply and the date of the VAT return, and
- the debt has been written off as a bad debt in the accounting records.

If the business receives a **repayment of the debt later,** it must make an adjustment to the VAT relief claimed.

The bad debt relief is entered in box 4 of the return along with the VAT on purchases.

Be very careful when computing the VAT on the bad debt. The amount of the bad debt will be VAT inclusive because the amount the debtor owes is the amount that includes VAT. To calculate the VAT you have to multiply the bad debt by 17.5/117.5.

Be careful also that the examiner may try and confuse you by giving you a purchases figure (which also goes into box 4) that is net of VAT – and you calculate the VAT on that by simply multiplying by 17.5/% ie 0.175.

O EXAMPLE

A business has made purchases of £237,000 (net of VAT) in the VAT quarter and has written off a bad debt of £750. Calculate the figure that will be entered on the VAT return for the quarter in Box 4.

Solution

	£	£
Purchases (net of VAT)	237,000	
VAT thereon (237,000 × 0.175)		41,475.00
Bad debt	750	
VAT thereon (750 × 17.5/117.5)		111.70
Total VAT for Box 4		41,586.70

3 VAT penalties

3.1 Late notification

If a trader **trades** in **excess of the registration limits** without informing HM Revenue and Customs, a penalty is levied for failing to register by the proper date.

This penalty is a **proportion of the net tax due** from the date registration should have taken place. The proportion percentage varies as follows:

Period of failure to register	*Percentage of tax*
9 months or less	5%
Over 9 months, but not over 18 months	10%
Over 18 months	15%

A **minimum penalty** of £50 exists. If the trader can show a reasonable excuse for not registering, the penalty may be mitigated.

3.2 Default surcharge

A **default** occurs when a trader submits his VAT return late or submits the return on time but pays the VAT late. On default, HM Revenue and Customs serve a **default liability notice** on the taxpayer which identifies a surcharge period which runs from the date of the notice until the anniversary of the end of the period for which the taxpayer is in default.

If a **second default** occurs in the surcharge period it is further extended until the anniversary of the end of the period to which the new default relates.

If **VAT is paid late in a surcharge period,** a surcharge is payable as follows:

Default involving late payment of VAT in the surcharge period	Surcharge, % of outstanding VAT
1st	2%
2nd	5%
3rd	10%
4th and above	15%

(The minimum charge is £30.)

3.3 Misdeclaration penalties

Making returns which **understate the trader's VAT liability** incurs a penalty of 15% of the lost tax. Errors of up to £2,000 can be rectified on the usual quarter-end VAT 100 return.

3.4 Default interest

Interest is charged on VAT due on an assessment from HM Revenue and Customs. Interest runs from the date the VAT should have been paid (up to a maximum of three years).

4 Test your knowledge

1. Company X is based in an EC Member State, in which the VAT rate is 8%, and sells goods worth £100 to Company Y, a VAT-registered company in the UK. How much VAT, if any, is payable and from whom is it collected?
2. Box 6 on the VAT return is for 'total value of sales and all other outputs excluding any VAT'. Does this include (i) zero-rated and/or (ii) exempt supplies?
3. Under what three conditions can bad debt relief be claimed?

[Answers on p. 223]

5 Summary

In this final chapter the actual completion of the VAT return was considered. A business should keep a VAT account which summarises all of the VAT from the accounting records and this can be used to complete the first five boxes on the VAT return. The figure for VAT due to or from HM Revenue and Customs on the VAT return should equal the balance on the VAT account.

In order to complete the remaining boxes on the VAT return information will be required from the accounting records of the business, normally in the form of the day books.

Answers to chapter activities & 'test your knowledge' questions

△ ACTIVITY 1

Panther

The two basic records needed are the sales day book and purchase day book for the **sales** and **purchases.**

For **cash sales** and **purchases** the cash book should be analysed.

Information about **credit notes received and issued** should be in the purchase returns and sales returns day books.

The **capital goods purchased and sold** will probably be in a separate assets account under plant and machinery unless the company maintains analysed purchase and sales day books which include asset purchases and disposals.

The goods taken for own use should be recorded in the sales day book and the drawings account.

The **bad debt relief** is generally found in the bad and doubtful debts account.

△ ACTIVITY 2

Part (a)

Long Supplies Ltd
VAT account 1 January to 31 March 20X1

	£		£
VAT on purchases	1,422.30	VAT on sales	2,709.98
EC acquisitions	117.08	EC acquisitions	117.08
	1,539.38		2,827.06
Less: credit notes received	163.70	Less: credit notes issued	284.50
Total tax deductible	1,375.68	Total tax payable	2,542.56
		Less: total tax deductible	1,375.68
		Payable to HM Revenue and Customs	1,166.88

Part (b)

Value Added Tax Return
For the period
1/1/X1 to 31/3/X1

For Official Use

Registration number: 285 3745 12
Period: 01X1

Long Supplies Ltd
Vale House
Lily Road
Trent
TR5 2KL

You could be liable to a financial penalty if your completed return and all the VAT payable are not received by the due date.

Due date: 30 April 20X1

Your VAT Office telephone number 0123-4567

For Official Use

Before you fill in this form please read the notes on the back and the VAT Leaflet 'Filling in your VAT return'. Fill in all boxes clearly in ink and write 'none' where necessary. Don't put a dash or leave any box blank. If there are no pence write '00' in the pence column. Do not enter more than one amount in any box.

For official use	Description	Box	£	p
	VAT due in this period on sales and other outputs	1	2,42[illegible]	48
	VAT due in this period on acquisitions from other EC Member States	2	11[illegible]	08
	Total VAT due (the sum of boxes 1 and 2)	3	2,54[illegible]	56
	VAT reclaimed in this period on purchases and other inputs (including acquisitions from the EC)	4	1,37[illegible]	68
	Net VAT to be paid to Customs or reclaimed by you (Difference between boxes 3 and 4)	5	[illegible]	88
	Total value of sales and all other outputs excluding any VAT. Include your box 8 figure.	6	15,25[illegible]	00
	Total value of purchases and all other inputs excluding any VAT. Include your box 9 figure.	7	8,76[illegible]	00
	Total value of all supplies of goods and related services excluding any VAT to other EC Member States.	8	Non[illegible]	00
	Total value of all acquisitions of goods and related services excluding any VAT, from other EC Member States.	9	66[illegible]	00

If you are enclosing a payment please tick this box. ✓

DECLARATION: You, or someone on your behalf, must sign below.
I .... declare that the information given
(Full name of signatory in BLOCK LETTERS)
above is true and complete.
Signature .... Date 20
A false declaration can result in prosecution.

VAT 100 (full) PT1 (April 2004)

Workings

Box 1

	£
VAT on sales	2,709.98
Less: VAT on credit notes	(284.50)
	2,425.48

Box 4

	£
VAT on purchases	1,422.30
EC Member States acquisitions	117.08
	1,539.38
Less: VAT on credit notes	(163.70)
	1,375.68

Box 6

	£
Standard-rated sales	15,485.60
Zero-rated sales	1,497.56
	16,983.16
Less: credit notes	
Standard-rated	(1,625.77)
Zero-rated	(106.59)
	15,250.80

Box 7

	£
Standard-rated purchases	8,127.45
Zero-rated purchases	980.57
EC acquisitions	669.04
	9,777.06
Less: credit notes	
Standard-rated	(935.47)
Zero-rated	(80.40)
	8,761.19

Test your knowledge

1 The VAT on transfers between EC Member States is payable at the rate prevalent in the buyer's country and is collected from the buyer. Thus, £17.50 will be payable by Company Y (via Box 2 on the VAT Return) and can be reclaimed (via Box 4).

2 It includes both zero-rated and exempt supplies.

3 Output tax was paid on original supply. There has been at least six months between the supply date and the VAT return date. The debt has been written off as a bad debt in the books.

KEY TECHNIQUES QUESTIONS

Chapter 1
Internal and external reports

▷ ACTIVITY 1

Management require various types of internal reports which aid them in achieving their objectives. These include:

- regular reports
- exception reports
- analysis
- forecasts.

Give an example of each type of report listed above, relating each one to labour cost and/or employee information.

▷ ACTIVITY 2

You work as an accounting technician for a young, expanding SME. Your managing director often sets you 'ad hoc' projects. He asks you to set up an information base of sources of secondary data, particularly those sources produced by government, including the ONS, Office for National Statistics.

Outline the general and specific digests you would include in your information base.

Chapter 2
Writing reports

(**Note:** only one brief question is included here. The other questions and skills tests contain numerous examples of report writing.)

▷ ACTIVITY 3

A typical formal report will include some or all of the following elements:

- Title and preliminaries
- Introduction/terms of reference
- Procedure
- Findings
- Conclusions
- Recommendations
- Appendices

Outline briefly the purpose of each of these elements.

Chapter 3
Tables and diagrams

▷ ACTIVITY 4

What principles need to be followed when constructing a table of data to be included in a report?

▷ ACTIVITY 5

Loftus Fertilisers Ltd manufactures three main products 'LF1', 'LF2' and 'LF3'.

Production in tonnes for the last three years was:

	Year		
	20X1	20X2	20X3
Products			
'LF1'	250,000	300,000	340,000
'LF2'	100,000	125,000	85,000
'LF3'	50,000	50,000	75,000
	400,000	475,000	500,000

Illustrate this information pictorially using:

- a component bar chart, and
- a compound bar chart.

What are the benefits of using each method?

▷ ACTIVITY 6

A company made sales of £119,880 for the quarter October to December 20X2. These were made up of sales of £37,440 in October, £41,040 in November and the remainder in December. Sales for the same quarter in 20X1 were £38,880 in October, £40,320 in November and £38,400 in December. The sales figures for July, August and September of 20X2 were £37,440, £41,040 and £42,000 respectively.

You are required to draw up a table showing the sales for the quarter to 31/12/X2, the preceding quarter and the corresponding quarter.

▷ ACTIVITY 7

Houses 'R' Us is an estate agent company that has four branches in Buckfordshire. The managing director is compiling a report for the employees to inform them about the branch and company results for the past quarter. He wishes to make the report as visually interesting as possible.

The value of houses sold by each branch over the past year were as follows:

Branch	Value of house sales
	£000
Buckford	458.2
New Milton	875.4
Wycfield	512.8
Chefford	690.1

Represent this information using (i) a pictogram and (ii) a pie chart. Which do you think provides the most useful information?

▷ ACTIVITY 8

Stainsacre Park is an agricultural museum and working farm.

During the month of July 20X1 the visitors to the centre (to the nearest 5) each day were:

520	525	515	515	520	560	525
530	535	520	525	535	555	
535	540	525	535	545	540	
550	555	530	555	545	525	
560	565	525	560	550	515	

(a) Produce a frequency distribution for this data.

(b) Using the frequency distribution calculated in part (a), calculate the median, mode and the mean values.

Chapter 4
Graphs, time series and index numbers

▷ ACTIVITY 9

Runswick Camp is a military museum situated in the North of England. You work as an accounting technician in the business and undertake a number of 'one off' exercises in addition to your routine accounting tasks. The museum keeps a record of visitor numbers per quarter but little analysis has been done on the figures.

The number of visitors to the museum for the past two years were:

20X1	Q	1	5,750
		2	8,950
		3	14,750
		4	6,250
20X2	Q	1	6,550
		2	9,750
		3	15,550
		4	7,050

(a) Calculate the centred four-point moving average trend figures.

(b) Prepare a graph showing the trend line and actual number of visitors per quarter to the museum.

(c) Comment on the trend in visitor numbers.

▷ ACTIVITY 10

Coastal Coaches run a number of services, one of which is a local community commuter run.

The following information shows revenue per passenger over the past three years, together with details of the retail price index for the periods. The total number of passengers per year has remained fairly constant.

Coastal Coaches

	Years		
	20X1	20X2	20X3
Revenue per passenger	£0.93	£1.10	£1.32
Retail price index	137.7	143.2	147.3

(a) Prepare a table to show the revenue per passenger for each of the three years and a comparative figure for each year but at year 20X3 prices.

(b) Present the original revenue per passenger and adjusted revenue per passenger for the three-year period in the form of a clearly labelled compound bar chart. If available, prepare your graph on graph paper.

▷ ACTIVITY 11

You are an accounting technician working for a group of companies. In one sector of the business there are two divisions, A and B.

Some concern has been expressed in recent years regarding the growth in administrative costs in the two divisions.

Details of administrative costs for the past five years are:

	20X1	**20X2**	**20X3**	**20X4**	**20X5**
	£m	**£m**	**£m**	**£m**	**£m**
Division A	2.7	3.0	3.4	3.6	4.0
Division B	1.7	2.1	2.5	3.0	3.6
Retail price index	130.2	135.6	137.7	143.2	146.7

(a) Prepare a table to show the actual administrative costs per year for each division and comparative figures for each year based on year 20X5 prices, i.e. converting the administrative costs for each year to 20X5 prices.

(b) Draw a line graph to show the administrative costs for both divisions at both original and adjusted prices for the period from 20X1 to 20X5.

(c) Write brief notes to the divisional managers explaining your findings from your graph.

▷ ACTIVITY 12

Sales forecast

(a) The following data shows the number of cash receipts per day for a company over four working weeks. Complete the following table to calculate the trend using five-day moving averages.

Week	Day				
	1	2	3	4	5
1	8	12	15	10	9
2	10	13	17	15	16
3	17	23	25	21	21
4	26	30	32	34	35

Week	Day	Receipts		Trend
1	1			
	2			
	3			
	4			
	5			
2	1			
	2			
	3			
	4			
	5			
3	1			
	2			
	3			
	4			
	5			
4	1			
	2			
	3			
	4			
	5			

(b) What useful information from the trend could you pass on to the management of this company?

▷ ACTIVITY 13

This scenario-based question is divided into four tasks, and contains a large amount of data which you may need to complete the tasks. You are advised to read the whole of the material before commencing the tasks.You are provided with proforma schedules and report forms for the tasks and these are included at the end of the question.

The situation

Business: Brompton Fertilisers and Chemicals Ltd

Location: North East of England

Personnel:
Owner manager – Zoe Swinglehurst
Production manager – William Morley
Warehouse manager – Sarah Buck
Accountant – Andrew Hill
Accounting technician – you

The business produces and distributes fertilisers and industrial and agricultural chemicals. It has a manufacturing unit near Scarborough and a distribution unit based in Middlesborough. Both these sites are considered as responsibility centres, i.e. profit centres.

The manufacturing unit transfers finished goods to the distribution centre at a transfer price based on full production cost. It also sells some products direct to customers.

The company's year end is 31 December 20X5 and today's date is 20 January 20X6.

Tasks to be completed

Task 1
Immediately following the tasks below you will find an analysis of the monthly sales for the two divisions for the last two years. The figures are exclusive of VAT.

Using these figures you are to complete the sales report form provided at the end of the question.

Task 2
Using the blank graph provided at the end of the question you are required to plot a graph for 20X5 to show, for the company as a whole:

- monthly total of external sales for each month
- cumulative total of external sales at the end of each month
- 12-month moving totals for each month.

Task 3
Refer to the incomplete table provided in the proformas at the end of the

question which shows a summary of turnover for the company over a five-year period.

Complete the report to incorporate the sales figures for the years 20X4 and 20X5.

Task 4

In the data below you will find details of a price index appropriate to the business sector in which the company operates.

You are required to calculate the indexed value of the annual sales at year 20X1 prices, and complete the schedule laid out at the end of the question.

Monthly sales over the last two years

	Manufacturing unit			Distribution unit
20X4	Total	External sales	To distribution	Total
	£000	£000	£000	£000
January	215	39	176	320
February	175	51	124	222
March	148	33	115	194
April	191	56	135	249
May	216	45	171	305
June	173	34	139	220
July	135	21	114	205
August	201	38	163	283
September	219	44	175	315
October	175	27	148	241
November	165	23	142	225
December	240	51	189	329
20X5				
January	245	45	200	343
February	158	51	107	194
March	127	22	105	223
April	258	47	211	288
May	226	51	175	275
June	177	39	138	262
July	131	11	120	225
August	222	44	178	318
September	223	42	181	307
October	184	33	151	277
November	195	24	171	257
December	239	51	188	320

Price index appropriate to the business sector

Year	Index
20X1	100.0
20X2	103.5
20X3	107.4
20X4	110.6
20X5	113.7

PROFORMA SCHEDULES AND REPORT FORMS FOR ANSWERS

Task 1

Sales report (external sales)
Period ended 31 December 20X5

Quarter	Manufacturing	Distribution	Total
	£000	£000	£000
January – March			
April – June			
July – September			
October – December			

Task 2

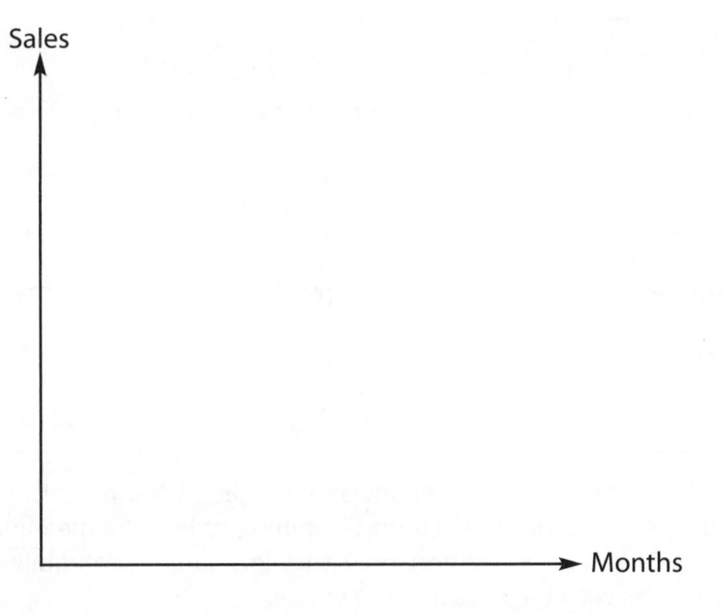

Task 3

Brompton Fertilisers and Chemicals Ltd Sales report – five-year review					
Year	20X1	20X2	20X3	20X4	20X5
Turnover (£000)	3,370	3,410	3,480		

Task 4

Sales report – five-year summary adjusted to 20X1 prices					
Year	**20X1**	**20X2**	**20X3**	**20X4**	**20X5**
Actual turnover (£000)					
Index					
Adjusted turnover (£000)					

Chapter 5
Performance assessment

▷ ACTIVITY 14

You work as an accounting technician for an SME in the agricultural feeds sector of business.

Your company is a member of a trade association and subscribes to the inter-firm comparison scheme.

You have recently received the following report from the trade association.

Agricultural feeds sector		
Ratio	**Company**	**Industry average**
Return on capital employed	26%	24%
Asset turnover	1.63	1.6
% net profit to sales	16%	15%
Current ratio	1.3 : 1	1.2 : 1
Acid test	0.99 : 1	1.01 : 1

Your managing director is a non-financial manager with a technical background and asks you to prepare a report outlining to him the meaning and purpose of each ratio and stating how the company's profitability and liquidity compares with the industry as a whole.

ACTIVITY 15

National Stores Group

The National Stores Group consists of four national chains of stores:

1. Brighter Homes are large department stores selling clothes, furniture and other household products.
2. Happy Life sell high quality furniture and other decorative items.
3. Kidsfair sells children's and babies' clothes and other baby equipment.
4. Roberts Stores sell smart, but affordable, clothes for women.

Results for the group for the financial years 20X1 and 20X2 were as follows:

20X1	Brighter Homes	Happy Life	Kidsfair	Roberts Stores
Number of stores	143	38	282	241
Total selling area (000m^2)	390	172	118	49
Turnover (excluding VAT) (£m)	623.4	207.4	237.9	94.3
Net profit (£m)	22.4	(12.7)	7.4	1.6
20X2				
Number of stores	135	37	283	241
Total selling area (000m^2)	385	164	119	50
Turnover (excluding VAT) (£m)	638.4	198.7	235.2	98.4
Net profit (£m)	26.4	(9.2)	(3.7)	0.8

Note: There was a negligible rise in the UK RPI between 20X1 and 20X2.

Task 1

The table below has been devised to show the following information relating to 20X1 and 20X2 for each of the four chains in the group:

(i) average store size in 000 m^2

(ii) average turnover per store

(iii) turnover per m^2

(iv) net profit/turnover ratio

(v) net profit per m^2.

This table has been completed for all four companies below for 20X1 and for Brighter Homes, Happy Life and Roberts Stores for 20X2.

National Stores Group – Profitability Analysis 20X1	Brighter Homes	Happy Life	Kidsfair	Roberts Stores
Average size of store (000m^2)	2.73	4.53	0.42	0.20
Turnover per store (£m)	4.36	5.46	0.84	0.39
Turnover per m^2	£1,598.4	£1,205.8	£2,016.1	£1,924.4
Net profit / turnover	3.59%	(6.12%)	3.11%	1.70%
Net profit per m^2	£57.44	(£73.84)	£62.71	£32.65

National Stores Group – Profitability Analysis 20X2				
	Brighter Homes	**Happy Life**	**Kidsfair**	**Roberts Stores**
Average size of store (000m²)	2.85	4.43		0.21
Turnover per store (£m)	4.73	5.37		0.41
Turnover per m²	£1,658.1	£1,211.5		£1,968
Net profit / turnover	4.14%	(4.63%)		0.81%
Net profit per m²	£68.57	(£56.10)		£16.00

Required

Complete the 20X2 table for Kidsfair.

Task 2

Calculate for the group as a whole:

(a) total turnover figures for 20X1 and 20X2

(b) percentage change in total turnover from 20X1 to 20X2

(c) total net profit figures for 20X1 and 20X2

(d) percentage change in total net profit from 20X1 to 20X2

(e) total net profit/turnover ratios for 20X1 and 20X2.

Present your answer in the form of a table.

▷ ACTIVITY 16

You are an accounting technician employed by Paper Products Limited, a manufacturing company which uses recycled paper and wood pulp to produce three products:

- toilet tissue
- paper handkerchiefs
- kitchen roll.

The company operates from three sites:

- East Factory, which has three production departments
- West Factory, which has one production department
- Head Office, which contains the selling, accounting and administration departments.You are employed at Head Office and are currently helping the company's management accountant compare the performance of the different departments and factories in the company.

Task 1

Complete the following table to analyse the performance of the departments and factories in the company. Show your figures to TWO decimal places.

Paper Products Limited
Performance Report year ended 31 October 20X5

	East Factory			West Factory	Total
	Toilet tissue	Paper hankerchiefs	Kitchen roll	Toilet tissue	
	£m	£m	£m	£m	£m
Sales	1.80	1.60	0.70	3.00	7.10
Costs:					
Recycled paper	0.15	0.18	0.08	0.22	0.63
Wood pulp	0.30	0.40	0.15	0.55	1.40
Labour	0.52	0.60	0.32	0.80	2.24
Factory overheads (Note 1)	0.20	0.20	0.20	0.50	1.10
Head office costs (Note 2)	0.10	0.10	0.10	0.10	0.40
Total costs	1.27	1.48	0.85	2.17	
Profit	0.53	0.12	(0.15)	0.83	
	£	£	£	£	£
Sales per £ recycled paper	12.00	8.89	8.75	13.64	
Sales per £ wood pulp	6.00	4.00	4.67	5.45	
Sales per £ labour					
Profit / sales (%)	29.44	7.50	(21.43)	27.67	

Company Accounting Policy

Notes:

1 The factory overheads at the East Factory are shared equally between the three departments.

2 The Head Office costs are shared equally between the four departments at the two factories.

Task 2

Prepare a report for the management accountant comparing the performance of the departments and factories within Paper Products Limited for the year ended 31 October 20X5.

Your report should be well presented and address the following issues:

- a brief assessment of the overall profitability of Paper Products Limited
- a comment on how useful the data is in assessing the overall profitability of the company.

- a comparison of the profitability and efficiency of the manufacturing departments at the East Factory: toilet tissue, paper handkerchiefs and kitchen roll.

Task 3

The sales, total cost and profit figures for Paper Products Limited over the last five years were as follows.

	20X1	20X2	20X3	20X4	20X5
	£m	£m	£m	£m	£m
Sales	6.00	6.40	6.58	7.40	7.10
Total cost	4.20	4.65	5.05	5.80	5.77
Profit	1.80	1.75	1.53	1.60	1.33
Profit / sales (%)					

Complete the table above by calculating the profit/sales (%) for each year. Your figures should be shown as percentages to one decimal place.

▷ ACTIVITY 17

Super Shops is a business which sells sweets, chocolates and souvenirs from shops in the tourist areas of London. It currently rents four shops: North, South, East and West. It also rents a small office for central administration purposes.

You are the accounting technician employed to assist the owner, Manish Shah.

The following information is available to you.

Business policy:

- all products are purchased centrally, therefore the purchase price is the same for products regardless of which shop they are sold in
- whilst the selling price of some products is controlled by the owner, the shop managers are free to reduce the price of other products to improve sales
- central administration costs are shared equally between the four shops.

Super Shops

Profit and loss account for the year ended 31 March 20X8

	North	South	East	West	Total
	£	£	£	£	£
Sales	973,000	824,000	1,240,000	456,000	3,493,000
Less Cost of goods sold	710,000	648,000	850,000	312,000	2,520,000
Gross profit	263,000	176,000	390,000	144,000	973,000
Less Expenses:					
Wages	48,000	42,000	102,000	20,000	212,000
Rent	128,000	92,000	153,000	67,000	440,000
Sundries	16,500	9,600	34,000	9,000	69,100
Share of central costs	45,000	45,000	45,000	45,000	180,000
	237,500	188,600	334,000	141,000	901,100
Net profit	25,500	(12,600)	56,000	3,000	71,900

Notes:

- Wages include the wages of the shop manager and shop assistants. The shop manager determines the number of shop assistants employed.
- Sundries include any other costs incurred by the shop managers for the benefit of their shops. These include electricity, local advertising and cleaning.

Task 1

Complete the performance ratio table below.

Show all ratios to two decimal places.

Super Shops
Shop performance ratio table for the year ended 31 March 20X8

	North	South	East	West	Total
Gross profit/sales (%)					
Net profit/sales (%)					
Expense ratios:					
Wages / sales (%)	4.93	5.10	8.23	4.39	
Rent / sales (%)	13.16	11.17	12.34	14.69	
Sundries / sales (%)	1.70	1.17	2.74	1.97	
Central costs / sales (%)	4.62	5.46	3.63	9.87	

Task 2

Prepare a well-presented report for Mr Shah, comparing the performance of the four shops, addressing the following:

- gross profit/sales ratio
- expense ratios (wages, rent, sundries and central costs)
- overall net profitability of the shops
- any limitations to your analysis.

Your report should relate the performance of individual shops to the other shops and to the business as a whole, offering explanations where you consider it appropriate. You should also consider the effect of business policy on the relative profitability of the shops.

▷ ACTIVITY 18

You are given the following scenario information:

Business: Brompton Fertilisers and Chemicals Ltd
Location: North East of England

The business produces and distributes fertilisers and industrial and agricultural chemicals. It has a manufacturing unit near Scarborough and a distribution unit based in Middlesborough. Both these sites are considered as responsibility centres, i.e. profit centres.

The manufacturing unit transfers finished goods to the distribution centre at a transfer price based on full production cost. It also sells some products direct to customers.

The company's year end is 31 December 20X5 and today's date is 20 January 20X6.

In the data below you will find an extract from the accounts of the company for the year ended 31 December 20X5.

Brompton Fertilisers and Chemicals Ltd
Extract from your accounts for year ended 31 December 20X5

	£m
Turnover	3.75
Cost of sales	2.06
Gross profit	1.69
Administration costs	0.15
Distribution costs	0.27
Other costs	0.01
	0.43
Net profit	1.26
Capital employed	£4.85m

Below you will find a schedule of profitability ratios. The figures for year 20X4 are already shown on the report.

PERFORMA RATIO SCHEDULE

Brompton Fertilisers and CHemicals Ltd
Profitability ratios for 20X4 and 20X5

Year	20X4	20X5
Ratio:		
Gross profit % of sales	44.15%	
Net profit % of sales	32.00%	
Return on capital employed	24.50%	

Required

Calculate the following ratios for 20X5:

- gross profit % of sales
- net profit % of sales
- return on capital employed.

Write a memo to Andrew Hill focusing on a brief review of performance for past the two years.

▷ ACTIVITY 19

This scenario-based question is divided into two tasks, and contains a large amount of data which you may need to complete the tasks. You are advised to read the whole of the material before commencing the tasks.You are provided with proforma schedules and report forms for the tasks and these are included at the end of the question.

The situation

Business: Redcar Foods Ltd

Location: Redcar, Cleveland

Personnel: Owner manager and director – Frank Smith
Warehouse manager – John Noble
Accountant – Susan Woodhouse
Accounting technician – you

The business is a wholesaler of foodstuffs to the catering trade across the North East of England. Its main customers are restaurants, hotels, boarding houses and pubs. The business has expanded in recent years and you have been employed by the company for almost a year.

The main site is based in Redcar, but the company also has a branch in Whitby, North Yorkshire. Most of the buying is done through Redcar; but the Whitby branch also buys in direct from suppliers.

Tasks to be completed

Today is early November 20X1 and the accounts for the year ended 30 September 20X1 have recently been finalised.

You will find an extract from the accounts for this period for each of the Redcar site and the Whitby site in the data below, immediately following the Tasks.

Task 1

You are required to consolidate this information (combine the accounts for both sites) so as to produce a profit and loss account for the company as a whole.

Note that transfers between the two sites are not to be treated as sales or purchases and are excluded when preparing this statement.

Use the proforma provided near the end of the question.

Also calculate the ratios incorporated into the report.

Task 2

Complete the summary sheet showing the main profitability ratios for each site and in total.

The blank schedule is provided at the end of the question.

Data

Extract from the accounts for the year ended 30 September 20X1 Redcar site

	£m	£m
Sales		9.45
Opening stock	1.21	
Purchases	6.72	
	7.93	
Less closing stock	1.73	
COst of goods sold		6.20
Gross profit		3.25
Wages and salaries	0.95	
Administration costs	0.61	
Distribution costs	0.65	
Other costs	0.10	
		2.31
Net profit		0.94
Capital employed		£3.10m

Included in the sales figure is an amount of £0.55m transferred at cost to the Whitby site.

Whitby site

	£m	£m
Sales		4.65
Opening stocks	0.64	
Purchases (including from Redcar site)	3.27	
	3.91	
Less closing stock	0.75	
Cost of goods sold		3.16
Gross profit		1.49
Wages and salaries	0.41	
Administration costs	0.32	
Distribution costs	0.33	
Other costs	0.04	
		1.10
Net profit		0.39
Capital employed		£2.4m

The average number of full-time equivalent employees in the company during the year was:

Redcar site	73
Whitby site	35

PROFORMA SCHEDULES FOR ANSWERS

Task 1

Consolidates profit and loss account for the eyear ended 30 September 20X1

	Redcar	Whitby	Total
	£m	£m	£m
Sales			
Cost of sales			
Gross profit			
Gross profit as % of sales	%	%	%
Costs:			
Wages and salaries			
Administration costs			
Distribution costs			
Other costs			

Net profit			
Net profit as % of sales	%	%	%
Capital employed			
Return on capital employed	%	%	%

Task 2

Redcar Foods Ltd
Summary of profitablility ratios - Year ended 30 September 20X1

	Responsibility Centre		
Ratio	Redcar	Whitby	Total
Return on capital employed			
Gross profit % of sales			
Net profit % of sales			

Chapter 6
Reporting to external agencies

▷ ACTIVITY 20

Many business systems make use of standard or pre-printed forms. Outline the principles of good form design.

▷ ACTIVITY 21

The following are external reports to outside agencies:
(a) Corporation tax return.
(b) Returns in relation to employees' PAYE and NI contributions.
(c) Annual return for a registered charity.
(d) VAT return.
(e) Planning application for a workshop extension.
(f) Annual return for a limited company.
(g) Return on accidents within the workplace.
(h) Return for inter-firm comparison purposes, for a business sector.

Identify the agencies to which such reports would be submitted.

▷ ACTIVITY 22

This scenario-based question is divided into two tasks, and contains a large amount of data which you may need to complete the tasks.

You are advised to read the whole of the material before commencing the tasks. You are provided with a proforma schedule for Task 1 at the end of the question.

The situation

Business:	Redcar Foods Ltd
Location:	Redcar, Cleveland
Personnel:	Owner manager and director – Frank Smith Warehouse manager – John Noble Accountant – Susan Woodhouse Accounting technician – you

The business is a wholesaler of foodstuffs to the catering trade across the North East of England. Its main customers are restaurants, hotels, boarding houses and pubs. The business has expanded in recent years and you have been employed by the company for almost a year.

The main site is based in Redcar, but the company also has a branch in Whitby, North Yorkshire. Most of the buying is done through Redcar; but the Whitby branch also buys in direct from suppliers.

Tasks to be completed

Task 1

The company subscribes to the Foods Federation Inter-firm Comparison scheme.

You have recently received the standard form which needs to be submitted annually. The form is shown at the end of the question.

Prepare the form ready for Susan Woodhouse's signature, using information provided by the consolidated profit and loss account immediately following the tasks.

Task 2

Once you have completed the form for Task 1, write a short memo to Susan Woodhouse asking her to sign the form, so that it can be sent to the Foods Federation.

Data

Consolidated profit and loss account for the year ended 30 September 20X1

	Total
	£m
Sales	13.55
Cost of sales	8.81
Gross profit	4.74
Gross profit as % of sales	34.98%
Costs:	
Wages and salaries	1.36
Administration costs	0.93
Distribution costs	0.98
Other costs	0.14
	3.41
Net profit	1.33
Net profit as % of sales	9.82%
Capital employed	£5.50m
Return on capital employed	24.18%

Average numbers of full-time equivalent employees in the company during the year were:

Redcar site	73
Whitby site	35

PROFORMA SCHEDULE FOR ANSWERS

Task 1

FOODS FEDERATION INTER-FIRM COMPARISON SCHEME
Annual return – 30 September 20X1
(Express the figures to nearest £000 and % to two decimal places)

Name of business:...

Financial year end: ....

	£000
Turnover	....
Cost of sales	....
Gross profit % of sales	......................%

Other operating costs	**£000**	**% of turnover**
Wages and salaries	-----------	-----------%
Administration costs	-----------	-----------%
Distribution costs	-----------	-----------%
Other costs	-----------	-----------%
Net profit % of sales	-----------%	
Capital employed (£)	-----------	
Number of employees (full-time equivalent)	-----------	
Turnover per employee (£)	-----------	
Average wages and salaries per employee (£)	-----------	

Chapter 7
Spreadsheets

▷ ACTIVITY 23

The manager of a small flower shop, Petalart, is preparing a cash flow forecast for the coming three months, and has gathered the following information:

Sales in September were £3,600, and are expected to be £3,750 in October and £4,800 in each of November and December. Most customers pay when they buy, but it is estimated that 20% of the sales are made to corporate customers, who pay in the month following that of sale.

The costs of flower and other purchases account for 50% of sales values, and are paid on a cash on delivery basis. The fixed costs of the shop, staff etc come to £1,200 per month, also paid in the month they are incurred.

The bank balance at 30 September is expected to be £450.

The cash flow forecast proforma is as follows:

	October	November	December	Total
	£	£	£	£
Sales	3,750	4,800	4,800	
Receipts - from currrent month's sales				
- from previous month's sales				
Total receipts				
Purchase costs				
Fixed costs				
Total payments				
Net cash flow				
Bank balance b/f				
Bank balance c/f				

Set up a spreadsheet to compute the end of month cash balances, which will also allow you to answer the query 'what would happen if sales were in fact only £3,000 in October and November, and £3,500 in December?'

▷ ACTIVITY 24 

Houses 'R' Us is an estate agent company that has four branches in Buckfordshire. The managing director is compiling a report for the employees to inform them about the branch and company results for the past quarter. He wishes to make the report as visually interesting as possible.

The value of houses sold by each branch over the past year were as follows:

Branch	**Value of houses sold**
	£000
Buckford	458.2
New Milton	875.4
Wycfield	512.8
Chefford	690.1

Use a spreadsheet program to produce two different visual representations of this data.

▷ ACTIVITY 25

Set up the stock data for Bridings Ltd below on a spreadsheet. Improve its general appearance and readability by adding titles and formats as you think fit. Add three more columns to show (i) expected closing stock (units), (ii) closing stock value, and (iii) stock turnover (total issues for period, divided by the average of stock held at the beginning and end of the period).

Comment on any unusual results.

Product code	Description	Standard cost price	Stock movements in period (units)		
			Op bal	Receipts	Issues
BRL102	Brown leather belts	8.5	4	10	11
BLL102	Black leather belts	8.25	18	24	16
REV205	Red vinyl bags	12.5	8	6	15
BLV205	Blue vinyl bags	12.5	12	18	22
GRV205	Green vinyl bags	14.8	25	0	4
MUL370	Multi purse	6.8	20	10	18
BLL458	Black leather wallet	15.6	7	6	5
BLL654	Black leather diary	8.45	12	40	36
BRV700	Keyring case	4.32	0	0	0
BLC865	Glasses case	5.75	8	6	9

Chapter 8
VAT

▷ ACTIVITY 26

You work as an accounting technician for a small firm of accountants. Much of your work centres on small and medium sized sole traders and partnerships. You are often involved with the preparation of VAT returns for small businesses.

When accepting new clients you are often asked what records HM Revenue and Customs require a registered business to keep.

Prepare a checklist of such detail which you can give to clients in answer to this question.

▷ ACTIVITY 27

The following are commonly used VAT terms:

- Supply of goods
- Supply of services
- Output tax
- Input tax
- Zero-rated item
- Exempt item
- Standard-rated

Define clearly each of the above VAT terms.

▷ ACTIVITY 28

HM Revenue and Customs do not specify a standard format of invoice for registered businesses. However, there are certain essential elements to be shown on a VAT invoice.

List these, explaining clearly the purpose of each.

▷ ACTIVITY 29

Some businesses, particularly retailers, are permitted to issue a 'less detailed tax invoice'.

List the elements which need to be shown on this type of document.

▷ ACTIVITY 30

You are a self-employed accounting technician and Duncan Bye, a motor engineer, is one of your clients. He is registered for VAT with registration number 131 7250 19.

His records for the quarter ended 30 June 20X1 showed the following:

Sales day book

	Gross	Net	VAT
	£	£	£
April	7,931.25	6,750.00	1,181.25
May	7,649.25	6,510.00	1,139.25
June	9,682.00	8,240.00	1,442.00
	25,262.50	21,500.00	3,762.50

Purchases day book

	Gross	Net	VAT
	£	£	£
April	3,701.25	3,150.00	551.25
May	3,842.25	3,270.00	572.25
June	3,149.00	2,680.00	469.00
	10,692.50	9,100.00	1,592.50

He also gives you some details of petty cash expenditure in the quarter.

	£
Net purchases	75.60
VAT	13.23
	88.83

He informs you that he used some parts on a job to repair his own car. The parts had previously cost him £120 (exclusive of VAT).

Prepare the following VAT 100 form for the period, ready for Duncan Bye's signature.

Value Added Tax Return
For the period
to

Duncan Bye
Low House
Low Green
Derbyshire
DE1 7XU

Your VAT Office telephone number 0123-4567

For Official Use

Registration number | Period

You could be liable to a financial penalty if your completed return and all the VAT payable are not received by the due date.

Due date:

For Official Use	
Dor only	

Before you fill in this form please read the notes on the back and the VAT Leaflet 'Filling in your VAT return'. Fill in all boxes clearly in ink and write 'none' where necessary. Don't put a dash or leave any box blank. If there are no pence write '00' in the pence column. Do not enter more than one amount in any box.

For official use				
	VAT due in this period on sales and other outputs	1		
	VAT due in this period on acquisitions from other EC Member States	2		
	Total VAT due (the sum of boxes 1 and 2)	3		
	VAT reclaimed in this period on purchases and other inputs (including acquisitions from the EC)	4		
	Net VAT to be paid to Customs or reclaimed by you (Difference between boxes 3 and 4)	5		
	Total value of sales and all other outputs excluding any VAT. Include your box 8 figure.	6		00
	Total value of purchases and all other inputs excluding any VAT. Include your box 9 figure.	7		00
	Total value of all supplies of goods and related services excluding any VAT to other EC Member States.	8		00
	Total value of all acquisitions of goods and related services excluding any VAT, from other EC Member States.	9		00

If you are enclosing a payment please tick this box.	DECLARATION: You, or someone on your behalf, must sign below. I .... declare that the information given (Full name of signatory in BLOCK LETTERS) above is true and complete. Signature .... Date 20 A false declaration can result in prosecution.

VAT 100 (full) PT1 (April 2004)

▷ ACTIVITY 31

This scenario-based question is divided into two tasks, and contains a large amount of data which you may need to complete the tasks. You are advised to read the whole of the material before commencing the tasks.
You are provided with proforma schedules and report forms for the tasks and these are included at the end of the question.

The situation

Business: Daniel and James, Licensed Accounting Technicians

Personnel: Partners – James Musgrave and Daniel Robb
Accounting technician senior – you
Junior technician – Brenda Peach
Administration assistant – Diane Kelly

Data and tasks

Your work involves bookkeeping and accounting services mainly to small businesses.

Mark Ambrose is one of your clients; he is a self-employed master joiner and this assessment focuses on his file. The time is mid October 20X1.

Tasks to be completed

Task 1

Refer to the memo from James Musgrave below, immediately following the Tasks, regarding Mark Ambrose, and prepare the VAT form for the quarter ended 30 September 20X1 – a blank VAT form is provided at the end of the question.

Task 2

Write a letter to Mark Ambrose enclosing his VAT return for signature and explain to him how you have dealt with the VAT on the bad debts listed on his schedule, and also the private use of the materials.

Write your letter on the blank notepaper provided at the end of the question.

Data

MEMO

To: Accounting Technician

From: James Musgrave

Date: 15 October 20X1

Subject: Mark Ambrose - VAT return and query

I attach a letter and details relating to Mark's VAT return for quarter ended 30 September 20X1.

Could you please complete the form, incorporating any necessary adjustments for VAT on bad debts queried in his letter.

Many thanks.

James

Mark Ambrose
Master Joiner
High Park House
High Melton
Doncaster
DN5 7EZ

13 October 20X1

Dear James

I attach two schedules you will need for completing my VAT return for this quarter.

I have suffered some loss from bad debts in recent months and would like you to claim back the VAT on these – if that is possible.

I look forward to hearing from you shortly.

Yours sincerely

Mark

MARK AMBROSE

Summary of day books and petty cash expenditure
Quarter ended 30 September 20X1

Sales day book

	Work done	VAT	Total
	£	£	£
July	12,900.00	2,257.50	15,157.50
August	13,200.00	2,310.00	15,510.00
September	12,300.00	2,152.50	14,452.50
	38,400.00	6,720.00	45,120.00

Purchase day book

	Net	VAT	Total
	£	£	£
July	5,250.00	918.75	6,168.75
August	5,470.00	957.25	6,427.25
September	5,750.00	1,006.25	6,756.25
	16,470.00	2,882.25	19,352.25

Petty cash expenditure for quarter (VAT inclusive)

July	£105.75
August	£94.00
September	£117.50

I have also used some materials from my stock, valued at £500 (exclusive of VAT), to repair my garage roof.

Bad debts list – 30 September 20X1

Date	Customer	Total (including VAT)
30 November 20X0	High Melton Farms	£293.75
3 January 20X1	Concorde Motors	£176.25
4 April 20X1	Bawtry Engineering	£117.50

These have now been written off as bad debts.

PROFORMAS FOR ANSWERS

Task 1

Value Added Tax Return
For the period
01/07/X1 to 03/09/X1

For Official Use

Registration number: 123 9872 17
Period: 09X1

Mark Ambrose
High Park House
High Melton
Doncaster
DN5 7EZ

You could be liable to a financial penalty if your completed return and all the VAT payable are not received by the due date.

Due date:

Your VAT Office telephone number 0123-4567

For Official Use	
DOR only	

Before you fill in this form please read the notes on the back and the VAT Leaflet 'Filling in your VAT return'. Fill in all boxes clearly in ink and write 'none' where necessary. Don't put a dash or leave any box blank. If there are no pence write '00' in the pence column. Do not enter more than one amount in any box.

For official use		Box	£	p
	VAT due in this period on sales and other outputs	1		
	VAT due in this period on acquisitions from other EC Member States	2		
	Total VAT due (the sum of boxes 1 and 2)	3		
	VAT reclaimed in this period on purchases and other inputs (including acquisitions from the EC)	4		
	Net VAT to be paid to Customs or reclaimed by you (Difference between boxes 3 and 4)	5		00
	Total value of sales and all other outputs excluding any VAT. Include your box 8 figure.	6		00
	Total value of purchases and all other inputs excluding any VAT. Include your box 9 figure.	7		00
	Total value of all supplies of goods and related services excluding any VAT to other EC Member States.	8		00
	Total value of all acquisitions of goods and related services excluding any VAT, from other EC Member States.	9		

If you are enclosing a payment please tick this box. ☐

DECLARATION: You, or someone on your behalf, must sign below.
I .... declare that the information given
(Full name of signatory in BLOCK LETTERS)
above is true and complete.
Signature .... Date 20
A false declaration can result in prosecution.

VAT 100 (full) PT1 (April 2004)

Task 2

DANIEL AND JAMES
LICENSED ACCOUNTING TECHNICIANS

Stonehill House
Stonehill Rise
Doncaster
DN5 9HB

Tel/Fax: 01302 786050

e-mail: danjames@virgin.net

Partners: James Musgrave FMAAT
Daniel Robb FMAAT

▷ ACTIVITY 32

This scenario-based question is divided into three tasks, and contains a large amount of data which you may need to complete the tasks. You are advised to read the whole of the material before commencing the tasks.You are provided with proforma schedules and report forms for the tasks and these are included at the end of the question.

The situation

Business: Simon White – self-employed accounting technician

Location: North East Coast of England

You are to adopt the role of Simon White.

Your work includes a bookkeeping and accounting service to small businesses, particularly small hotels and guesthouses, restaurants and public houses.

One of your clients is Crescent Hotel which has 40 bedrooms, a small restaurant and bar. The hotel is owned by John and Norma Thistle. The time is mid October 20X1 and you are currently working on their bookkeeping and VAT records for the quarter ended 30 September 20X1.

Tasks to be completed

Task 1

Immediately following these tasks you will find a summary of the records from the day books for the period ended 30 September, together with other relevant notes.

There is also a short note attached from John Thistle regarding a bad debt.

Using the blank VAT form provided at the end of the question, prepare the return ready for John Thistle's signature.

Task 2

When you have completed the form, John is not around to see you.

Prepare a note for John explaining briefly how you have adjusted the return to account for the matters brought to your attention. Use the space provided at the end of the question for your note.

Task 3

A few days later you receive a phone call from Norma who informs you that she is considering the purchase of a newsagents' shop close to the hotel.

She says that she has heard that special VAT schemes apply to the retail trade.

Before responding fully to her, you decide to write to the VAT office for clarification of the scheme or schemes which apply to this type of business.

Write a letter to the VAT office at:

Customs House
Bright Street
Scarborough
North Yorkshire YO33 23J

regarding this issue. Use the blank notepaper provided at the end of the question.

Data

CRESCENT HOTEL

Summary of day books for quarter ended 30 September 20X1

Hotel sales day book

	Net	VAT	Gross
	£	£	£
July	17,300.00	3,027.50	20,327.50
August	20,200.00	3,535.00	23,735.00
September	17,600.00	3,080.00	20,680.00
	55,100.00	9,642.50	64,742.50

Sales – Gross takings in cash

	Bar	Restaurant
	£	£
July	3,877.50	6,873.75
August	4,935.00	6,638.75
September	3,466.25	6,168.75
	12,278.75	19,681.25

Purchases day book

	Net	VAT	Gross
	£	£	£
July (Hotel)	5,190.00	908.25	6,098.25
August (Hotel)	6,060.00	1,060.50	7,120.50
September (Hotel)	5,280.00	924.00	6,204.00
	16,530.00	2,892.75	19,422.75
July - September (bar and restaurant)	10,800.00	1,890.00	12,690.00

Petty cash expenditure

Gross for period £481.75

NOTE

To: Simon

From: John

Date: 16 October 20X1

Simon, you are aware that we had three residents last year (December 20X0) from a company working in the area. This company has now gone into liquidation and we have been informed that we will not receive any funds against this debt.

Could you please, if possible, claim back the VAT from HM Revenue and Customs.

The gross value of the invoice was £587.50.

Also, in mid-August it was Norma's birthday and we 'put on' a surprise party for her. We used £300 worth of stock from the restaurant and the bar (ex VAT).

Do we need to adjust any figures for VAT?

Value Added Tax Return

For the period
01/07/X1 to 03/09/X1

For Official Use

John Thistle
T/A Crescent Hotel
High Street
Whitby
YO21 37L

Registration number	Period
179 6421 27	09X1

You could be liable to a financial penalty if your completed return and all the VAT payable are not received by the due date.

Due date:

For Official Use	
DOR only	

Your VAT Office telephone number 0123-4567

Before you fill in this form please read the notes on the back and the VAT Leaflet 'Filling in your VAT return'. Fill in all boxes clearly in ink and write 'none' where necessary. Don't put a dash or leave any box blank. If there are no pence write '00' in the pence column. Do not enter more than one amount in any box.

For official use		Box	£	p
	VAT due in this period on sales and other outputs	1		
	VAT due in this period on acquisitions from other EC Member States	2		
	Total VAT due (the sum of boxes 1 and 2)	3		
	VAT reclaimed in this period on purchases and other inputs (including acquisitions from the EC)	4		
	Net VAT to be paid to Customs or reclaimed by you (Difference between boxes 3 and 4)	5		
	Total value of sales and all other outputs excluding any VAT. Include your box 8 figure.	6		00
	Total value of purchases and all other inputs excluding any VAT. Include your box 9 figure.	7		00
	Total value of all supplies of goods and related services excluding any VAT to other EC Member States.	8		00
	Total value of all acquisitions of goods and related services excluding any VAT, from other EC Member States.	9		00

If you are enclosing a payment please tick this box.

DECLARATION: You, or someone on your behalf, must sign below.
I .... declare that the information given
(Full name of signatory in BLOCK LETTERS)
above is true and complete.
Signature .... Date 20
A false declaration can result in prosecution.

VAT 100 (full) PT1 (April 2004)

Task 2

NOTE

To: John Thistle

From: Simon White

Date: 18 October 20X1

Task 3

Simon White FMAAT
Accounting Technician
Bay Farm
High Street
Hawsker
YO21 3EJ

Date: ……………………..

PRACTICE SIMULATION 1 QUESTIONS

Dunsley Pubs and Restaurants Ltd

This simulation is designed to test your ability to prepare reports and returns. You are allowed **1½ hours** to complete your work.

The simulation covers the following performance criteria:

Element 7.1 Prepare and present periodic performance reports Performance criteria

- A Consolidate information derived from different units of the organisation into the appropriate form
- B Reconcile information derived from different information systems within the organisation
- C Compare results over time using an appropriate method that allows for changing price levels
- D Account for transactions between separate units of the organisation in accordance with the organisation's procedures
- E Calculate ratios and performance indicators in accordance with the organisation's procedures
- F Prepare reports in the appropriate form and present them to management within the required timescales

Range Statement

Performance in this element relates to the following contexts:

Information:
- Costs
- Revenue

Ratios:
- Gross profit margin
- Net profit margin
- Return on capital employed

Performance indicators:
- Productivity
- Cost per unit
- Resource utilisation
- Profitability

Method of presenting information:
- Written report containing diagrams
- Table

Element 7.2 Prepare reports and returns for outside agencies Performance Criteria

A Identify, collate and present relevant information in accordance with the conventions and definitions used by outside agencies
B Ensure calculations of ratios and performance indicators are accurate
C Obtain authorisation for the despatch of completed reports and returns from the appropriate person
D Present reports and returns in accordance with outside agencies' requirements and deadlines

Range Statement

Performance in this element relates to the following contexts:

Ratios:
- Gross profit margin
- Net profit margin
- Return on capital employed

Reports and returns:
- Written report
- Return on standard form

Data and tasks

The situation and tasks to be completed are set out on the following pages.

The simulation is divided into five tasks.

The simulation contains a large amount of data which you may need to complete the tasks. You are advised to read the whole of the material before commencing your tasks.

Documents provided

You are provided with proforma schedules and report forms for each task and these are included in the answer booklet.

The situation

Business: Dunsley Pubs and Restaurants Ltd

Location: North East England

Personnel: Owner manager – Pauline Dunn
Development manager – Philip Rose
Accountant – Claire Daly
Accounting technician – you

The business owns a group of 12 pubs, all with restaurant facilities attached. The business sites are all located in and around the North East Coast, ranging from York inland up to Whitby and Scarborough.

The business has expanded in recent years and you have been employed by the company for the past two years.

Tasks to be completed

Today is early February 20X6 and the accounts for the year ended 31 December 20X5 have recently been finalised.

You will find an extract from these accounts immediately following the tasks below.

TASK 1

In the data below you will find an analysis of company turnover for each quarter for years ended 31 December 20X4 and 20X5.

You are required to calculate the four-point moving average trend figures for the period, and construct a graph showing the trend line and actual turnover, by quarter, for presentation to the accountant.

Use the proforma schedule provided in the answer booklet.

TASK 2

In the data below is a five-year summary of company turnover, together with a price index appropriate to the business sector in which Dunsley operates.

Using the schedule provided in the answer booklet, restate each year's turnover in terms of 20X1 prices and calculate the year-on-year annual increase in sales based on actual and adjusted turnover.

TASK 3

Set out in the answer booklet is a schedule of profitability ratios for the year ended 31 December 20X5.

You are required to calculate these ratios using the accounts shown in the data below and complete the schedule.

TASK 4

The company is a member of a trade association and subscribes to its inter-firm comparison scheme.

In the answer booklet you will find an annual return for the scheme. You are required to complete this ready for Claire Daly's signature and submission to the trade association.

TASK 5

On completing the above return in Task 4, draft a short memo to Claire Daly requesting her signature and commenting briefly on the ratios calculated.

Extract from accounts for year ended 31 December 20X5
Dunsley Pubs and Restaurants Ltd

	£m	£m
Turnover		3.10
Cost of sales		1.36
Gross profit		1.74
Wages and salaries	0.81	
Other operating costs	0.25	
		1.06
Net profit		0.68
Capital employed		£2.90m
Number of full-time equivalent employees		72

Dunsley Pubs and Restaurants Ltd
Analysis of sales per quarter – years 20X4 and 20X5

Year		Turnover
		£m
20X4	Q1	0.40
	Q2	0.44
	Q3	1.02
	Q4	0.89
		2.75
20X5	Q1	0.45
	Q2	0.49
	Q3	1.15
	Q4	1.01
		3.10

Five-year summary of turnover

Year	Turnover	Index
	£m	
20X1	2.10	100.0
20X2	2.25	103.1
20X3	2.51	106.2
20X4	2.75	110.2
20X5	3.10	113.1

PRACTICE SIMULATION 1 ANSWER BOOKLET

TASK 1

Centred four-point moving average trend figures

Year	Quarter	Turnover	Moving annual total	Moving average	Centred average trend
		£m	£m	£m	£m
20X4	1				
	2				
	3				
	4				
20X5	1				
	2				
	3				
	4				

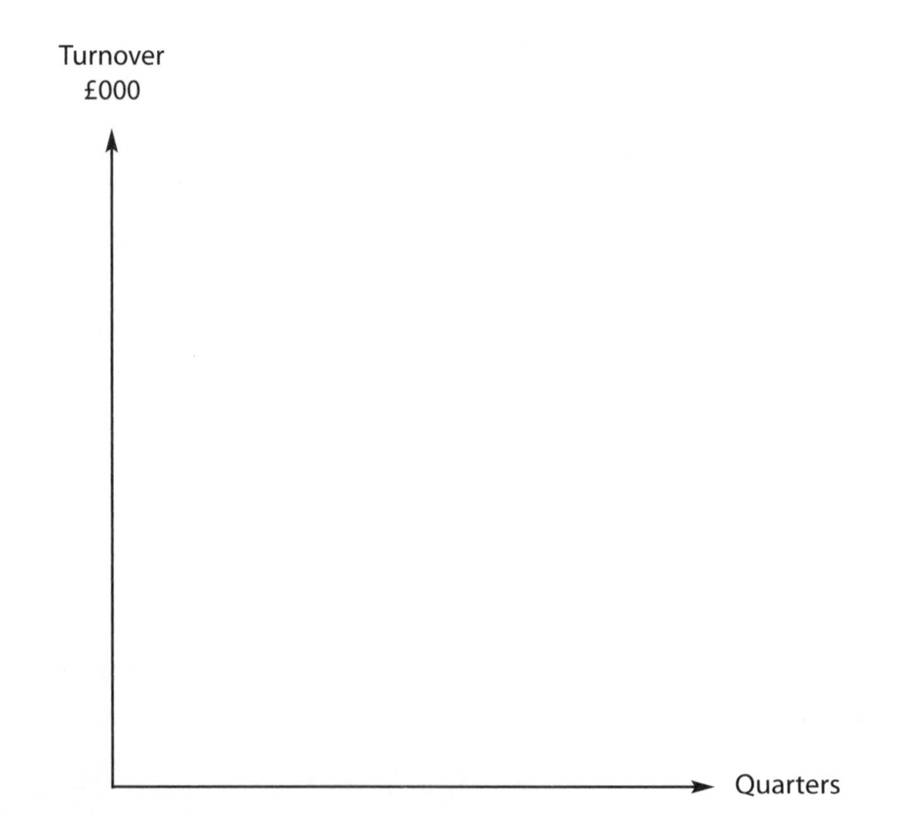

TASK 2

Dunsley Pubs and Restaurants Ltd

Year	20X1	20X2	20X3	20X4	20X5
	£m	£m	£m	£m	£m
Actual turnover					
% increase year on year					
Index					
Adjusted turnover					
% increase year on year					

TASK 3

Dunsley Pubs and Restaurants Ltd
Profitability ratios for 20X5

Ratio

Return on capital employed ....%
Gross profit as a % of turnover ....%
Net profit as a % of turnover ....%

TASK 4

TRADE ASSOCIATION INTER-FIRM COMPARISON SCHEME
Annual return – 31 December 20X5

Business name:..

Year end: ....

(**Note:** figures are to be shown to nearest £000 and % to two decimal places.)

£000

Turnover
Cost of sales
Gross profit as a % of sales __________%

£000

Wages and salaries
Other operating costs
Net profit as a % of sales __________%

Number of full-time equivalent employees ____________

Turnover per employee – full-time equivalent (£000) £____________

Wages and salaries per employee (£000) £____________

Signature: .... Date: ....

TASK 5

MEMO

To:

From:

Date:

Subject:

....

....

....

....

....

....

....

....

....

....

....

....

....

....

....

....

....

....

....

....

....

....

....

....

....

....

....

....

....

PRACTICE SIMULATION 2 QUESTIONS

COLEMAN LIMITED

This practice simulation is designed to test your ability to prepare reports and returns, and deals with a number of criteria in Element 7.2 and Element 7.3 of the Unit.

Performance criteria

Element 7.2 Prepare reports and returns for outside agencies

A Identify, collate and present relevant information in accordance with the conventions and definitions used by outside agencies
B Ensure calculations of ratios and performance indicators are accurate
C Obtain authorisation for the despatch of completed reports and returns from the appropriate person
D Present reports and returns in accordance with outside agencies' requirements and deadlines

Element 7.3 Prepare VAT returns

A Complete and submit VAT returns correctly, using data from the appropriate recording systems within the statutory time limits
B Correctly identify and calculate relevant inputs and outputs
C Ensure submissions are made in accordance with current legislation
D Ensure guidance is sought from the VAT Office when required in a professional manner.

Data and tasks

Instructions

The simulation is designed to test your ability to prepare reports and returns.

The situation and tasks to be completed are set out on the following pages.

The simulation contains a volume of data which you will require in order to complete the tasks.

The information you require is provided as far as possible in the sequence in which you will need to deal with it. However, you are advised to look quickly through all of the material before you begin. This will help you to familiarise yourself with the situation and the information available.

Your answers should be set out in the answer booklet using the answer sheets provided. If you require additional answer pages, ask the person in charge.

You are allowed 90 minutes to complete your work.

A high level of accuracy is required. Check your work before handing it in.

Correcting fluid may be used but it should be used in moderation. Errors should be crossed out neatly and clearly. You should write in black ink, not pencil.

You are reminded that you should not bring any unauthorised material, such as books or notes, into the simulation. If you have any such material in your possession, you should surrender it to the assessor immediately.

Any instances of misconduct will be brought to the attention of the AAT and disciplinary action may be taken.

The situation

Your name is Dennis Viollet and you work as an accounts assistant for Coleman Limited, 58 Elizabethan Street, Woodray, MU3 3RS. The company manufactures and distributes a product called the 'thain'.

The operations of Coleman Limited are conducted through two divisions: Manufacturing and Distribution. Each division is a profit centre. Manufacturing transfers finished goods to Distribution at full production cost, and Distribution sells them on to external customers. For historical reasons, Manufacturing also sells a small part of its output to external customers direct (i.e. without going through Distribution).

Most of Coleman's customers are based in the UK, but sales are also made to other countries in the European Union (EU). There are no exports to countries outside the EU.

Coleman Limited is registered for VAT and its sales to UK customers are all standard-rated. All sales to other EU countries qualify as zero-rated. The company's local VAT office is at Rayment House, 17 Crickmer Road, Whalley, WY4 8EW.

The company's year end is 31 December and today's date is 13 January 20X9.

The tasks to be completed

TASK 1

You are given the following information about Coleman Limited in 20X8.

Sales in the year (excluding VAT):	
Manufacturing - To Distribution	£1,817,000
- External	£432,000
Distribution	£3,109,000
Production cost of 'thains' produced and sold in the year	£2,070,000
Administration costs for the year	£523,000
Distribution costs for the year	£401,000
Total of all other costs for the year	£151,000
Capital employed	£5,983,000
Number of 'thains' produced and sold in the year	181,000
Average number of employees in the year	117

Turnover (external customers) in 20X7 was £3,427,000.

Coleman Limited is a member (membership number 441238) of the Northern Manufacturers Association (NMA). Each year the Association requires members to complete a standard form presenting statistical information relating to their most recent accounting period.

In the answer booklet you will find the form sent to Coleman by the NMA. You are required to complete the form in relation to Coleman's accounting year ended 31 December 20X8.

TASK 2

You are required to write a memo to the accounts supervisor, Roger Byrne, presenting the following ratios for his information:

- the gross profit percentage for 20X8
- the net profit percentage for 20X8
- the production cost per 'thain' produced and sold in 20X8
- the value of sales earned in 20X8 per employee.

Use the memo form in the answer booklet.

Ratios should be calculated to two decimal places; monetary amounts should be calculated to the nearest penny.

In your memo you should note that you are enclosing the NMA form from Task 4 and seeking authorisation for its despatch.

TASK 3

You are required to complete a VAT return for Coleman Limited in respect of the quarter ended 31 December 20X8. You are given the following information to assist you in this task:

- Of the external sales of £916,000 made during the quarter ended 31 December 20X8, a total of £65,000 relates to exports to EU countries. The remainder of this quarter's sales were to UK customers. You are reminded that all sales figures given exclude VAT.

- Total purchases by the company in the quarter amounted to £310,000 of standard-rated inputs, and £23,000 of zero-rated inputs (both figures stated are exclusive of VAT). All of these purchases were from within the UK.

- The sales figures for October 20X8 include an invoice for standard-rated goods with a value, excluding VAT, of £3,200. These goods were actually despatched in September 20X8 and should have been accounted for in the VAT return for the previous quarter, but were omitted in error.

- A debt of £611, inclusive of VAT, was written off as bad during the month of December 20X8. The related sale was made in February 20X8. Bad debt relief is now to be claimed.

- The return is to be signed by the accounts supervisor, Roger Byrne. Payment of any balance due to HM Revenue and Customs will be made by cheque.

A blank VAT return is printed in the answer booklet.

TASK 4

The company recently made a gift of some obsolete computer equipment to a local charity. You have belatedly realised that this transaction may give rise to a liability for output VAT.

You are required to write to your local VAT office requesting clarification of this point. Your objective is to ascertain whether such a liability exists and, if so, how it should be calculated. Use the letterhead in the answer booklet.

PRACTICE SIMULATION 2 ANSWER BOOKLET

COLEMAN LIMITED

TASK 1

NORTHERN MANUFACTURERS ASSOCIATION

23 Pegg Street, Edwardston, EN2 1WY

Dear Member

Please supply the following information in respect of your most recent accounting period. The information should be prepared in accordance with the notes below.

Name of company ____________________

NMA membership number ____________________

Financial year end date ____________________

1 Turnover for year ____________________
  Percentage change on previous year (+/-) ____________________
2 Production costs as percentage of sales ____________________
3 Administration costs as percentage of sales ____________________
4 Distribution costs as percentage of sales ____________________
5 Return on capital employed ____________________

Notes

1 Turnover should be stated net of VAT
2 Return on capital employed should be calculated as net profit divided by total capital employed.
3 Percentages and ratios should be stated to two decimal places.

Please return the completed form to Thomas Taylor at the above address by 31 January 20X9. Thank you for your assistance.

TASK 2

M E MO

To:

From:

Date:

Subject:

TASK 3

Value Added Tax Return
For the period
01 10 X8 to 31 12 X8

For Official Use

COLEMAN LIMITED
58 Elizabethan Street
Woodray
MU3 3RS

Your VAT Office telephone number 0123-4567

Registration number	Period
578 406019	12 X8

You could be liable to a financial penalty if your completed return and all the VAT payable are not received by the due date.

Due date: 31 01 X9

For Official Use	
DOR only	

Before you fill in this form please read the notes on the back and the VAT Leaflet 'Filling in your VAT return'. Fill in all boxes clearly in ink and write 'none' where necessary. Don't put a dash or leave any box blank. If there are no pence write '00' in the pence column. Do not enter more than one amount in any box.

For official use		Box	£	p
	VAT due in this period on sales and other outputs	1		
	VAT due in this period on acquisitions from other EC Member States	2		
	Total VAT due (the sum of boxes 1 and 2)	3		
	VAT reclaimed in this period on purchases and other inputs (including acquisitions from the EC)	4		
	Net VAT to be paid to Customs or reclaimed by you (Difference between boxes 3 and 4)	5		
	Total value of sales and all other outputs excluding any VAT. Include your box 8 figure.	6		00
	Total value of purchases and all other inputs excluding any VAT. Include your box 9 figure.	7		00
	Total value of all supplies of goods and related services excluding any VAT to other EC Member States.	8		00
	Total value of all acquisitions of goods and related services excluding any VAT, from other EC Member States.	9		00

If you are enclosing a payment please tick this box.

DECLARATION: You, or someone on your behalf, must sign below.
I .... declare that the information given
(Full name of signatory in BLOCK LETTERS)
above is true and complete.
Signature .... Date 20
A false declaration can result in prosecution.

VAT 100 (full) PT1 (April 2004)

TASK 4

COLEMAN LIMITED

58 Elizabethan Street, Woodray, MU3 3RS

Telephone 01423 335128

Registered in England, number 2234156
Registered office: 58 Elizabethan Street, Woodray, MU3 3RS

MOCK SIMULATION 1 QUESTIONS

Data and tasks

Instructions

This simulation is designed to test your ability to prepare reports and returns. The situation and the tasks to be performed are set out below.

The simulation also contains a large volume of data which you will require in order to complete the tasks.

Your answers should be set out in the answer booklet, using the answer sheets provided.

You are allowed three hours to complete your work.

A high level of accuracy is required. Check your work before handing it in.

Correcting fluid may be used but it should be used in moderation. Errors should be crossed out neatly and clearly. You should write in black ink, not pencil.

The information you require is provided as far as possible in the sequence in which you will need to deal with it. However, you are advised to look quickly through all the material before you begin. This will help you to familiarise yourself with the situation and the information available.

The situation

Your name is Sol Bellcamp and you work as an accounts assistant for a printing company, Hoddle Limited. Hoddle Limited is owned 100% by another printing company, Kelly Limited. You report to the Group Accountant, Sherry Teddingham.

Hoddle Limited manufactures a wide range of printed materials such as cards, brochures and booklets. Most customers are based in the UK, but sales are also made to other countries in the European Union (EU). There are no exports to countries outside the EU. All of the company's purchases come from businesses within the UK.

Hoddle Limited is registered for VAT and it makes both standard-rated and zero-rated supplies to its UK customers. All sales to other EU countries qualify as zero-rated. The company's local VAT office is at Brendon House, 14 Abbey Street, Pexley PY2 3WR.

Kelly Limited is separately registered for VAT; there is no group registration in force. Both companies have an accounting year ending on 31 March. There are no other companies in the Kelly group.

Hoddle Limited is a relatively small company and sometimes suffers from shortage of capacity to complete customers' jobs. In these cases, the printing work is done by Kelly Limited. Kelly then sells the completed products to Hoddle for onward sale to the customer. The sale from Kelly to Hoddle is recorded in the books of each company at cost; Kelly does not charge a profit margin.

In this simulation you are concerned with the accounting year ended 31 March 20X8.

- To begin with you will be required to prepare the VAT return for Hoddle Limited in respect of the quarter ended 31 March 20X8.
- You will then be required to prepare certain reports, both for internal use and for an external inter-firm comparison scheme, covering the whole accounting year ended 31 March 20X8. These reports will treat the two companies as a single group; they will contain consolidated figures, not figures for either of the two companies separately.

Today's date is 9 April 20X8.

Tasks to be completed

TASK 1

Refer to the three invoices immediately following these tasks, which have been received from Hoddle Ltd's suppliers during March 20X8. No entries have yet been made in Hoddle Ltd's books of account in respect of these documents. You are required to explain how you will treat each one of these documents when preparing Hoddle Ltd's VAT return for the period January to March 20X8. Set out your answer in the space provided in the answer booklet.

TASK 2

Refer to the sales day book summary, purchases day book summary, cash book summary and petty cash book summary in the data below. These have been printed out from Hoddle Ltd's computerised accounting system for the period January to March 20X8. (You are reminded that these summaries do not include the documents dealt with in Task 1.) Refer also to the memo dated 6 April in the data below. Using this information you are required to complete the VAT return of Hoddle Ltd for the quarter ended 31 March 20X8. A blank return is provided for this purpose in the answer booklet.

TASK 3

The Group Accountant is considering adoption of the cash accounting scheme for VAT. He believes that Hoddle Ltd (though not Kelly Ltd) might qualify for the scheme. He has asked you to draft a letter to the VAT office, in his name, requesting certain details of the scheme. He is interested in the turnover limit for the scheme, particularly since Hoddle is a member of a group of companies, and in the effect of the scheme in dealing with bad debts. Draft a letter in the space provided in the answer booklet.

TASK 4

Refer to the profit and loss account of Kelly Ltd in the data below which covers the period 1 January to 31 March 20X8. You are required to prepare a profit and loss account for the same period in which the results of Hoddle and Kelly are consolidated. Prepare your answer as follows, using the schedule provided in the answer booklet.

- Enter the results of Kelly in the first column.

- Using the information already provided for earlier tasks, construct the results of Hoddle Ltd and enter them in the second column. Note that Hoddle Ltd's stock at 1 January 20X8 was valued at £14,638, while stock at 31 March 20X8 was valued at £16,052.

- Make appropriate adjustments in the third column to eliminate the effects of trading between Kelly and Hoddle.

- Calculate the consolidated figures and enter them in the fourth column.

TASK 5

Refer to the consolidated balance sheet, and the memo dated 2 April in the data below. Using these, and the information already provided for earlier tasks, you are required to prepare a report for the accountant on the group results for the year ended 31 March 20X8. Your report should contain the following:

- the completed quarterly consolidated profit and loss accounts located in the answer booklet.
- Key ratios: gross profit margin; net profit margin; return on shareholders capital employed.
- Sales revenue for each quarter, both in actual terms and indexed to a common base.
- A pie chart showing the proportion of annual (unindexed) sales earned in each quarter.

Note: You are not required to comment on the results for the year, merely to present them according to the instructions above. Use the space provided in the answer booklet.

TASK 6

You are required to complete an inter-firm comparison as set out in the answer booklet.

Data

Engineering Supplies Limited

Haddlefield Road, Blaysley, CG6 6AW
Tel/Fax: 01376 44531

Hoddle Limited
22 Formguard Street
Pexley
PY6 3QW

SALES INVOICE NO: 2155

Date: 27 March 20X8

	£
VAT omitted in error from invoice no 2139	
£2,667.30 @ 17.5%	466.77
Total due	466.77

Terms: net 30 days

VAT registration: 318 1827 58

Alpha Stationery

Aindsale Centre, Mexton, EV1 4DF
Telephone: 01392 43215

26 March 20X8

1 box transparent folders : red

Total incl VAT @ 17.5%	14.84
Amount tendered	20.00
Change	5.16

VAT registration: 356 7612 33

JAMIESON & CO

Jamieson House, Baines Road, Gresham, GM7 2PQ
Telephone: 01677 35567 Fax: 01677 57640

PROFORMA SALES INVOICE

VAT registration: 412 7553 67

Hoddle Limited
22 Formguard Street
Pexley
PY6 3QW

For professional serices in connection with debt collection	£
Our fees	350.00
VAT	61.25
Total due	411.25

A VAT invoice will be submitted when the total due is paid in full.

HODDLE LIMITED : SALES DAY BOOK SUMMARY
JANUARY TO MARCH 20X8

	JAN	FEB	MAR	TOTAL
	£	£	£	£
UK: ZERO-RATED	20,091.12	22,397.00	23,018.55	65,506.67
UK: STANDARD-RATED	15,682.30	12,914.03	15,632.98	44,229.31
OTHER EU	874.12	4,992.66	5,003.82	10,870.60
VAT	2,744.40	2,259.95	2,735.77	7,740.12
TOTAL	39,391.94	42,563.64	46,391.12	128,346.70

HODDLE LIMITED : PURCHASES DAY BOOK SUMMARY
JANUARY TO MARCH 20X8

	JAN	FEB	MAR	TOTAL
	£	£	£	£
PURCHASES	14,532.11	20,914.33	15,461.77	50,908.21*
DISTRIBUTION EXPENSES	4,229.04	3,761.20	5,221.43	13,211.67
ADMIN EXPENSES	5,123.08	2,871.45	3,681.62	11,676.15
OTHER EXPENSES	1,231.00	1,154.99	997.65	3,383.64
VAT	4,027.97	4,543.22	4,119.34	12,690.53
TOTAL	29,143.20	33,245.19	29,481.81	91,870.20

*This figure includes £18,271 of purchases from Kelly Limited.

HODDLE LIMITED : CASH BOOK SUMMARY
JANUARY TO MARCH 20X8

	JAN	FEB	MAR	TOTAL
	£	£	£	£
PAYMENTS:				
TO CREDITORS	12,901.37	15,312.70	18,712.44	46,926.51
TO PETTY CASH	601.40	555.08	623.81	1,780.29
WAGES/SALARIES	5,882.18	6,017.98	6,114.31	18,014.47
TOTAL	19,384.95	21,885.76	25,450.56	66,721.27
RECEIPTS:				
VAT FROM HM REVENUE AND				
CUSTOMS	2,998.01			2,998.01
FROM CUSTOMERS	29,312.44	34,216.08	36,108.77	99,637.29
TOTAL	32,310.45	34,216.08	36,108.77	102,635.30
SURPLUS FOR MONTH	12,925.50	12,330.32	10,658.21	
BALANCES B/F	-8,712.41	4,213.09	16,543.41	
BALANCE C/F	4,213.09	16,543.41	27,201.62	

HODDLE LIMITED : PETTY CASH BOOK SUMMARY JANUARY TO MARCH 20X8

	JAN	FEB	MAR	TOTAL
	£	£	£	£
PAYMENTS:				
STATIONERY	213.85	80.12	237.58	531.55
TRAVEL	87.34	76.50	102.70	266.54
OFFICE EXPENSES	213.66	324.08	199.51	737.25
VAT	86.55	74.38	84.02	244.95
TOTAL	601.40	555.08	623.81	1,780.29
RECEIPTS:				
FROM CASH BOOK	601.40	555.08	623.81	1,780.29
SURPLUS FOR MONTH	0.00	0.00	0.00	
BALANCES B/F	200.00	200.00	200.00	
BALANCE C/F	200.00	200.00	200.00	

MEMO

To: Sol Bellcamp

From: Sherry Teddingham

Date: 6 April 20X8

Subject: Bad debt – Batty Limited

As you probably know, we have had great difficulty in persuading the above customer to pay what he owes us. We invoiced him in July 20X7 for £420 plus VAT at the standard rate, but he has always disputed the debt and it looks as though we will never recover it. We wrote it off to the bad debt account in March of this year, so you should take this into account when preparing the VAT return for the quarter just ended.

Kelly Limited
Profit and loss account for the three months ended 31 March 20X8

	£	£
Sales to external customers		275,601
Sales to Hoddle Limited at cost		20,167*
Total sales		295,768
Opening stock	28,341	
Purchases	136,095	
	164,436	
Closing stock	31,207	
Cost of sales		133,229
Gross profit		162,539
Wages and salaries	47,918	
Distribution expenses	28,341	
Administration expenses	30,189	
Stationery	2,541	
Travel	2,001	
Office expenses	3,908	
Interest payable	12,017	
Other expenses	11,765	
		138,680
Net profit for the period		23,859

*This figure includes £1,896 in respect of a job completed on 31 March 20X8 but not delivered to Hoddle Limited until 1 April 20X8. It is not included in Hoddle Ltd's purchases for the period ended 31 March.

Kelly and Hoddle
Consolidated balance sheet at 31 March 20X8

	£	£
Fixed assets at net book value		1,229,348
Current assets		
Stock	49,155	
Trade debtors	223,009	
VAT recoverable	13,451	
Cash at bank and in hand	40,088	
	325,703	
Current liabilities		
Trade creditors	136,531	
Other creditors	11,740	
	148,271	

Net current assets	177,432
Total assets less current liabilities	1,406,780
Long-term liability	
Loan repayable in 20Y4	372,072
	1,034,708
Capital and reservces	
Called up share capital	234,167
Retained profits	800,541
	1,034,708

MEMO

To: Sol Bellcamp

From: Sherry Teddingham

Date: 2 April 20X8

Subject: Adjusting for the effects of price rises

When presenting your quarterly reports on group results please include an item of information additional to that which you normally present. As well as noting sales revenue by quarter, please present quarterly sales revenue adjusted to take account of price rises.

I have identified a suitable index as follows:

First quarter 20X6/X7 (base period)	231.8
First quarter 20X7/X8	239.3
Second quarter 20X7/X8	241.5
Third quarter 20X7/X8	244.0
Fourth quarter 20X7/X8	241.8

I will keep you informed of future movements in this index.

MOCK SIMULATION 1 ANSWER BOOKLET

TASK 1

TASK 2

Value Added Tax Return
For the period
to

For Official Use

Mr Sherry Teddingham
Hoddle Limited
22 Formguard Street
Pexley
PY6 3QW

Registration number: 5 6 3 4 1 7 2 2 1

Period

You could be liable to a financial penalty if your completed return and all the VAT payable are not received by the due date.

Due date: 30 04 X8

Your VAT Office telephone number 0123-4567

For Official Use	
DOR only	

Before you fill in this form please read the notes on the back and the VAT Leaflet 'Filling in your VAT return'. Fill in all boxes clearly in ink and write 'none' where necessary. Don't put a dash or leave any box blank. If there are no pence write '00' in the pence column. Do not enter more than one amount in any box.

For official use		Box	£	p
	VAT due in this period on sales and other outputs	1		
	VAT due in this period on acquisitions from other EC Member States	2		
	Total VAT due (the sum of boxes 1 and 2)	3		
	VAT reclaimed in this period on purchases and other inputs (including acquisitions from the EC)	4		
	Net VAT to be paid to Customs or reclaimed by you (Difference between boxes 3 and 4)	5		
	Total value of sales and all other outputs excluding any VAT. Include your box 8 figure.	6		00
	Total value of purchases and all other inputs excluding any VAT. Include your box 9 figure.	7		00
	Total value of all supplies of goods and related services excluding any VAT to other EC Member States.	8		00
	Total value of all acquisitions of goods and related services excluding any VAT, from other EC Member States.	9		00

If you are enclosing a payment please tick this box.

DECLARATION: You, or someone on your behalf, must sign below.
I .... declare that the information given
(Full name of signatory in BLOCK LETTERS)
above is true and complete.
Signature .... Date 20
A false declaration can result in prosecution.

VAT 100 (full) PT1 (April 2004)

TASK 3

Hoddle Limited
22 Formguard Street, Pexley, PY6 3QW
Telephone 01682 431256

Registered office: 22 Formguard Street, Pexley, PY6 3QW
Registered in England, number 2314561

TASK 4

	Kelly	Hoddle	Adjustments	Consolidated
	£	£	£	£
Sales				
Opening stock				
Purchases				
Closing stock				
Cost of sales				
Gross profit				
Wages and salaries				
Distribution expenses				
Administration expenses				
Stationery				
Travel				
Office expenses				
Interest payable				
Other expenses				
Net profit for the period				

TASK 5

Quarterly consolidated profit and loss accounts for the year ended 31 March 20X8

	1 Apr X7 to 30 Jun X7	1 Jul X7 to 30 Sep X7	1 Oct X7 to 31 Dec X7	1 Jan X8 to 31 Mar X8	Totals for year 1 Apr X7 to 31 Mar X8
	£	£	£	£	£
Sales	325,719	275,230	306,321		
Cost of sales	134,861	109,421	121,358		
Gross profit	190,858	165,809	184,963		
Wages and salaries	63,314	61,167	64,412		
Distribution expenses	34,217	30,135	31,221		
Admin expenses	34,765	33,012	36,415		
Stationary	2,981	2,671	3,008		
Travel	1,975	1,876	2,413		
Office expenses	4,412	4,713	3,083		
Interest payable	12,913	12,714	12,432		
other expenses	10,981	16,421	15,431		
	165,558	162,709	168,415		
Net profit for the period	25,300	3,100	16,548		

Note for candidates: you are advised to complete the above schedule by filling in the figures for the final quarter in the fourth column and totalling the figures for the year in the final column.

Report

To:

From:

Date:

Subject:

TASK 6

Inter-firm comparison data (extracts)

Name of company ……………………………………………..

Year ended ……………………………………………..

Data

	£	% of sales	Industry best	Industry average
Sales				
Gross profit			62.1%	57.3%
Net profit			10.4%	5.8%
Fixed assets				
Current assets				
Current liabilities				
Return on capital employed			10.3%	9.0%

Important note

Before completing this form you should read the explanatory notes below:

Note 1

'Sales' means sales to external customers. Inter-company, inter-divisional or inter-branch sales should be excluded.

Note 2

Fixed assets should be stated at net book value.

Note 3

Return on capital employed is net profit before interest charges, divided by capital employed.

MOCK SIMULATION 2 QUESTIONS

Houillier Ltd

Data and tasks

Instructions

This simulation is designed to test your ability to prepare reports and returns. The situation and the tasks to be completed are set out below.

The simulation also contains data which you will require in order to complete the tasks.

Your answers should be set out in the answer booklet, using the answer sheets provided. If you require additional answer pages, ask the person in charge.

You are allowed **three hours** to complete your work.

A high level of accuracy is required. Check your work before handing it in.

Correcting fluid may be used, but it should be used in moderation. Errors should be crossed out neatly and clearly. You should write in black ink, not pencil.

The information you require is provided as far as possible in the sequence in which you will need to deal with it. However, you are advised to look quickly through all of the material before you begin. This will help you to familiarise yourself with the situation and the information available.

The situation

Your name is Stevie Real and you work as an accounts assistant for Houillier Limited, a wholesaling company based in Liverpool. Operations are conducted through two outlets: the City Centre branch and the District branch. Along with all other office staff in Houillier you work in office accommodation housed in the City Centre branch. You report to Janice Knapper, the accounts supervisor.

Houillier's most recent accounting period is the year ended 30 September 20X9. Part of the work facing you at the moment is to prepare consolidated information relating to costs and revenues arising in that year. ('Consolidated' information means total information relating to the two branches combined.)

Houillier is a member of the Federation of North Western Wholesalers (FNWW), a trade body. Members of FNWW submit an annual report to the Federation which includes summarised financial information. The Federation uses this to prepare comparative information for use by members. The second main task on your agenda at present is to complete the annual report ready for submission to FNWW.

Finally, you are also responsible for preparing the company's VAT return. The return for the quarter ended 30 September 20X9 is to be prepared in good time for submission to HM Revenue and Customs by 31 October 20X9.

In relation to VAT, Houillier's sales to UK customers are all standard-rated. All sales to other EU countries qualify as zero-rated. The company's local VAT office is at 38 Bergerac Road, Babbtown, Liverpool, L16 3NV. The company settles its quarterly VAT liability by enclosing a cheque along with its VAT 100 return.

Tasks to be completed

TASK 1

Immediately following the tasks below, you will find cost and revenue data for the year ended 30 September 20X9 for both the City Centre branch and the District Branch (a profit and loss account and other information for each).

You are required to consolidate this information (i.e. combine the information for the two branches) so as to produce a profit and loss account for the company as a whole for the year ended 30 September 20X9. Note that transfers between the two branches are not to be treated as sales or purchases and must instead be excluded from the consolidated figures.

Use the proforma provided in the answer booklet to set out your answer.

TASK 2

Reproduced in the answer booklet you will find the company's consolidated profit and loss account for the year ended 30 September 20X8. A price index appropriate to the company had an average value of 161.2 during year ended 30 September 20X8 and an average value of 168.8 during year ended 30 September 20X9.

You are required to restate the 20X8 profit and loss account in terms of 20X9 prices using the average values of the price index given above, and to show the percentage change from 20X8 (restated) to 20X9 in each line of the profit and loss account. Your calculations of the percentage should be accurate to one decimal place. (You may find it helpful to enter the 20X9 figures calculated in Task 1 on the schedule provided for Task 2 in the answer booklet.)

TASK 3

You are required to write a memo, dated 11 October 20X9, to your accounts supervisor.

In the memo you should:

(a) set out the following ratios for the year ended 30 September 20X9:
- gross profit margin
- net profit margin
- return on capital employed (the average capital employed by Houillier Limited during the year ended 30 September 20X9 was £21,600,000)

(b) include a pie chart showing the total sales revenue for the year broken down into slices for:
- cost of goods sold
- wholesaling wages and salaries
- administration wages and salaries
- other costs
- net profit.

Your pie chart should clearly indicate the percentage of sales revenue represented by each of these items.

Use the blank memo form provided in the answer booklet.

(This task relates entirely to the consolidated results for 20X8/X9, i.e. the results for the two branches combined, not to the results of each branch singly.)

TASK 4

You are required to enter the relevant details on the FNWW annual report set out in the answer booklet. You should then send a memo dated 12 October 1999, enclosing the completed form for the attention and approval of your accounts supervisor prior to its despatch to FNWW. Use the blank memo form provided in the answer booklet.

TASK 5

Refer to the sales day book summary, purchases day book summary, and petty cash book summary in the data below. Using this information you are required to complete the VAT return of Houillier Limited for the quarter ended 30 September 20X9 ready for signature by the accounts supervisor. A blank VAT return is provided in the answer booklet.

TASK 6

Your accounts supervisor believes that the company may be eligible to account for VAT using the special schemes designed for retail businesses. You are required to draft a letter to your local VAT office requesting details of these schemes. Use the blank letterhead provided in the answer booklet and date your letter 12 October 20X9.

Data

CITY CENTRE BRANCH
Profit and loss account for the year ended 30 September 20X9

	£	£
Sales to external customers		8,672,130
Transfer to District branch (valued at cost)		387,160
		9,059,290
Opening stock	934,120	
Purchases	6,521,540	
	7,455,660	
Less closing stock	1,065,410	
Cost of goods sold		6,390,250
Gross profit		2,669,040
Wholesaling wages and salaries*	856,120	
Administration wages and salaries **	549,780	
Other costs	574,000	
		1,979,900
Net profit for the year		689,140

* Average number of employees (full-time equivalents) = 79

** Average number of employees (full-time equivalents) = 41

Note: A consignment of goods, costing £26,550, was despatched to the District branch on 30 September 20X9, but was not recorded in District's stock until 1 October 20X9.

DISTRICT BRANCH
Profit and loss account for the year ended 30 September 20X9

	£	£
Sales to external customers		6,241,100
Opening stock	518,710	
Purchases	4,111,900	
Transfers from City Centre branch at cost	360,610	
	4,991,220	
Less closing stock	597,230	
Cost of goods sold		47,393,990
Gross profit		1,847,110
Wholesaling wages and salaries*	801,980	
Other costs	423,170	
		1,225,150
Net profit for the year		621,960

* Average number of employees (full-time equivalents) = 71

Note: A consignment of goods, from the City Centre branch, despatched on 30 September 20X9, was not recorded in District's stock until 1 October 20X9. The cost of these goods was £26,550.

HOUILLIER LIMITED
Sales day book summary – July to September 20X9

	July	August	September	Total
	£	£	£	£
UK: STANDARD RATED	890,543	912,453	798,125	2,601,121
OTHER EU	100,871	123,009	98,137	322,017
VAT	155,845	159,679	139,672	455,196
TOTAL	1,147,259	1,195,141	1,035,934	3,378,334

HOUILLIER LIMITED
Purchases day book summary – July to September 20X9

	July	August	September	Total
	£	£	£	£
PURCHASES	781,235	861,200	900,125	2,542,560
OTHER COSTS	68,901	76,432	77,988	223,321
VAT	133,608	150,005	155,432	439,045
TOTAL	983,744	1,087,637	1,133,545	3,204,926

HOUILLIER LIMITED
Petty cash book payments – July to September 20X9

	July	August	September	Total
	£	£	£	£
OTHER COSTS	1,237	1,509	1,180	3,926
VAT	201	249	188	638
TOTAL	1,438	1,758	1,368	4,564

MOCK SIMULATION 2
ANSWER BOOKLET

TASK 1

Consolidated profit and loss account for the year ended 30 September 20X9

	City Centre	District	Consolidated
	£	£	£
Sales to external customers			
Opening stock			
Purchases			
Less closing stock			
Cost of goods sold			
Gross profit			
Wholesaling wages and salaries			
Administration wages and salaries			
Other costs			
Net profit for the year			

TASK 2

Consolidated profit and loss accont for the years ended 30 Septemeber 20X8 and X9

	20X8 (actual)	20X8 (restated)	20X9	Change in year
	£	£	£	%
Sales to external customers	12,247,318			
Opening stock	1,225,671			
Purchases	9,206,783			
	10,432,454			
Less closing stock	1,452,830			
Cost of goods sold	8,979,624			
Gross profit	3,267,694			
Wholesaling wages and salaries	(1,236,519)			
Administration wages and salaries	(483,512)			
Other costs	(852,090)			
Net profit for the year	695,573			

TASK 3

MEMO

To:

From:

Date:

Subject:

TASK 3 (continued)

TASK 4

FEDERATION OF NORTH WESTERN WHOLESALERS
Annual report to be completed by members (extract)

Please supply the information requested below as soon as possible after the end of your accounting period. The ratios and statistics should be calculated in accordance with the conventions and definitions explained in the notes.

Name of member ....Year end ....

Gross margin (Note 2) ....

Net margin (Note 3) ....

Return on capital employed (Note 4) ....

Total of direct salaries (Note 5) ....

Total of indirect salaries (Note 6) ....

Average salary per employee (Note 7) ....

Notes

1. All ratios and statistics should be calculated to one decimal place. Monetary amounts should be stated to the nearest thousand pounds. Members trading through more than one branch or division should submit consolidated information only, i.e. information for all branches combined as a single entity.

2. Gross margin is the ratio of gross profit to sales, expressed as a percentage.

3. Net margin is the ratio of net profit to sales, expressed as a percentage.

4. Return on capital employed is the ratio of net profit to average capital employed during the accounting period, expressed as a percentage.

5. Direct salaries are those of staff engaged directly in wholesaling activities.

6. Indirect salaries are those of all other staff, including administration staff.

7. Average salary per employee is the total wages and salaries for the year, divided by the number of full-time equivalent staff employed during the year.

TASK 4 (continued)

MEMO

To:

From:

Date:

Subject:

TASK 5

Value Added Tax Return
For the period
01/07/X9 to 30/09X9

For Official Use

HOUILLIER LIMITED
39 CARRAGHER ROAD
JAMESTOWN
LIVERPOOL
L15 3NP

Registration number: 578 4060 19
Period: 09 X9

You could be liable to a financial penalty if your completed return and all the VAT payable are not received by the due date.

Due date:

For Official Use	
DOR only	

Your VAT Office telephone number 0123-4567

Before you fill in this form please read the notes on the back and the VAT Leaflet 'Filling in your VAT return'. Fill in all boxes clearly in ink and write 'none' where necessary. Don't put a dash or leave any box blank. If there are no pence write '00' in the pence column. Do not enter more than one amount in any box.

For official use		Box	£	p
	VAT due in this period on sales and other outputs	1		
	VAT due in this period on acquisitions from other EC Member States	2		
	Total VAT due (the sum of boxes 1 and 2)	3		
	VAT reclaimed in this period on purchases and other inputs (including acquisitions from the EC)	4		
	Net VAT to be paid to Customs or reclaimed by you (Difference between boxes 3 and 4)	5		
	Total value of sales and all other outputs excluding any VAT. Include your box 8 figure.	6		00
	Total value of purchases and all other inputs excluding any VAT. Include your box 9 figure.	7		00
	Total value of all supplies of goods and related services excluding any VAT to other EC Member States.	8		00
	Total value of all acquisitions of goods and related services excluding any VAT, from other EC Member States.	9		00

If you are enclosing a payment please tick this box. ☐

DECLARATION: You, or someone on your behalf, must sign below.
I .... declare that the information given
(Full name of signatory in BLOCK LETTERS)
above is true and complete.
Signature .... Date 20
A false declaration can result in prosecution.

VAT 100 (full) PT1 (April 2004)

TASK 6

HOUILLIER LIMITED

39 Carragher Road, Jamestown, Liverpool, L15 3NP
Telephone: 0151 623 4671

Registered in England. Registration number 2314567

KEY TECHNIQUES ANSWERS

Chapter 1
Internal and external reports

△ ACTIVITY 1

- Regular reports are those which relate to a cycle of activities. The weekly analysis of payroll and labour cost (both direct and indirect) to cost centres is an example of a regular report.
- Exception reports are prepared to highlight some unusual occurrence. For example, if during a winter period a 'flu' epidemic occurred, then reporting on sick leave and hours lost could form the basis of an exception report.
- Analysis is the examination and carrying out of further work on balances and trends in order to gain a better understanding. The reporting and analysis of labour productivity and efficiency per cost centre is an example of such a report.
- Forecasts are projections of future activity for expense centres, profit centres and investment centres. These form the basis of forward looking plans, both in terms of short-term budgets and longer-term strategy. A business would prepare a forecast of employee numbers required in six months' time in order to ensure that sufficient new employees were recruited before they were required.

△ ACTIVITY 2

General digests would include:

- Monthly Digest of Statistics
- Annual Abstract of Statistics
- Social Trends

Specific digests would include:

- Economic Trends
- British Business (DTI)
- Employment Gazette
- National accounts
- Overseas trade statistics
- New earnings survey.

Chapter 2
Writing reports

△ ACTIVITY 3

The purpose of each element includes:

Title and preliminaries
Report title, to and from including job titles and also date.

Introduction/terms of reference
The need for and scope of the report. What does it cover, why is it being written, for whom is it written and its timing.

Procedure
The source of the data and/or information and how it is used.

Findings
The results are set out and analysed.

Conclusions
The summary of the findings with comments.

Recommendations
The recommendations are based on the conclusions reached.

Appendices
Extra data or references are included here.

Chapter 3
Tables and diagrams

△ ACTIVITY 4

The following guidelines should be adhered to when constructing a table:

- Give the table a title and suitable headings.
- If it contains a number of categories, use a two-way table.
- Give columns sub-totals where appropriate.
- State the source of the data.
- The units in the table should be manageable.
- Where appropriate include percentages.

ACTIVITY 6

Loftus Fertilisers Ltd

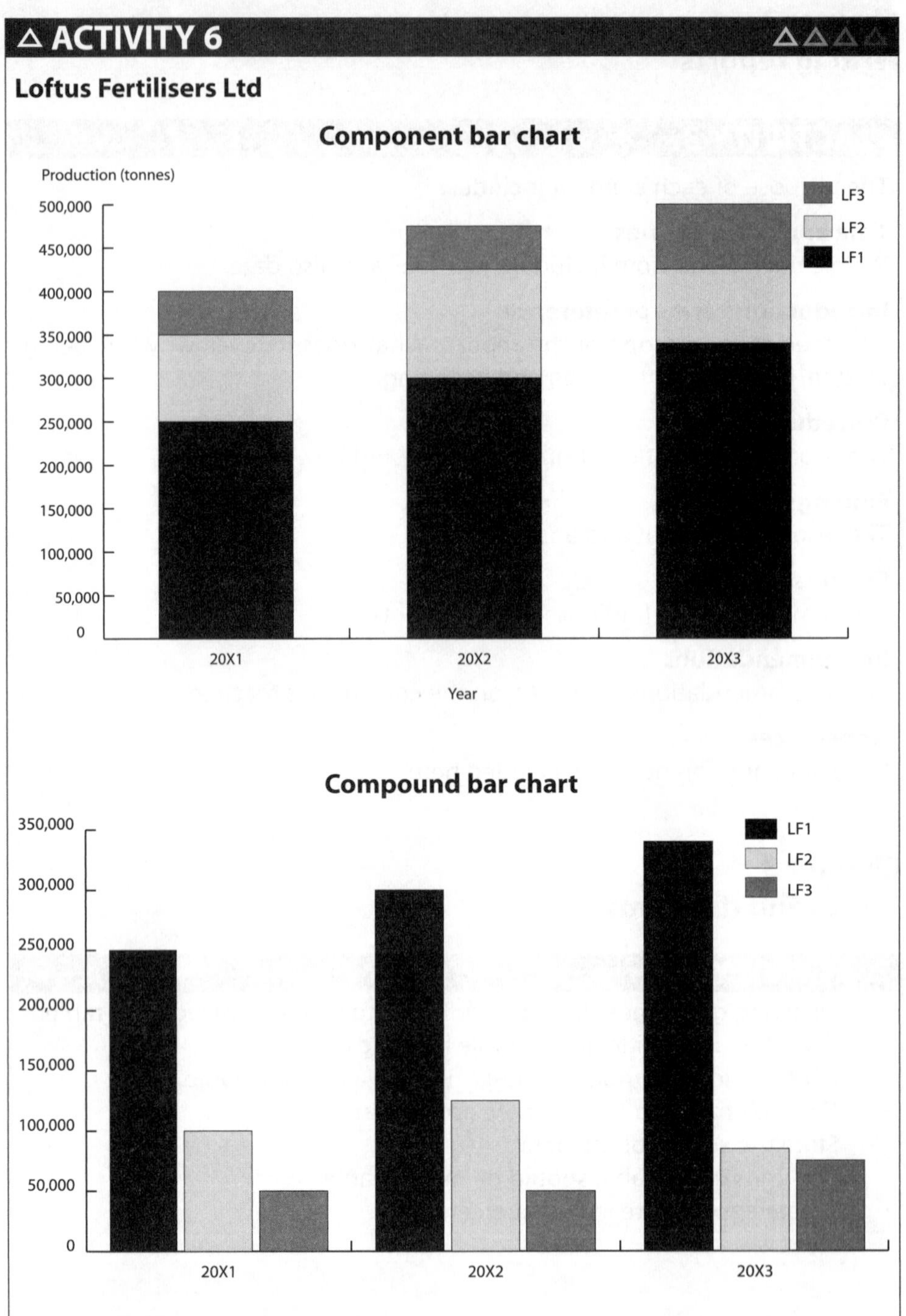

The benefits of each chart are:

- the component bar chart shows the total tonnage for each year
- the compound bar chart shows the trend or change between the years.

△ ACTIVITY 6

FOURTH QUARTER SALES			
	Previous quarter	**Current quarter**	*Corresponding quarter*
	July–Sep 20X2	**Oct–Dec 20X2**	*Oct–Dec 20X1*
	£	**£**	*£*
Month 1	37,440	**37,440**	*38,880*
Month 2	41,040	**41,040**	*40,320*
Month 3	42,000	**41,400**	*38,400*
TOTAL	120,480	**119,880**	*117,600*

△ ACTIVITY 7

Pictogram

Key

= £100,000 sales for the quater

Buckford

New Milton

Wycfield

Chefford

Pie chart

We need to compute the proportions of total sales each branch has generated, and convert these to angles by applying that proportion to 360°:

Branch	Value of houses sold	Proportion	Angle
	£000	%	°
Buckford	458.2	18.06	65
New Milton	875.4	34.51	124
Wycfield	512.8	20.22	73
Chefford	690.1	27.21	98
	2,536.5	100.00	360

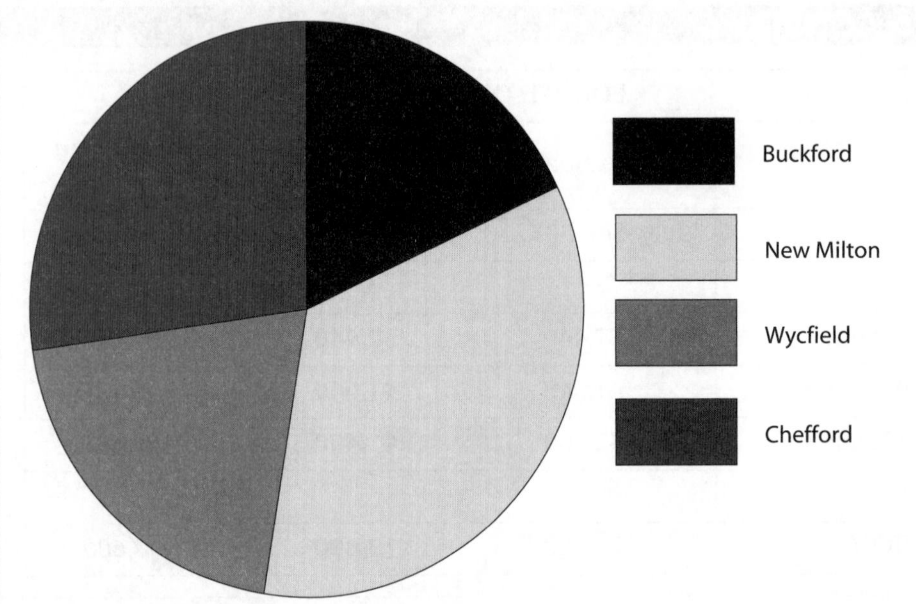

Both diagrams show the individual sales of each branch; the pictogram allows easier direct comparison between branches, whilst the pie chart shows the proportions to sales as a whole. The latter would probably be of greater interest to central management, whilst individual branch managers might prefer the pictogram (particularly the manager of New Milton!).

△ ACTIVITY 8

Stainsacre Park

(a)

Number of visitors	Tally	Frequency
515	|||	3
520	|||	3
525	~~||||~~ |	6
530	||	2
535	||||	4
540	||	2
545	||	2
550	||	2
555	|||	3
560	|||	3
565	|	1
		31

(b) The median value is the 16th item when the items are ranked in order.

Median = 535 visitors

$$\text{Mean} = \frac{\text{Sum of all values}}{\text{Total number of items}} = \frac{16,635}{31} = 537 \text{ visitors}$$

Mode = 525 visitors

Chapter 4
Graphs, time series and index numbers

ACTIVITY 9

(a)

Runswick Camp
Centred four-point moving average

Year	Quarter	Visitors	Moving annual total	Moving average	Centred average trend
20X1	1	5,750			
	2	8,950			
	3	14,750	35,700	8,925	9,025
	4	6,250	36,500	9,125	9,225
20X2	1	6,550	37,300	9,325	9,425
	2	9,750	38,100	9,525	9,625
	3	15,550	38,900	9,725	
	4	7,050			

(b)

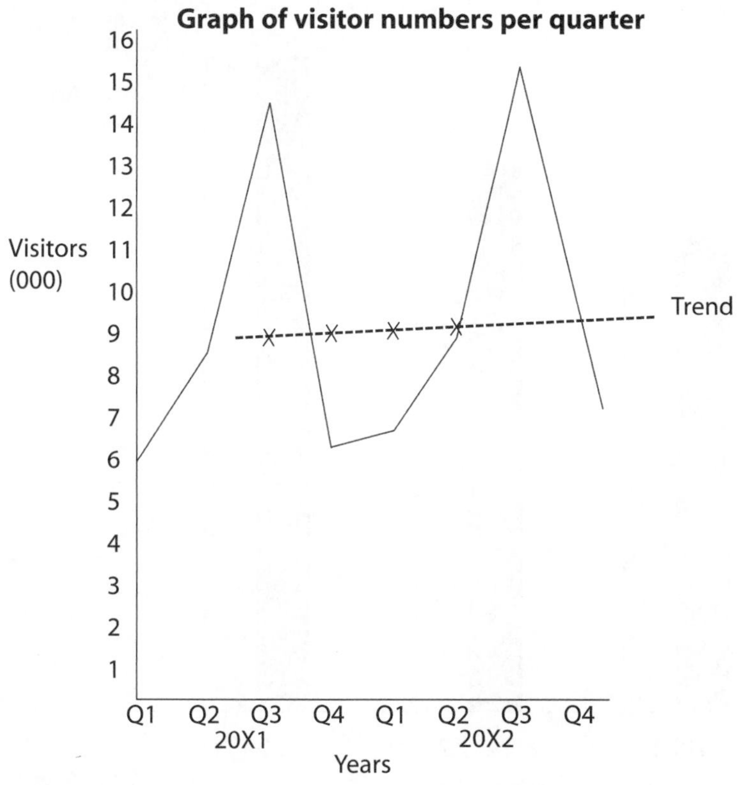

Graph of visitor numbers per quarter

(c) The trend is upward and increases by 200 visitors per quarter.

△ ACTIVITY 10

Coastal Coaches

(a)

	Years		
	20X1	**20X2**	**20X3**
Revenue per passenger	£0.93	£1.10	£1.32
Retail price index	137.7	143.2	147.3
Revenue per passenger at 20X3 prices	£0.99	£1.13	£1.32

(b)

Compound bar chart

Revenue per passenger
Actual and adjusted to 20X3 prices

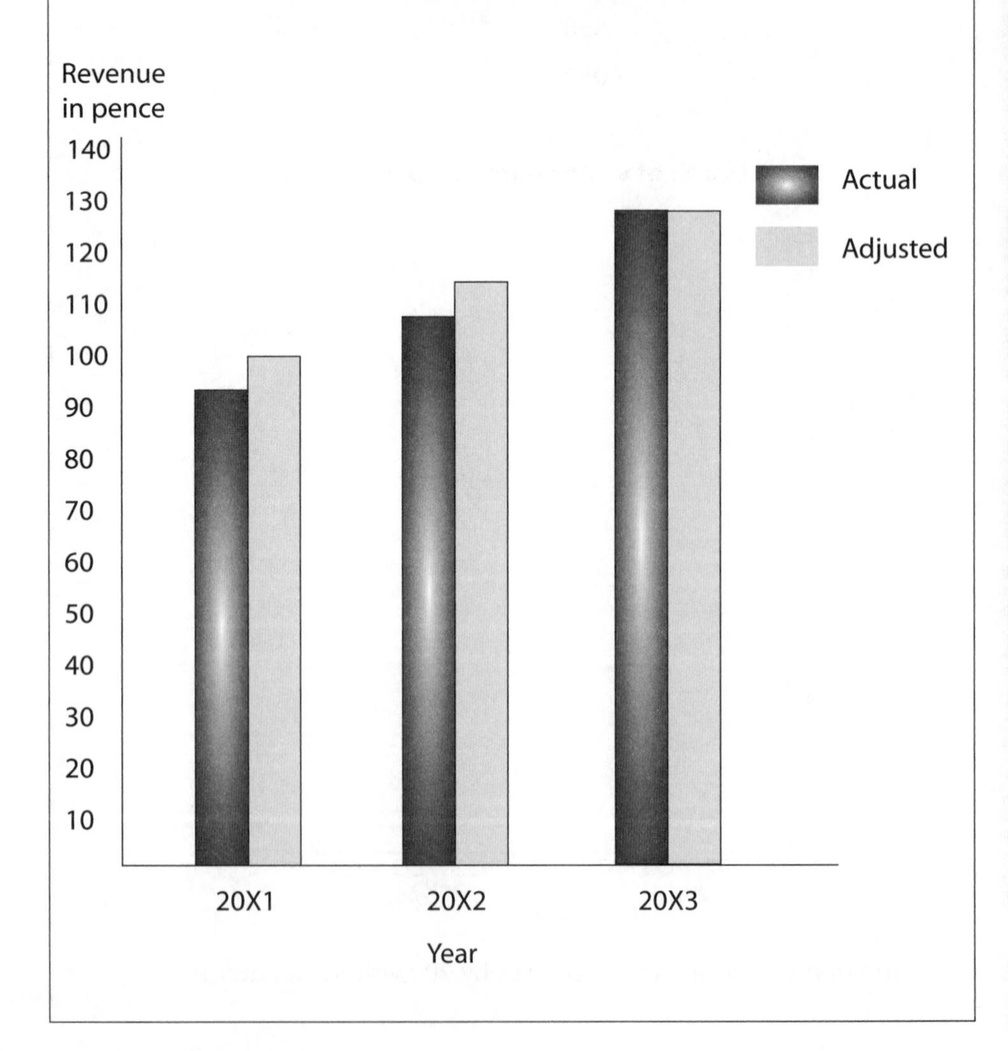

ACTIVITY 11

(a) Administrative costs

	Year				
	X1	X2	X3	X4	X5
Price index	130.2	135.6	137.7	143.2	146.7
Division A					
	£m	£m	£m	£m	£m
Actual cost	2.70	3.00	3.40	3.60	4.00
Adjusted cost X5 prices	3.04	3.25	3.62	3.69	4.00
Division B					
	£m	£m	£m	£m	£m
Actual cost	1.70	2.10	2.50	3.00	3.60
Adjusted cost X5 prices	1.92	2.27	2.66	3.07	3.60

(b)

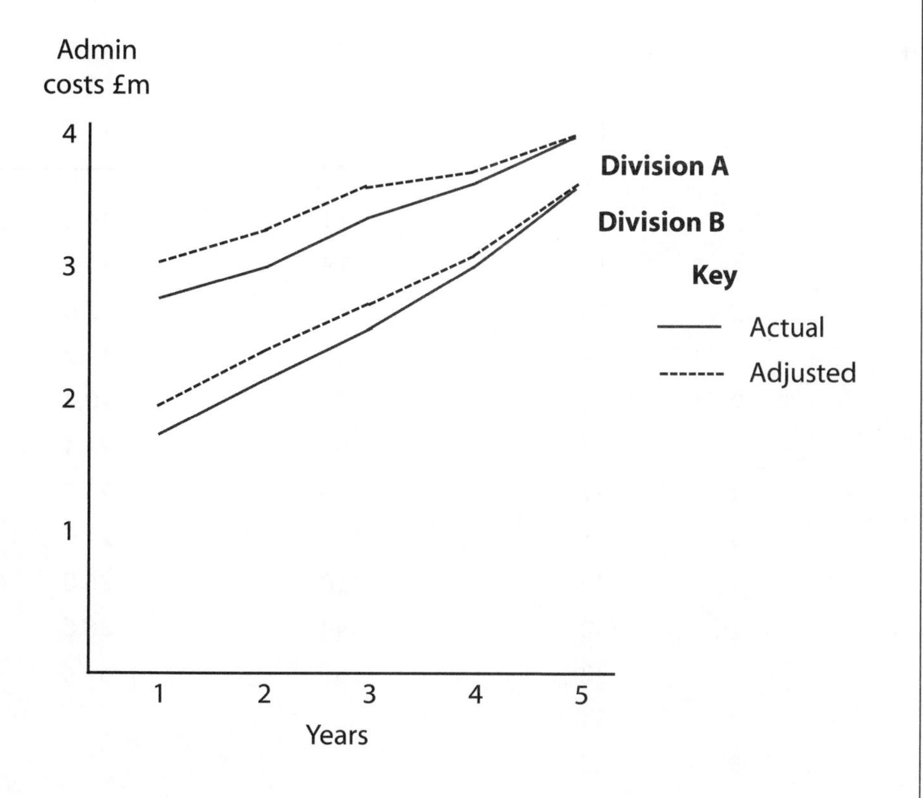

(c)

Division A

The % increase in actual cost between years X1 and X5 was 48%, however in real terms this represents a 31.5% increase.

Division B

There had been a rise of 112% between years X1 to X5, however in real terms this was a rise of 87.5%.

From the graph, it can be seen that the rise in Division B costs is steeper than in A, in both the actual and adjusted costs.

ACTIVITY 12

Sales forecast

(a)

Week	Day	Receipts	Five-day moving total	Trend
1	1	8		
	2	12		
	3	15	54	10.8
	4	10	56	11.2
	5	9	57	11.4
2	1	10	59	11.8
	2	13	64	12.8
	3	17	71	14.2
	4	15	78	15.6
	5	16	88	17.6
3	1	17	96	19.2
	2	23	102	20.4
	3	25	107	21.4
	4	21	116	23.2
	5	21	123	24.6
4	1	26	130	26.0
	2	30	143	28.6
	3	32	157	31.4
	4	34		
	5	35		

(b) Within a four-week period trend has risen from 10.8 to 31.4.
Implications for management:
- may require more stock
- may require more staff
- may require other resources.

△ ACTIVITY 13

TASK 1

Sales report (external sales)
Period ended 31 December 20X5

Quarter	Manufacturing	Distribution	Total
	£000	£000	£000
January – March	118	760	878
April – June	137	825	962
July – September	97	850	947
October – December	108	854	962
	460	3,289	3,749

TASK 2

Workings for graph

20X5	External sales for each month	Cumulative monthly total
	£000	£000
January	388	388
February	245	633
March	245	878
April	335	1,213
May	326	1,539
June	301	1,840
July	236	2,076
August	362	2,438
September	349	2,787
October	310	3,097
November	281	3,378
December	371	3,749
	3,749	

12-month moving annual total

		£000
January (February 20X4 to January 20X5)		3,599
February	3,599 – 273 + 245	3,571
March	3,571 – 227 + 245	3,589
April	3,589 – 305 + 335	3,619
May	3,619 – 350 + 326	3,595
June	3,595 – 254 + 301	3,642
July	3,642 – 226 + 236	3,652
August	3,652 – 321 + 362	3,693
September	3,693 – 359 +349	3,683
October	3,683 – 268 + 310	3,725
November	3,725 – 248 +281	3,758
December	3,758 – 380 +371	3,749

Graph of sales for 20X5

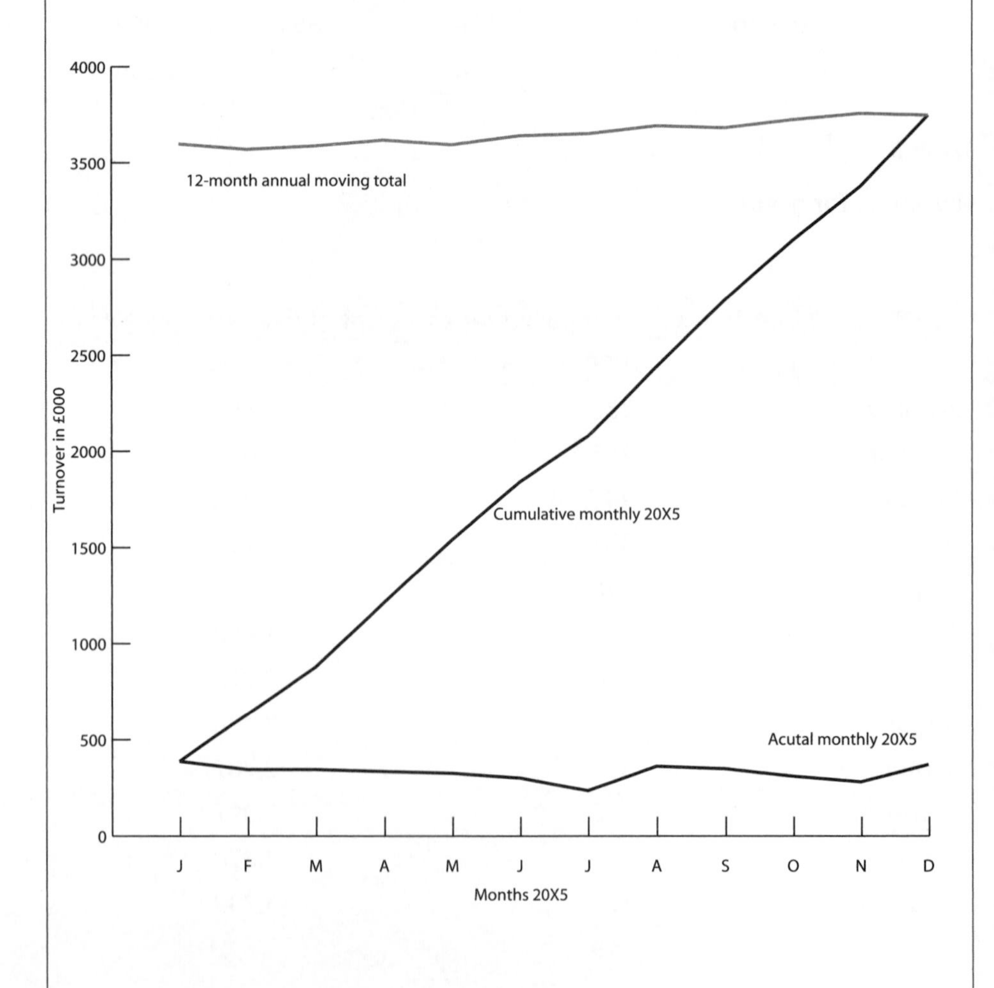

TASK 3

Brompton Fertilisers and Chemicals Ltd
Sales report – five-year review

	£000				
Year	**20X1**	**20X2**	**20X3**	**20X4**	**20X5**
Turnover	3,370	3,410	3,480	3,570	3,749

TASK 4

Sales report – five-year summary
adjusted to 20X1 prices

Year	20X1	20X2	20X3	20X4	20X5
Actual turnover (£000)	3,370	3,410	3,480	3,570	3,749
Index	100.00	103.5	107.4	110.6	113.7
Adjusted turnover (£000)	3,370	3,295	3,240	3,228	3,297

Chapter 5
Performance assessment

△ ACTIVITY 14 △△△△

REPORT

To: Managing Director

From: Accounting Technician

Date: X – X– XX

Subject: Inter-firm comparison – agricultural feeds sector

Introduction

We have recently received the following summary from the trade association inter-firm comparison scheme.

Agricultrual feeds sector

Ratio	Company	Industry average
Return on capital employed	26%	24%
Asset turnover	1.63	1.6
% net profit to sales	16%	15%
Current ratio	1.3:1	1.2:1
Acid test	0.99:1	1.01:1

Return on capital employed

The return on capital employed is the primary profitability ratio. It is expressed as:

$$\frac{\text{Net profit before interest and tax}}{\text{Capital employed}} \times 100\%$$

It represents, in percentage terms, the amount of profit being generated from the capital base in the company.

Our current return is slightly higher than that of the industry as a whole as we are generating more profit per '£' of capital employed than our major competitors.

It can be said that we are more profitable.

Asset turnover

This is a measure of how well the company is utilising its assets. It represents the volume of sales achieved in relation to the capital employed in the business.

It is expressed as:

$$\frac{\text{Turnover}}{\text{Capital employed}}$$

We are generating £1.63 in the form of turnover (i.e. sales exclusive of VAT) for each £1 invested in net assets.

The industry has a ratio of 1.6, so our volume of activity, in relation to capital invested, is slightly greater than our competitors.

We are utilising our assets to a greater capacity.

% **net profit to sales**

This represents, in percentage terms, the net profit in relation to sales. It is the profit margin.

We have a return of 16% on sales compared with an industry average of 15%.

It may be that our sales mix is more profitable or that we are controlling our other operating costs more effectively than the industry as a whole.

Current ratio

This is a measure of liquidity and is expressed as:

Current assets : Current liabilities

We currently have £1.30 in the form of current assets (i.e. cash, or other assets to be turned into cash in the near future) to each £1 worth of current liabilities (i.e. debts due to be paid in the near future).

This means that in the short-run the company should be able to meet its demands from creditors.

This is marginally better than the industry figure of 1.2.

Acid test

This is a stricter test of liquidity as it eliminates stocks from the current ratio calculation; stocks take time to convert to cash. The acid test ratio is expressed as:

(Current assets – Stocks) : Current liabilities

Our ratio is 0.99 : 1, ideally in the short-run this should be around 1 : 1. We see that both our ratio and the industry average ratio are close to this figure.

In the short-term we can meet the demands from creditors.

Conclusion

Our return on capital employed is greater than our competitors as is the asset turnover and profit margin.

We are therefore considered to be more profitable than the industry as a whole.

Our liquidity position is strong and compares well with the sector average.

△ ACTIVITY 15

Task 1

National Stores Group

National Stores Group – Profitability Analysis 20X2

	Brighter Homes	Happy Life	Kidsfair	Roberts Stores
Average size of store (000m^2)	2.85	4.43	0.42	0.21
Turnover per store (£m)	4.73	5.37	0.83	0.41
Turnover per m^2	£1,658.1	£1,211.5	£1,976.5	£1,968
Net profit / turnover	4.14%	(4.63%)	(1.57%)	0.81%
Net profit per m^2	£68.57	(£56.10)	(£31.09)	£16.00

Task 2

	20X1	20X2
Total turnover (£m)	1,163	1,170.7
% increase		0.66%
Total net profit (£m)	18.7	14.3
% decrease		23.53%
Total net profit/turnover	1.61%	1.22%

△ ACTIVITY 16

Task 1

Paper Products Limited
Performance Report year ended 31 October 20X5

	East Factory			West Factory	Total
	Toilet tissue	Paper handkerchiefs	Kitchen roll	Toilet tissue	
	£m	£m	£m	£m	£m
Sales	1.80	1.60	0.70	3.00	7.10
Costs:					
Recycled paper	0.15	0.18	0.08	0.22	0.63
Wood pulp	0.30	0.40	0.15	0.55	1.40
Labour	0.52	0.60	0.32	0.80	2.24
Factory overheads (Note 1)	0.20	0.20	0.20	0.50	1.10
Head office costs (Note 2)	0.10	0.10	0.10	0.10	0.40
Total costs	1.27	1.48	0.85	2.17	**5.77**
Profit	0.53	0.12	(0.15)	0.83	**1.33**
	£	£	£	£	£
Sales per £ recycled paper	12.00	8.89	8.75	13.64	**11.27**
Sales per £ wood pulp	6.00	4.00	4.67	5.45	**5.07**
Sales per £ labour	**3.46**	**2.67**	**2.19**	**3.75**	**3.17**
Profit / sales (%)	29.44	7.50	(21.43)	27.67	**18.73**

Task 2

REPORT

To: Management accountant

From: A Technician

Date: 1 December 20X5

Subject: Paper Products Limited: Analysis of performance for year ended 31 Oct 20X5

Overall profitability

The company as a whole made a profit of £1.33m which represented a return of 18.7% on sales of £7.1m.

Usefulness of the data

It is difficult to comment on the level of this return without knowledge of the capital employed. To prepare a real assessment of overall profitability it would be necessary to have performance data related to previous years and inter-firm comparison data.

Relative profitability and efficiency of manufacturing departments

In terms of profitability the performance of the separate units at the East Factory ranges significantly from a profit of £530,000 in the Toilet Tissue department to a loss of £150,000 in the Kitchen Roll department. Profit/sales ratios show a similar pattern.

In terms of using resources the production of toilet tissue is shown to be more efficient than both paper handkerchiefs and kitchen roll. Toilet tissue production is more efficient than average for all three resources: recycled paper, wood pulp and labour. Paper handkerchiefs and kitchen roll show similar efficiency to each other and below average for the usage of each of the three resources.

Task 3

	20X1	20X2	20X3	20X4	20X5
	£m	£m	£m	£m	£m
Sales	6.00	6.40	6.58	7.40	7.10
Total cost	4.20	4.65	5.05	5.80	5.77
Profit	1.80	1.75	1.53	1.60	1.33
Profit / sales (%)	30.0	27.3	23.3	21.6	18.7

△ ACTIVITY 17 △△△△

Task 1

Sugar Shops
Shop performance ratio table for the year ended 31 March X8

	North	South	East	West	Total
Gross profit / sales (%)	27.03	21.36	31.45	31.58	27.86
Net profit / sales (%)	2.62	–1.53	4.52	0.66	2.06
Expenses ratios:					
Wages / sales (%)	4.93	5.10	8.23	4.39	6.07
Rent / sales (%)	13.16	11.17	12.34	14.69	12.60
Sundries / sales (%)	1.70	1.17	2.74	1.97	1.98
Central costs / sales (%)	4.62	5.46	3.63	9.87	5.15

Task 2

REPORT

To: M Shah

From: A Technician

Date: 16 June X8

Subject: Shop performance year ended 31 March X8

This report shows a comparison of the performance of our retail shop units: North, South, East and West, in terms of profitability and cost control. The report is based on the operating statement and performance ratios for the year ended 31 March X8.

Gross profit/sales ratio

The units as a whole show an average gross return of 27.86% to sales. East and West had ratios above the business' average, whereas North was very slightly below the average and South significantly below the average. It may be that the selling prices charged in the South unit may be lower overall than in other areas. Otherwise there might have been a change in sales mix which results in a lower margin or an increase in pilferage within the shop.

Wages/sales ratio

There is quite a significant difference between the figure for East and the figures for the other three units. Whilst East is above average, the other units are below average. Since the employment of shop assistants appears to be the responsibility of the shop managers then there may be a case for the manager of East reducing the number of staff he/she employs and thereby improving the overall profitability of the business.

Rent/sales ratio

West seems to be somewhat above average and South somewhat below, the other two units being close to the average. Rent is a fixed cost out of the managers' scope of control.

Sundries/sales ratio

East is above average with South below average and the other two units close to average. Again, where the manager has the responsibility to spend money, the manager of East appears to have less control on this area of expenditure than other managers.

Central costs/sales ratio

West is well above average and East well below average with the others close to average, but the figures here are controlled by company policy. To divide the central costs equally between the four shops is extremely arbitrary. To judge the performance of the shops fairly, the distribution of the central costs between shops should be made according to their usage of the central resources, or else the figures should be omitted from the profit statement for individual shops – some form of activity based costing would be useful here for apportioning central overheads.

△ ACTIVITY 18

Brompton Fertilisers and Chemicals Ltd
Profitability ratios for 20X4 and 20X5

Year	20X4	20X5
Ratio:		
Gross profit % of sales	44.15%	45.07%
Net profit % of sales	32.00%	33.60%
Return on capital employed	24.50%	25.98%

MEMO

To: Andrew Hill

From: Accounting Technician

Date: 20 January 20X6

Subject: Profitability ratios for 20X4 and 20X5

I have calculated the following measures of profitability for the year ended 31 December 20X5:

- gross profit as % of sales
- net profit as % of sales
- return on capital employed

and compared and contrasted these measures with those for the previous year. The results are as follows.

Year	20X4	20X5
Ratio:		
Gross profit % of sales	44.15%	45.07%
Net profit % of sales	32.00%	33.60%
Return on capital employed	24.50%	25.98%

The principal profitability ratio, return on capital employed, shows that our return increased over the two-year period and indicates that we have, in the second year, achieved a greater percentage of net profit to total investment.

Likewise both the gross and net profit margins have increased and indicate that we have achieved a higher level of profitability in the second year.

Please contact me if you wish to discuss these matters further.

△ ACTIVITY 19

Task 1

Consolidated profit and loss account
for the year ended 30 September 20X1

	Redcar	Whitby	Total
	£m	£m	£m
Sales (W1)	8.90	4.65	13.55
Cost of sales (W2)	6.20	2.61	8.81
Gross profit	2.70	2.04	4.74
Gross profit as % of sales	30.34%	43.87%	34.98%

	Redcar	Whitby	Total
	£m	£m	£m
Costs:			
Wages and salaries	0.95	0.41	1.36
Administration costs	0.61	0.32	0.93
Distribution costs	0.65	0.33	0.98
Other costs	0.10	0.04	0.14
	2.31	1.10	3.41
Net profit	0.39	0.94	1.33
Net profit as % sales	4.38%	20.22%	9.82%
Capital employed	£3.10m	£2.40m	£5.50m
Return on capital employed	12.58%	39.17%	24.18%

Workings

(1) Redcar sales include £0.55m transferred at cost to the Whitby site.

Redcar sales = £9.45m – £0.55m = £8.90m

(2) Whitby cost of sales include £0.55m transferred from Redcar.

Whitby cost of sales = £3.16m – £0.55m = £2.61m

Task 2

Redcar Foods Ltd

Summary of profitability ratios
Year ended 30 September 20X1

	Responsibility Centre		
Ratio:	**Redcar site**	**Whitby site**	**Total**
Return on capital employed	12.58%	39.17%	24.18%
Gross profit % of sales	30.34%	43.87%	34.98%
Net profit % of sales	4.38%	20.22%	9.82%

Chapter 6
Reporting to external agencies

△ ACTIVITY 20 △△△△

The principles of good form design include:

(a) Requirements must be clearly explained and unambiguous.
- Terminology must be standardised.
- Order of completion must be logical.
- Calculations must be clearly explained.
- Level of accuracy, e.g. to nearest '£', must be stated.

(b) The amount of writing should be kept to a minimum.
- As much information as possible should be pre-printed.
- Use boxes to be ticked for a choice of answers.

(c) The destination of the completed form should be clearly indicated.
- The name and address of the department or person to whom the form is to be returned should be clearly shown.

(d) The information requested must be in a format that is easy to process.
- To facilitate computer analysis of responses.
- If judgements are required then a range of responses to questions should be included.

(e) The form should be uniquely identifiable from others.
- Include title, and colour code the form.

△ ACTIVITY 21 △△△△

The external agencies include:

(a) HM Revenue and Customs
(b) HM Revenue and Customs
(c) Charity Commissioners
(d) HM Revenue and Customs
(e) Local Authority Planning Department
(f) Companies House
(g) Health and Safety Executive
(h) Trade Association

△ ACTIVITY 22 △△△△

Task 1

FOODS FEDERATION INTER-FIRM COMPARISON SCHEME
Annual return – 30 September 20X1
(Express the figures to nearest £000 and % to two decimal places)

Name of business: Redcar Foods Ltd
Financial year end: 30 September 20X1

	£000	
Turnover	13,550	
Cost of sales	8,810	
Gross profit % of sales	34.98%	
Other operating costs	£000	% of turnover
Wages and salaries	1,360	10.04%
Administration costs	930	6.86%
Distribution costs	980	7.23%
Other costs	140	1.03%

Net profits % of sales	9.82%
Capital employed (£)	£5,500,000
Number of employees (full-time equivalent)	108
Turnover per employee (£)	£125,000
Average wages and salaries per employee (£)	£13,000

Task 2

MEMO

To: Susan Woodhouse

From: Accounting Technician

Date: 5 November 20X1

Subject: Inter-firm comparison return

I attach the Foods Federation Inter-firm Comparison Form for your attention and signature.

I have used the consolidated figures recently prepared for the year ended 30 September 20X1.

Please contact me if you have any queries.

A Technician

Chapter 7
Spreadsheets

△ ACTIVITY 23

Microsoft Excel - Book1 [Read-Only]

	A	B	C	D	E	F	G	H
1	PETALART FLOWER SHOP							
2	Cash flow forecast for the three months to 31 December							
3								
4		**Sept**		**October**	**November**	**December**		**Total**
5		£		£	£	£		£
6								
7	Sales	3,600		3,750	4,800	4,800		13,350
8								
9	Receipts: from current month's sales			3,000	3,840	3,840		10,680
10	Receipts: from previous month's sales			720	750	960		2,430
11	**Total receipts**			3,720	4,590	4,800		13,110
12								
13	Purchase costs			1,875	2,400	2,400		6,675
14	Fixed costs			1,200	1,200	1,200		3,600
15	**Total payments**			3,075	3,600	3,600		10,275
16								
17	**Net cash flow**			645	990	1,200		2,835
18	Balance b/f			450	1,095	2,085		450
19	**Balance c/f**			£1,095	£2,085	£3,285		£3,285
20								
21								

Note: formulae used (November column given as example)

E9: =0.8*E7
E10: =0.2*D7
E11: =E9+E10
E13: =0.5*E7
E15: =E13+E14
E17: =E11-E15
E18: =D19
E19: =E17+E18

If sales were to change as suggested in the query, the new balances can be computed by entering the new values in D7, E7 and F7 and letting the spreadsheet do the rest:

Microsoft Excel - Book1

File Edit View Insert Format Tools Data Window Help Acrobat

D2 =

	A	B	C	D	E	F	G	H
1	PETALART FLOWER SHOP							
2	Cash flow forecast for the three months to 31 December							
3								
4		**Sept**		**October**	**November**	**December**		**Total**
5		£		£	£	£		£
6								
7	Sales	3,600		3,000	3,000	3,500		9,500
8								
9	Receipts: from current month's sales			2,400	2,400	2,800		7,600
10	Receipts: from previous month's sales			720	600	600		1,920
11	**Total receipts**			3,120	3,000	3,400		9,520
12								
13	Purchase costs			1,500	1,500	1,750		4,750
14	Fixed costs			1,200	1,200	1,200		3,600
15	**Total payments**			2,700	2,700	2,950		8,350
16								
17	**Net cash flow**			420	300	450		1,170
18	Balance b/f			450	870	1,170		450
19	**Balance c/f**			£870	£1,170	£1,620		£1,620
20								
21								
22								

△ ACTIVITY 24

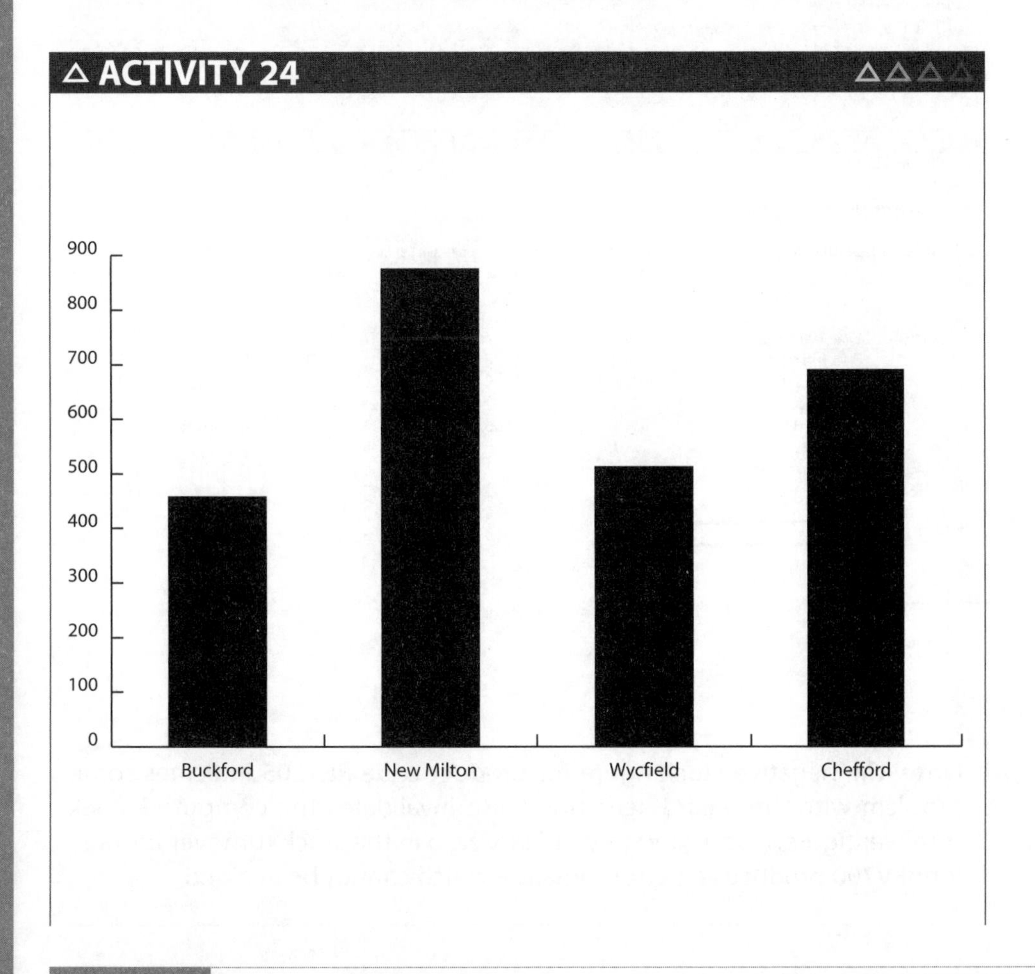

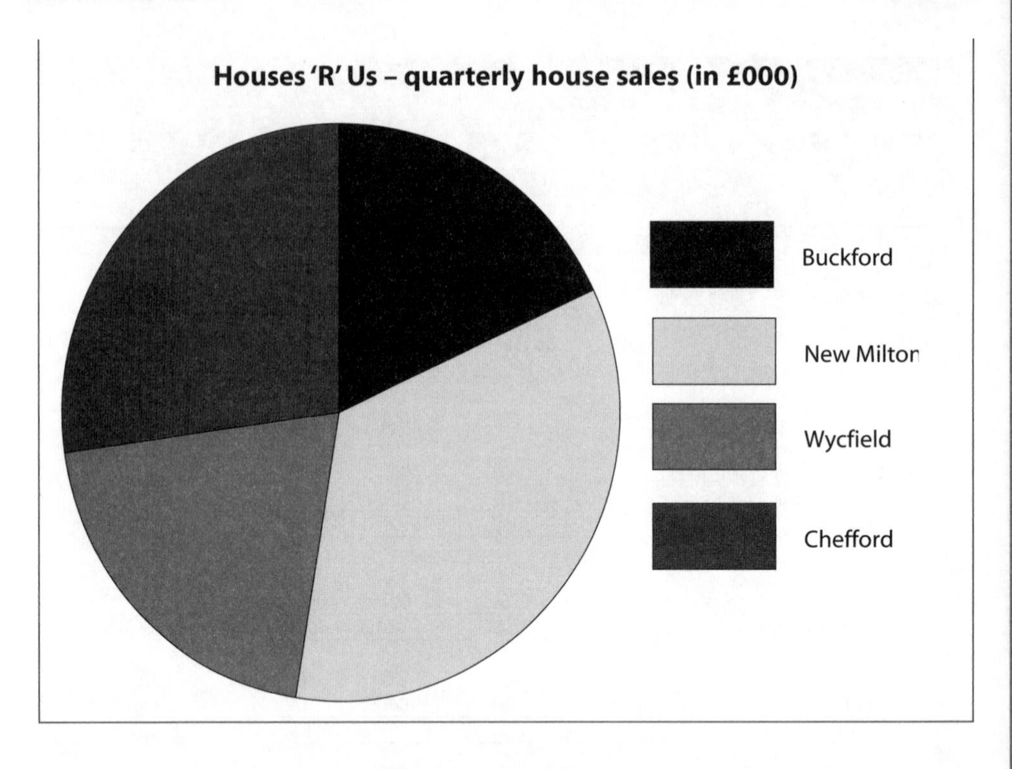

△ ACTIVITY 25

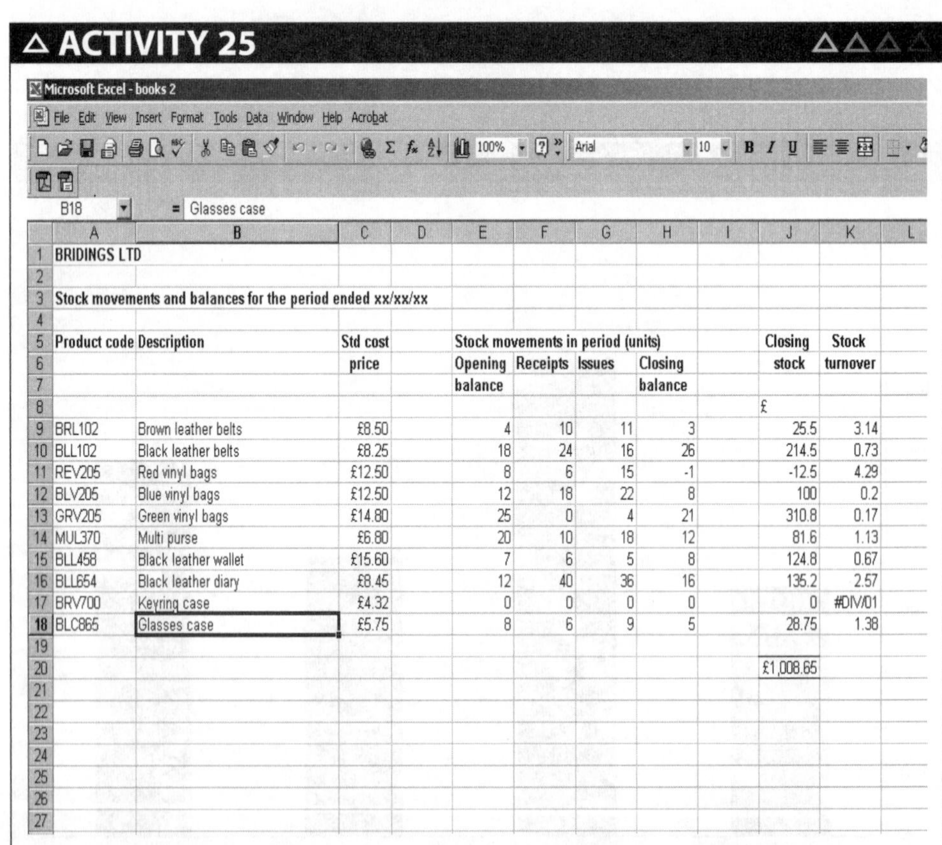

Microsoft Excel - books 2

B18 = Glasses case

BRIDINGS LTD

Stock movements and balances for the period ended xx/xx/xx

Product code	Description	Std cost price	Opening balance	Receipts	Issues	Closing balance	Closing stock £	Stock turnover
BRL102	Brown leather belts	£8.50	4	10	11	3	25.5	3.14
BLL102	Black leather belts	£8.25	18	24	16	26	214.5	0.73
REV205	Red vinyl bags	£12.50	8	6	15	-1	-12.5	4.29
BLV205	Blue vinyl bags	£12.50	12	18	22	8	100	0.2
GRV205	Green vinyl bags	£14.80	25	0	4	21	310.8	0.17
MUL370	Multi purse	£6.80	20	10	18	12	81.6	1.13
BLL458	Black leather wallet	£15.60	7	6	5	8	124.8	0.67
BLL654	Black leather diary	£8.45	12	40	36	16	135.2	2.57
BRV700	Keyring case	£4.32	0	0	0	0	0	#DIV/0!
BLC865	Glasses case	£5.75	8	6	9	5	28.75	1.38
							£1,008.65	

(Opening balance, Receipts, Issues and Closing balance: Stock movements in period (units))

Note: the negative stock figure for product code REV205 indicates some problem with the record keeping. It also invalidates the computed stock turnover figure. Also, trying to divide by zero in the stock turnover formula for BRV700 produces an error message which cannot be avoided.

Chapter 8
VAT

△ ACTIVITY 26

VAT records – checklist

The form of records must be such that HM Revenue and Customs can check VAT returns easily.

A business must keep a record of:

- all taxable and exempt supplies made in the course of business
- all taxable supplies received in the course of business
- a summary of total output tax and input tax for each period – the VAT account.

The business must keep records to verify figures shown on VAT returns for the previous six years.

These might include:

- Orders and delivery notes
- Business correspondence
- Appointment and job books
- Purchases and sales books
- Cash books and other account books
- Copy purchase and sales invoices
- Record of daily takings including till rolls
- Import and export documents
- VAT accounts
- Credit notes, issued and received.

△ ACTIVITY 27

VAT terminology definitions

- Supply of goods – the passing of exclusive ownership of goods to another person.
- Supply of services – doing something, other than supplying goods, for consideration.
- Output tax – tax collected from customers and clients.
- Input tax – tax paid to suppliers of goods and services.
- Zero-rated item – these relate to specific items listed in the VAT Act 1994 (e.g. food).
- Exempt item – specific items listed in the VAT Act 1994 (e.g. education).
- Standard-rated – items which are not zero-rated, taxable at the reduced rate (e.g. domestic fuel and power), or exempt from VAT.

△ ACTIVITY 28

Invoices must show (unless it is a less detailed tax invoice) the following:

- Identification number
- Date of supply (the 'tax point')
- Date of issue of the invoice
- Supplier's name and address and VAT registration number
- Name and address of customer
- Type of supply, e.g. sale, hire
- Description of the goods or services supplied
- Quantity of goods or extent of service rendered
- Rate of tax and amount payable for each item excluding tax
- Total amount payable (excluding tax)
- Rate of any cash discount
- Amount of tax chargeable
- Separate rate and tax charged for each rate of VAT

△ ACTIVITY 29

Less detailed tax invoice

Retailers often take advantage of this facility.

Where the tax-inclusive price does not exceed £100, a retailer may issue a 'less detailed tax invoice'.

It must contain the following elements:

- Supplier's name and address
- Supplier's VAT number
- Date of supply
- Description of goods
- Amount payable including VAT
- Rate of VAT

NB: All retailers must keep a record of their daily gross takings so that the output tax can be determined.

△ ACTIVITY 30

Value Added Tax Return
For the period
01/04/X1 to 30/06/X1

For Official Use

Duncan Bye
Low House
Low Green
Derbyshire
DE1 7XU

Registration number | Period

You could be liable to a financial penalty if your completed return and all the VAT payable are not received by the due date.

Due date: 31/07/X1

For Official Use

DOR only

Your VAT Office telephone number 0123-4567

Before you fill in this form please read the notes on the back and the VAT Leaflet 'Filling in your VAT return'. Fill in all boxes clearly in ink and write 'none' where necessary. Don't put a dash or leave any box blank. If there are no pence write '00' in the pence column. Do not enter more than one amount in any box.

For official use		Box	£	p
	VAT due in this period on sales and other outputs	1	3,783	50
	VAT due in this period on acquisitions from other EC Member States	2	None	
	Total VAT due (the sum of boxes 1 and 2)	3	3,783	50
	VAT reclaimed in this period on purchases and other inputs (including acquisitions from the EC)	4	1,605	73
	Net VAT to be paid to Customs or reclaimed by you (Difference between boxes 3 and 4)	5	2,177	77
	Total value of sales and all other outputs excluding any VAT. Include your box 8 figure.	6	21,620	00
	Total value of purchases and all other inputs excluding any VAT. Include your box 9 figure.	7	9,176	00
	Total value of all supplies of goods and related services excluding any VAT to other EC Member States.	8	None	00
	Total value of all acquisitions of goods and related services excluding any VAT, from other EC Member States.	9	None	00

If you are enclosing a payment please tick this box. ✓

DECLARATION: You, or someone on your behalf, must sign below.
I ....Duncan Bye.. declare that the information given
(Full name of signatory in BLOCK LETTERS)
above is true and complete.
Signature ....DBye.. Date 20
A false declaration can result in prosecution.

VAT 100 (full) PT1 (April 2004)

Workings for VAT return

		£
Box 1:	From SDB	3,762.50
	Goods for own use	21.00*
		3,783.50

* £120 x 0.175 = £21

		£
Box 4:	From PDB	1,592.50
	Petty cash	13.23
		1,605.73

		£
Box 6:	From SDB	21,500
	Goods for own use	120
		21,620

		£
Box 7:	From PDB	9,100
	Petty cash (£75.60 rounded up)	76
		9,176

△ ACTIVITY 31

Task 1

Value Added Tax Return
For the period
01/07/X1 to 30/09/X1

For Official Use

Mark Ambrose
High Park House
High Melton
Doncaster
DN5 7EZ

Registration number	Period
123 9 872 17	09/X1

You could be liable to a financial penalty if your completed return and all the VAT payable are not received by the due date.

Due date: 31/10/X1

Your VAT Office telephone number 0123-4567

For Official Use	
DOR only	

Before you fill in this form please read the notes on the back and the VAT Leaflet 'Filling in your VAT return'. Fill in all boxes clearly in ink and write 'none' where necessary. Don't put a dash or leave any box blank. If there are no pence write '00' in the pence column. Do not enter more than one amount in any box.

For official use		Box	£	p
	VAT due in this period on sales and other outputs	1	6,807	50
	VAT due in this period on acquisitions from other EC Member States	2	None	
	Total VAT due (the sum of boxes 1 and 2)	3	6,807	50
	VAT reclaimed in this period on purchases and other inputs (including acquisitions from the EC)	4	2,999	50
	Net VAT to be paid to Customs or reclaimed by you (Difference between boxes 3 and 4)	5	3,808	00
	Total value of sales and all other outputs excluding any VAT. Include your box 8 figure.	6	38,900	00
	Total value of purchases and all other inputs excluding any VAT. Include your box 9 figure.	7	16,740	00
	Total value of all supplies of goods and related services excluding any VAT to other EC Member States.	8	None	00
	Total value of all acquisitions of goods and related services excluding any VAT, from other EC Member States.	9	None	00

If you are enclosing a payment please tick this box. ☑

DECLARATION: You, or someone on your behalf, must sign below.
I ....Mark Ambrose... declare that the information given
(Full name of signatory in BLOCK LETTERS)
above is true and complete.
Signature ....M Ambrose.. Date 20
A false declaration can result in prosecution.

VAT 100 (full) PT1 (April 2004)

Task 2

DANIEL AND JAMES
LICENSED ACCOUNTING TECHNICIANS

Stonehill House
Stonehill Rise
Doncaster
DN5 9HB

Tel/Fax: 01302 786050

e-mail: danjames@virgin.net

25 October 20X1

Dear Mr Ambrose

Re: VAT return quarter ended 30 September 20X1

I enclose your completed VAT form for signature and submission to HM Revenue and Customs. You need to pay £3,808 for this period.

I have adjusted your output and input tax for the quarter to take account of both the bad debt relief and the goods for own use. Relief can be claimed on bad debts which are over six months old at the date of the return. I have therefore adjusted your input tax by £70, being bad debt relief claimed on both High Melton Farms and Concorde Motors. The bad debt relief for Bawtry Engineering will be claimed next quarter.

The use of materials for private purposes has to be treated as an output and attracts VAT on the cost of the items. I have therefore added a further £87.50 to your output tax for the period, to account for this item, which will be treated as drawings when your accounts are drafted.

If you wish to raise any of the issues above with me, please don't hesitate to give me a call.

Yours sincerely

A Technician

Partners: James Musgrave FMAAT
Daniel Robb FMAAT

Workings for VAT return

		£
Box 1:	From SDB	6,720.00
	Goods for own use	87.50
		6,807.50

VAT on goods for own use = £500 x 17.5% = £87.50

		£
Box 4:	From PDB	2,882.25
	Petty cash	47.25
	Bad debts	70.00
		2,999.50

Total petty cash expenditure = £(105.75 + 94.00 + 117.50)
= £317.25

VAT on £317.25 = 17.5/117.5 x £317.25 = £47.25

Bad debts more than six months old = £(293.75 + 176.25) = £470

VAT on £470 = 17.5/117.5 x £470 = £70

△ ACTIVITY 32

Task 1

Value Added Tax Return
For the period
01/07/X1 to 30/09/X1

John Thistle
T/A Crescent Hotel
High Street
WHitby
YO21 37L

Your VAT Office telephone number 0123-4567

For Official Use

Registration number: 179 6421 27

Period: 09/X1

You could be liable to a financial penalty if your completed return and all the VAT payable are not received by the due date.

Due date: 31/10/X1

For Official Use	
DOR only	

Before you fill in this form please read the notes on the back and the VAT Leaflet 'Filling in your VAT return'. Fill in all boxes clearly in ink and write 'none' where necessary. Don't put a dash or leave any box blank. If there are no pence write '00' in the pence column. Do not enter more than one amount in any box.

For official use

	Box	£	p
VAT due in this period on sales and other outputs	1	14,455	00
VAT due in this period on acquisitions from other EC Member States	2	None	
Total VAT due (the sum of boxes 1 and 2)	3	14,455	00
VAT reclaimed in this period on purchases and other inputs (including acquisitions from the EC)	4	4,942	00
Net VAT to be paid to Customs or reclaimed by you (Difference between boxes 3 and 4)	5	9,513	00
Total value of sales and all other outputs excluding any VAT. Include your box 8 figure.	6	82,600	00
Total value of purchases and all other inputs excluding any VAT. Include your box 9 figure.	7	27,740	00
Total value of all supplies of goods and related services excluding any VAT to other EC Member States.	8	None	00
Total value of all acquisitions of goods and related services excluding any VAT, from other EC Member States.	9	None	00

If you are enclosing a payment please tick this box. ✓

DECLARATION: You, or someone on your behalf, must sign below.
I ....John Thistle... declare that the information given
(Full name of signatory in BLOCK LETTERS)
above is true and complete.
Signature ....J Thistle.. Date 20
A false declaration can result in prosecution.

VAT 100 (full) PT1 (April 2004)

Task 2

NOTE

To: John Thistle

From: Simon White

Date: 18 October 20X1

I have completed the VAT return for the quarter ended 30 September ready for your signature.

I have made adjustments to account for both the bad debt written off and the goods for own use.

The VAT element of the bad debt, £87.50, has been added to the input tax for the period.

The VAT element on the goods at cost, £52.50, has been added to the output tax as the £300 is treated as an output.

The £352.50 will be charged to your drawings account.

Task 3

Simon White FMAAT
Accounting Technician
Bay Farm
High Street
Hawsker
YO21 3EJ

Date: 22 October 20X1

VAT Office
Customs House
Bright Street
Scarborough
YO33 23J

Dear Sirs

Re: Special Retail Schemes

One of my clients is planning to purchase a retail business. I understand that there are special VAT schemes that apply to such businesses.

Could you please send me any relevant information or standard publications you have which cover this matter.

Yours faithfully

S White

Workings for VAT return

		£
Box 1:	From SDB	9,642.50
	From cash takings (W1)	4,760.00
	Goods for own use (W2)	52.50
		14,455.00

(W1) Total cash takings (gross) = £(12,278.75 + 19,681.25)
= £31,960
VAT on £31,960 x 17.5/117.5 = £4,760

(W2) Goods for own use = £300 net
VAT on £300 = £300 x 17.5% = £52.50

Box 4:	From PDB	2,892.75
	Bar and restaurant	1,890.00
	Petty cash (W3)	71.75
	Bad debt (W4)	87.50
		4,942.00

(W3) Gross petty cash expenditure = £481.75
VAT on £481.75 = £481.75 x 17.5/117.5 = £71.75

(W4) Gross bad debt = £587.50
VAT on £587.50 = £587.50 x 17.5/117.5 = £87.50

PRACTICE SIMULATION 1 ANSWERS

Dunsley Pubs and Restaurants Ltd

TASK 1

Centred four-point moving average trend figures

Year	Quarter	Turnover	Moving annual total	Moving average	Centred average trend
		£m	£m	£m	£m
20X4	1	0.40			
	2	0.44			
			2.75	0.69	
	3	1.02			0.695
			2.80	0.70	
	4	0.89			0.705
			2.85	0.71	
20X5	1	0.45			0.730
			2.98	0.75	
	2	0.49			0.765
			3.10	0.78	
	3	1.15			
	4	1.01			

Graph of sales performance

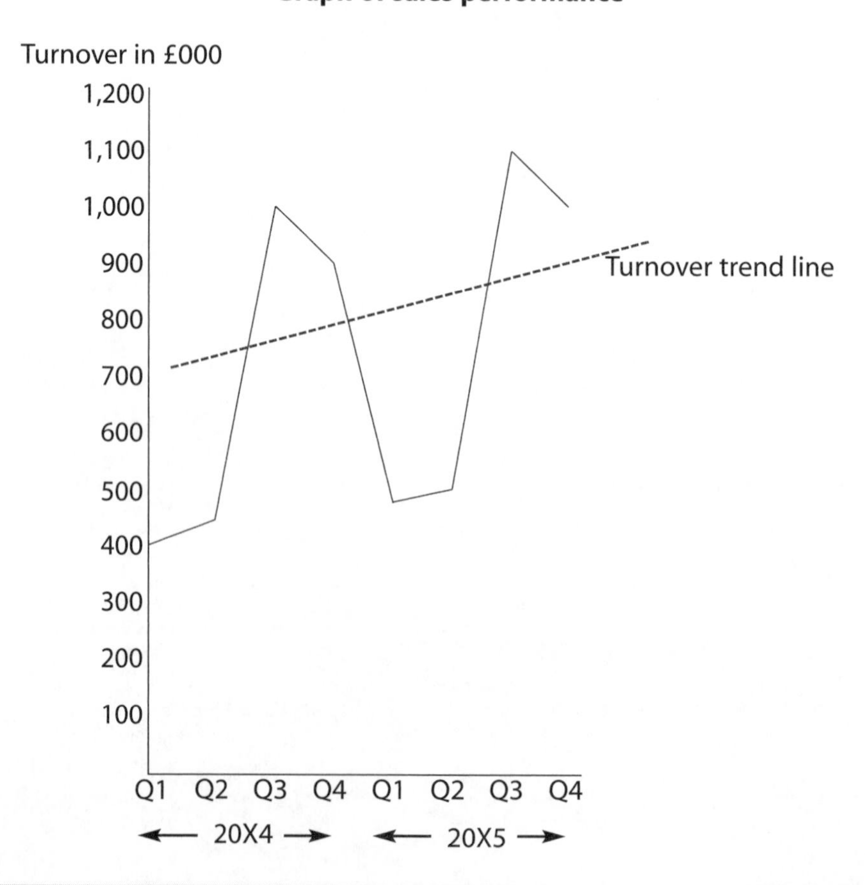

TASK 2

Dunsley Pubs and Restaurants Ltd

Year	20X1	20X2	20X3	20X4	20X5
	£m	£m	£m	£m	£m
Actual turnover	2.10	2.25	2.51	2.75	3.10
% increase year on year	–	7.14%	11.56%	9.56%	12.73%
Index	100.0	103.1	106.2	110.2	113.1
Adjusted turnover	2.10	2.18	2.36	2.50	2.74
% increase year on year	–	3.81%	8.26%	5.93%	9.60%

TASK 3

Dunsley Pubs and Restaurants Ltd
Profitability ratios for 20X5

Ratio	
Return on capital employed	23.45%
Gross profit as a % of turnover	56.13%
Net profit as a % of turnover	21.94%

TASK 4

TRADE ASSOCIATION INTER-FIRM COMPARISON SCHEME
Annual return – 31 December 20X5

Business name: Dunsley Pubs and Restaurants Ltd

Year end: 31 December 20X5

(Note: figures are to be shown to nearest £1,000 and % to two decimal places.)

Turnover	£3,100,000
Cost of sales	£1,360,000
Gross profit as a % of sales	56.13%
Wages and salaries	£810,000
Other operating costs	£250,000
Net profit as a % of sales	21.94%
Number of full-time equivalent emplyees	72
Turnover per employee – full-time equivalent	£43,000
Wages and salaries per employee	£11,000

Signature:.................................. Date:...........................

TASK 5

MEMO

To:	Claire Daly
From:	Accounting Technician
Date:	3 February 20X6
Subject:	Trade Association Inter-firm Comparison Scheme

I attach for your attention and signature the annual return for the above scheme. I have based this on the accounts for the year ended 31 December 20X5.

The gross profit as a percentage of sales is our gross margin, out of which we provide for both other costs and net profit.

The net profit as a percentage of sales represents our net profit margin, out of which we must provide tax, dividends and retention for future expansion.

The turnover per employee indicates the efficiency of our workforce in generating sales. Each employee can be associated with generating £43,000 of sales last year.

The wages and salaries per employee indicates the average amount we paid our employees last year. This was £11,000.

PRACTICE SIMULATION 2 ANSWERS

TASK 1

NORTHERN MANUFACTURERS ASSOCIATION

23 Pegg Street, Edwardston, EN2 1WY

Dear Member

Please supply the following information in respect of your most recent accounting period. The information should be prepared in accordance with the notes below.

Name of company	COLEMAN LTD
NMA membership number	441238
Financial year end date	31 DECEMBER 20X8

1	Turnover for year (W1)	£3,541,000
	Percentage change on previous year (+/-) (W2)	+ 3.33%
2	Production costs as percentage of sales (W3)	58.46%
3	Administration costs as percentage of sales (W4)	14.77%
4	Distribution costs as percentage of sales (W5)	11.32%
5	Return on capital employed (W6)	0.07

Notes

1 Turnover should be stated net of VAT
2 Return on capital employed should be calculated as net profit divided by total capital employed.
3 Percentages and ratios should be stated to two decimal places.

Please return the completed form to Thomas Taylor at the above address by 31 January 20X9. Thank you for your assistance.

Workings:

(W1) Turnover

	£
Manufacturing – External	432,000
Distribution	3,109,000
	3,541,000

(W2) Turnover 20X8 = £3,541,000

Turnover 20X7 = £3,427,000

$$\% \text{ change} = \frac{3{,}541{,}000 - 3{,}427{,}000}{3{,}427{,}000} \times 100\%$$

= 3.33%

(W3) Production costs = £2,070,000

$$\text{Production costs as \% of sales} = \frac{2{,}070{,}000}{3{,}541{,}000} \times 100\%$$

= 58.46%

(W4) Administration costs = £532,000

$$\text{Administration costs as \% of sales} = \frac{523{,}000}{3{,}541{,}000} \times 100\%$$

= 14.77%

(W5) Distribution costs = £401,000

$$\text{Distribution costs as \% of sales} = \frac{401{,}000}{3{,}541{,}000} \times 100\%$$

= 11.32%

$$\text{(W6) Return on capital} = \frac{\text{Net profit}}{\text{Capital employed}}$$

	£	£
Turnover		3,541,000
Cost of sales	2,070,000	
Administration costs	523,000	
Distribution costs	401,000	
Other costs	151,000	
		3,145,000
Net project		396,000

$$\text{Return on capital employed} = \frac{396{,}000}{5{,}983{,}000}$$

= 0.07

TASK 2

MEMO

To: Roger Byrne, Accounts Supervisor

From: Dennis Viollet, Accounts Assistant

Date: 13 January 20X9

Subject: 20X8 financial performance

For your information, the company's performance for the year ended 31 December 20X8 is summarised in the following key ratios and other statistics:

Gross profit percentage $\frac{£3,541,000 - £2,070,000}{£3,541,000} = 41.54\%$

Net profit percentage $\frac{£3,541,000 - £3,145,000}{£3,541,000} = 11.18\%$

Production cost per 'thain' produced and sold $\frac{£2,070,000}{181,000} = £11.44$

Sales earned per employee $\frac{£3,541,000}{117} = £30,264.96$

I also enclose the NMA annual return which I have completed. If you are happy with this, I will despatch it immediately.

TASK 3

Value Added Tax Return
For the period
01/10/X8 to 31/12/X8

COLEMAN LIMITED
58 Elizabethan Street
Woodray
MU3 3RS

Your VAT Office telephone number 0123-4567

For Official Use

Registration number: 578 4060 19

Period: 12/X8

You could be liable to a financial penalty if your completed return and all the VAT payable are not received by the due date.

Due date: 31/01/X9

For Official Use	
DOR only	

Before you fill in this form please read the notes on the back and the VAT Leaflet 'Filling in your VAT return'. Fill in all boxes clearly in ink and write 'none' where necessary. Don't put a dash or leave any box blank. If there are no pence write '00' in the pence column. Do not enter more than one amount in any box.

For official use

	Box	£	p
VAT due in this period on sales and other outputs	1	148,925	00
VAT due in this period on acquisitions from other EC Member States	2	None	
Total VAT due (the sum of boxes 1 and 2)	3	148,925	00
VAT reclaimed in this period on purchases and other inputs (including acquisitions from the EC)	4	54,341	00
Net VAT to be paid to Customs or reclaimed by you (Difference between boxes 3 and 4)	5	94,584	00
Total value of sales and all other outputs excluding any VAT. Include your box 8 figure.	6	916,000	00
Total value of purchases and all other inputs excluding any VAT. Include your box 9 figure.	7	333,000	00
Total value of all supplies of goods and related services excluding any VAT to other EC Member States.	8	65,000	00
Total value of all acquisitions of goods and related services excluding any VAT, from other EC Member States.	9	None	00

If you are enclosing a payment please tick this box. ✓

DECLARATION: You, or someone on your behalf, must sign below.
I ....ROGER BYRNE... declare that the information given
(Full name of signatory in BLOCK LETTERS)
above is true and complete.
Signature ....R Bryne.. Date 20
A false declaration can result in prosecution.

VAT 100 (full) PT1 (April 2004)

Workings for VAT return

Box 1:

	£
External sales	916,000
Exports to EU countries	(65,000)
	851,000

VAT on £851,000 = 17.5% x £851,000 = £148,925

Box 4: Purchases = £310,000

VAT on £310,000 = 17.5% x £310,000 = £54,250

VAT on bad debt relief = 17.5/117.5 x £611 = £91

	£
Purchases	54,250
Bad debt relief	91
	54,341

Box 7:

	£
Standard-rated inputs	310,000
Zero-rated inputs	23,000
	333,000

TASK 4

COLEMAN LIMITED

58 Elizabethan Street, Woodray, MU3 3RS
Telephone 01423 335128

13 January 20X9

HM Revenue and Customs
Rayment House
17 Crickmer Road
Whalley
WY4 8EW

Dear Sirs

VAT registration number 578 4060 19

Our company manufactures and distributes thains. We have recently made a gift of some obsolete computer equipment to a local charity. I am writing to enquire whether this gives rise to a liability for output VAT.

Should such a liability exist, I would be grateful for any guidance you can give me on the calculation of the amount of the liability.

I look forward to hearing from you.

Yours faithfully

Dennis Viollet
Accounts Assistant

Registered in England, number 2234156
Registered office: 58 Elizabethan Street, Woodray, MU3 3RS

MOCK SIMULATION 1 ANSWERS

TASK 1

Engineering Supplies Limited

This is a valid VAT-only invoice. It should be processed as a March input and the VAT should be reclaimed in the quarter January to March 20X8.

Alpha Stationery

This is a valid VAT invoice of the less detailed kind. It should be processed as a March input and the VAT should be reclaimed in the quarter January to March 20X8.

Jamieson and Co

This is merely a proforma invoice. The service provided by Jamieson & Co cannot be regarded as an input until a valid invoice is received. The VAT should not be reclaimed at this stage.

TASK 2

Value Added Tax Return

For the period
01/01/X8 to 31/03/X8

For Official Use

Mr Sherry Teddingham
Hoddle Limited
22 Formguard Street
Pexley
PY6 3QW

Registration number	Period
5 6 3 4 1 7 2 2 1	03/X8

You could be liable to a financial penalty if your completed return and all the VAT payable are not received by the due date.

Due date: 30/04/X8

For Official Use	
DOR only	

Your VAT Office telephone number 0123-4567

Before you fill in this form please read the notes on the back and the VAT Leaflet 'Filling in your VAT return'. Fill in all boxes clearly in ink and write 'none' where necessary. Don't put a dash or leave any box blank. If there are no pence write '00' in the pence column. Do not enter more than one amount in any box.

For official use	Description	Box	£	p
	VAT due in this period on sales and other outputs	1	7,740	12
	VAT due in this period on acquisitions from other EC Member States	2	None	
	Total VAT due (the sum of boxes 1 and 2)	3	7,740	12
	VAT reclaimed in this period on purchases and other inputs (including acquisitions from the EC)	4	13,477	96*
	Net VAT to be paid to Customs or reclaimed by you (Difference between boxes 3 and 4)	5	5,737	84
	Total value of sales and all other outputs excluding any VAT. Include your box 8 figure.	6	120,606	00
	Total value of purchases and all other inputs excluding any VAT. Include your box 9 figure.	7	80,727	00
	Total value of all supplies of goods and related services excluding any VAT to other EC Member States.	8	10,870	00
	Total value of all acquisitions of goods and related services excluding any VAT, from other EC Member States.	9	None	00

If you are enclosing a payment please tick this box. ☐

DECLARATION: You, or someone on your behalf, must sign below.
I ....SHERRY TEDDINGHAM.............................. declare that the information given
(Full name of signatory in BLOCK LETTERS)
above is true and complete.
Signature ....S. Teddingham.. Date 20
A false declaration can result in prosecution.

VAT 100 (full) PT1 (April 2004)

*See workings sheet at the end of answers to this assessment.

TASK 3

Hoddle Limited

22 Formguard Street, Pexley, PY6 3QW
Telephone 01682 431256

9 April 20X8

HM Revenue and Customs
Brendon House
14 Abbey Street
Pexley
PY2 3WR

Dear Sirs

Registration number 563417221

This company at present accounts for VAT on the basis of invoices raised and received. We are considering the idea of changing to the cash accounting scheme, and I would be grateful if you could provide some information on this. Perhaps there is a leaflet setting out details of the scheme?

The particular points of which we are uncertain are as follows.

- What turnover limits apply to the scheme? Are these limits affected by the fact that this company is part of a group consisting of the company itself and its parent company?

- How are bad debts accounted for under the cash accounting scheme?

I would be grateful for any assistance you are able to give on these points, and generally about the workings of the scheme.

Yours faithfully

Sherry Teddingham
Accountant

Registered office: 22 Formguard Street, Pexley, PY6 3QW
Registered in England, number 2314561

TASK 4

Consolidated profit and loss account
for the three months ended 31 March 20X8

	Kelly	Hoddle	Adjustments	Consolidated
	£	£	£	£
Sales	295,768	120,607	(20,167)	396,208
Opening stock	28,341	14,638		42,979
Purchases	136,095	50,908	(18,271)	168,732
	164,436	65,546		211,711
Closing stock	31,207	16,052	1,896	49,155
Cost of sales	133,229	49,494*		162,556
Gross profit	162,539	71,113		233,652
Wages and salaries	47,918	18,014		65,932
Distribution expenses	28,341	13,212		41,553
Administration expenses	30,189	11,676		41,865
Stationery	2,541	544*		3,085
Travel	2,001	267		2,268
Office expenses	3,908	737		4,645
Interest payable	12,017			12,017
Other expenses	11,765	3,384		15,149
	138,680	47,834		186,514
Net profit for the period	23,859	23,279		47,138

*See workings sheet at the end of this assessment answers.

TASK 5

Quarterly consolidated profit and loss accounts for the year ended 31 March 20X8

	1 Apr 20X7 – 30 Jun 20X7	1 Jul 20X7 – 30 Sep 20X7	1 Oct 20X7 – 31 Dec 20X7	1 Jan 20X8 – 31 Mar 20X8	*Totals for year* 1 Apr 20X7 – 31 Mar 20X8
Sales	325,719	275,230	306,321	396,208	1,303,478
Cost of sales	134,861	109,421	121,358	162,556	528,196
Gross profit	190,858	165,809	184,963	233,652	775,282
Wages & salaries	63,314	61,167	64,412	65,932	254,825
Distribution expenses	34,217	30,135	31,221	41,553	137,126
Administration expenses	34,765	33,012	36,415	41,865	146,057
Stationery	2,981	2,671	3,008	3,085	11,745
Travel	1,975	1,876	2,413	2,268	8,532
Office expenses	4,412	4,713	3,083	4,645	16,853
Interest payable	12,913	12,714	12,432	12,017	50,076
Other expenses	10,981	16,421	15,431	15,149	57,982
	165,558	162,709	168,415	186,514	683,196
Net profit for the period	25,300	3,100	16,548	47,138	92,086

TASK 5

REPORT

To: Sherry Teddingham

From: Sol Bellcamp

Date: 9 April 20X8

Subject: Report on group results for the year ended 31 March 20X8

Introduction

This report contains the usual information on group results for the year, plus the additional information requested in your memo to me of 2 April 20X8.

Key ratios

Gross profit margin	= £775,282 ÷ £1,303,478	= 59.5%
Net profit margin	= £92,086 ÷ £1,303,478	= 7.1%
Return on shareholders' capital employed	= £92,086 ÷ £1,034,708	= 8.9%

Note: This is return on shareholders' capital employed so doesn't include long-term loans in the capital employed.

Sales revenue by quarter

Quarter	Unindexed	Indexed (base period = first quarter 20X6/X7)
	£	£
April – June 20X7	325,719 (x 231.8 ÷ 239.3)	315,511
July – September 20X7	275,230 (x 231.8 ÷ 241.5)	264,175
October – December 20X7	306,321 (x 231.8 ÷ 244.0)	291,005
January – March 20X8	396,208 (x 231.8 ÷ 241.8)	379,822

Pie chart showing sales by quarter

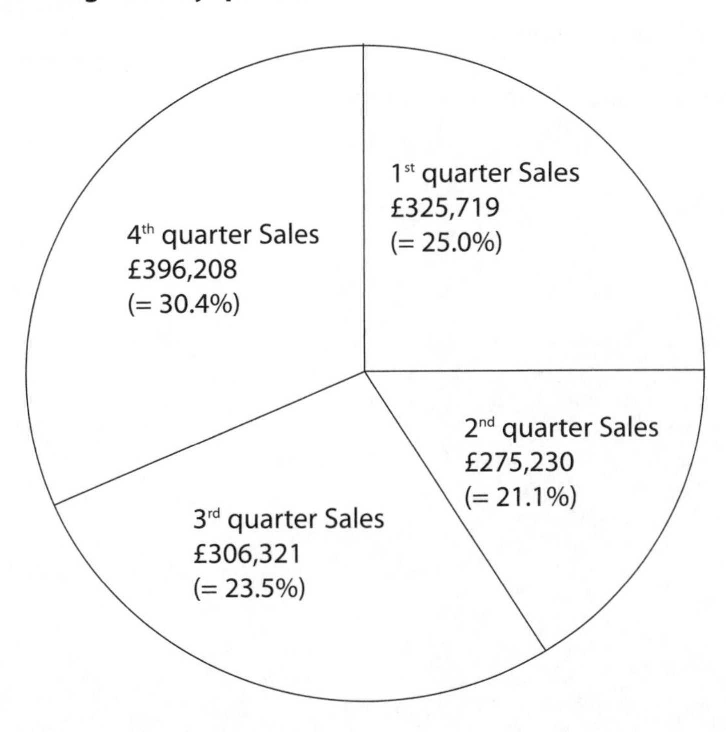

TASK 6

Inter-firm comparison data (extracts)

Name of company Kelly Limited and subsidiary

Year ended 31 March 20X8

Data

	£	% of sales	Industry best	Industry average
Sales	1,303,478			
Gross profit	775,282	59.5%	62.1%	57.3%
Net profit	92,086	7.1%	10.4%	5.8%
Fixed assets	1,229,348			
Current assets	325,703			
Current liabilities	148,271			
Return on capital employed		10.1%*	10.3%	9.0%

*See workings sheet at the end of this assessment answers.

Workings

Task 2

		£
Box 4	PDB	12,690.53
	Petty cash	244.95
	Bad debt (£420 x 17.5%)	73.50
	Engineering Supplies invoice	466.77
	Alpha Stationery invoice (£14.84 x 17.5/117.5)	2.21
		13,477.96

Box 6 £128,346.70 – £7,740.12 = £120,606.58

		£
Box 7		
	PDB (91,870.20 – 12,690.53)	79,179.67
	Petty cash (1,780.29 – 244.95)	1,535.34
	Apha Stationery invoice (14.84 – 2.21)	12.63
		80,727.64

Task 4

Hoddle's stationery costs, Jan – Mar 20X8

	£
Petty cash book	531.55
Alpha Stationery invoice (net of VAT)	12.63
	544.18

Task 6

Return on capital employed

	£
Net profit	92,086
Interest	50,076
	142,162 ÷ £1,406,780 = 10.1%

MOCK SIMULATION 2 ANSWERS

Houillier Ltd

TASK 1

Consolidated profit and loss account
for the year ended 30 September 20X9

	City Centre	District	Consolidated
	£	£	£
Sales to external customers	8,672,130	6,241,100	14,913,230
Opening stock	934,120	518,710	1,452,830
Purchases	6,521,540	4,111,900	10,633,440
Less closing stock	(1,065,410)	(623,780)*	(1,689,190)
Cost of goods sold	6,390,250	4,006,830	10,397,080
Gross profit	2,281,880	2,234,270	4,516,150
Wholesaling wages and salaries	(856,120)	(801,980)	(1,658,100)
Administration wages and salaries	(549,780)		(549,780)
Other costs	(574,000)	(423,170)	(997,170)
Net profit for the year	301,980	1,009,120	1,311,100

* £597,230 + £26,550 (unrecorded stock) = £623,780

TASK 2

Consolidated profit and loss account
for the years ended 30 September 20X8 and 20X9

	20X8 (actual)	20X8 (restated)	20X9	Change in year
	£	£	£	%
Sales to exteranl customers	12,247,318	12,824,735	14,913,230	16.3
Opening stock	1,225,671	1,283,457	1,452,830	13.2
Purchases	9,206,783	9,640,850	10,633,440	10.3
	10,432,454	10,924,307	12,086,270	10.6
Less closing stock	1,452,830	1,521,326	1,689,190	11.0
Cost of goods sold	8,979,624	9,402,981	10,397,080	10.6
Gross profit	3,267,694	3,421,754	4,516,150	32.0
Wholesaling wages and salaries	(1,236,519)	(1,294,816)	(1,658,100)	28.1
Administration wages and salaries	(483,512)	(506,308)	(549,780)	8.6
Other costs	(852,090)	(892,263)	(997,170)	11.8
Net profit for the year	695,573	728,367	1,311,100	80.0

TASK 3

MEMO

To: Janice Knapper, Accounts Supervisor

From: Stevie Real, Accounts Assistant

Date: 11 October 20X9

Subject: Results for year ended 30 September 20X9

I have analysed the consolidated accounts for the year ended 30 September 20X9 and calculated the following performance measures in the form of ratios:

- Gross profit margin (W1) 30.3%
- Net profit margin (W2) 8.8%
- Return on capital employed (W3) 6.1%

The elements of sales revenue are shown pictorially below.

Pie Chart
Sales revenue showing elements of cost and profit

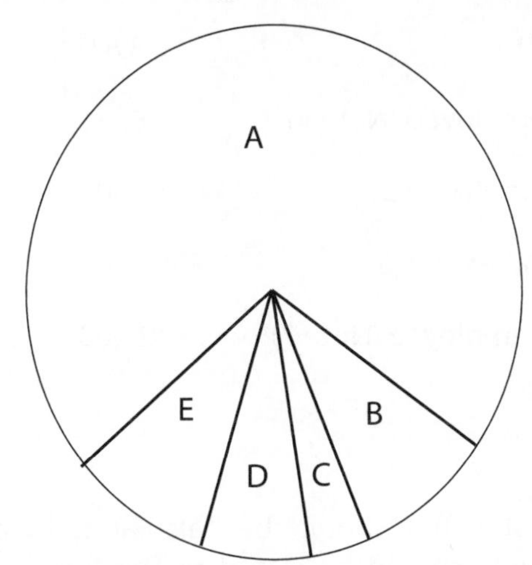

Key

A = Cost of goods sold = 10,397,080 ÷ 14,913,230 x 100% = 69.7% of sales

B = Wholesaling wages and salaries = 1,658,100 ÷ 14,913,230 x 100% = 11.1% of sales

C = Administration wages and salaries = 549,780 ÷ 14,913,230 x 100% = 3.7% of sales

D = Other costs = 997,170 ÷ 14,913,230 x 100% = 6.7% of sales

E = Net profit = 1,311,100 ÷ 14,913,230 x 100% = 8.8% of sales

Workings

(W1) Gross profit margin = $\frac{4,516,150}{14,913,230}$ x 100% = 30.3%

(W2) Net profit margin = $\frac{1,311,100}{14,913,230}$ x 100% = 8.8%

(W3) Return on capital employed = $\frac{1,311,100}{21,600,000}$ = 6.1%

TASK 4

FEDERATION OF NORTH WESTERN WHOLESALERS
Annual report to be completed by members (extract)

Please supply the information requested below as soon as possible after the end of your accounting period. The ratios and statistics should be calculated in accordance with the conventions and definitions explained in the notes.

Name of member	Houillier Ltd	Year end	30/09/X9
Gross margin (Note 2)	30.3%		
Net margin (Note 3)	8.8%		
Return on capital employed (Note 4)	6.1%		
Total of direct salaries (Note 5)	£1,658,000		
Total of indirect salaires (Note 6)	£550,000		
Average salary per employee (Note 7)	£12,000		

Notes

1 All ratios and statistics should be calculated to one decimal place. Monetary amounts should be stated to the nearest thousand pounds. Members trading through more than one branch or division should submit consolidated information only, i.e. information for all branches combined as a single entity.

2 Gross margin is the ratio of gross profit to sales, expressed as a percentage.

3 Net margin is the ratio of net profit to sales, expressed as a percentage.

4 Return on capital employed is the ratio of net profit to average capital employed during the accounting period, expressed as a percentage.

5 Direct salaries are those of staff engaged directly in wholesaling activities.

6 Indirect salaries are those of all other staff, including administration staff.

7 Average salary per employee is the total wages and salaries for the year, divided by the number of full-time equivalent staff employed during the year.

MEMO

To: Janice Knapper, Accounts Supervisor

From: Stevie Real, Accounts Assistant

Date: 12 October 20X9

Subject: FNWW annual report

I enclose the FNWW annual report based on our accounts for the year ended 30 September 20X9, for your attention and approval prior to despatch to the Federation.

TASK 5

Value Added Tax Return
For the period
01/07/X9 to 30/09/X9

For Official Use

HOUILLIER LIMITED
39 Carragher road
Jamestown
Liverpool
LI5 3NP

Registration number: 578 4060 19
Period: 09/X9

You could be liable to a financial penalty if your completed return and all the VAT payable are not received by the due date.

Due date: 31/10/X9

Your VAT Office telephone number 0123-4567

For Official Use	
DOR only	

Before you fill in this form please read the notes on the back and the VAT Leaflet 'Filling in your VAT return'. Fill in all boxes clearly in ink and write 'none' where necessary. Don't put a dash or leave any box blank. If there are no pence write '00' in the pence column. Do not enter more than one amount in any box.

For official use		Box	£	p
	VAT due in this period on sales and other outputs	1	455,196	00
	VAT due in this period on acquisitions from other EC Member States	2	None	
	Total VAT due (the sum of boxes 1 and 2)	3	455,196	00
	VAT reclaimed in this period on purchases and other inputs (including acquisitions from the EC)	4	439,683	00
	Net VAT to be paid to Customs or reclaimed by you (Difference between boxes 3 and 4)	5	15,513	00
	Total value of sales and all other outputs excluding any VAT. Include your box 8 figure.	6	2,923,138	00
	Total value of purchases and all other inputs excluding any VAT. Include your box 9 figure.	7	2,769,807	00
	Total value of all supplies of goods and related services excluding any VAT to other EC Member States.	8	322,017	00
	Total value of all acquisitions of goods and related services excluding any VAT, from other EC Member States.	9	None	00

If you are enclosing a payment please tick this box. ✓

DECLARATION: You, or someone on your behalf, must sign below.
I ....JANICE KNAPPER......................... declare that the information given
(Full name of signatory in BLOCK LETTERS)
above is true and complete.
Signature ....J. Knapper...................... Date 20
A false declaration can result in prosecution.

VAT 100 (full) PT1 (April 2004)

TASK 6

HOUILLIER LIMITED

39 Carragher Road, Jamestown, Liverpool, L15 3NP

Telephone: 0151 623 4671

12 October 20X9

HM Revenue and Customs
38 Bergerac Road
Babbtown
Liverpool
L16 3NV

Dear Sirs

VAT registration number: 578 4060 19

I believe that as a company engaged in retailing we may be eligible to account for VAT under the special retail schemes category.

Could you please forward me details and any relevant publications you may have covering this matter.

Yours faithfully

S Real

Stevie Real

Accounts Assistant

Registered in England. Registration number 2314567

GLOSSARY

Term	Description
Annual accounting scheme	A scheme whereby small businesses can make an annual VAT return
Asset turnover	A measure of the rate at which sales revenue is being generated from the assets of the business: $\text{Asset turnover} = \dfrac{\text{Sales}}{\text{Capital employed}}$
Cash accounting scheme	A scheme for small businesses whereby VAT can be accounted for on the basis of cash paid/received rather than on an accruals basis.
Component bar chart	A simple bar chart with each category bar being proportionately split horizontally into sub-categories or components.
Compound (multiple) bar chart	Each category is represented by a set of sub-category bars whose height or length is proportionate to the size of the sub-category.
Consolidation	The combining of units' results with elimination of inter-unit transactions.
Controllable costs	Traceable costs over which the organisational unit's manager has control or can influence, used in manager evaluation.
Cost unit	A measure of the activity level/output of a business, activity or process to which costs are attributed for performance evaluation.
External (outside) agencies	Individuals and organisations outside of the business that require information from within the business from time to time, e.g. HM Revenue and Customs, DTI, Office for National Statistics, banks.
Fixed format report	Of a fixed length and style, e.g. insurance claim, customer questionnaire.
Flat rate accounting scheme	A scheme for small businesses whereby VAT liability is calculated as a percentage of total turnover rather than by reference to individual transactions.
Formal report	Findings of more complex investigations, generally including sections giving an introduction, approach to the investigation, detailed findings, conclusions and recommendations.
Grant awarding organisations	Government and privately funded schemes that award grants to businesses, e.g. the DTI's Enterprise Initiative Scheme.
Graph	A diagram representing the relationship between two variables, x and y, represented on the horizontal and vertical axes respectively.
Gross profit margin	A measure of the profitability of the direct production/service activity of the business: $\text{Gross profit margin} = \dfrac{\text{Gross profit}}{\text{Sales}} \times 100\%$
HM Revenue and Customs	The government department responsible for administering VAT in the UK.

Term	Description
Index numbers	A means of comparing the relative values (prices, quantities, etc) of a time series over time, by expressing the value of each period's data as a percentage of that of a basis period.
Information	Processed data.
Information-collecting organisations	Such as Office for National Statistics, market survey organisations.
Input VAT	The VAT paid by a business on its purchases and expenses.
Internal information systems	The accounting and administrative systems that produce data and information for management and reporting purposes
Less detailed tax invoice	May be issued by a retailer if the VAT inclusive supply value does not exceed £100.
Management levels: operational	Day-to-day running of the business.
Management levels: strategic	Long-term planning and decision making with a view to achieving corporate objectives.
Management levels: tactical	Short-term planning for the most effective use of available resources.
Memorandum report	Internal communication, often on standardised stationery, for routine reporting.
Moving average	A series of averages, computed from consecutive sets of time series data, which results in a 'smoothed' set of data upon which the trend estimate can be based.
Net profit margin	A measure of the profitability of the whole business relative to sales: $\text{Net profit margin} = \frac{\text{Net profit}}{\text{Sales}} \times 100\%$
One-way table	Summarises data by one characteristic (e.g. customers' ages, invoice values, etc).
Organisation chart	A diagrammatic representation of the hierarchy of responsibilities of the management of an enterprise.
Output VAT	A part of a business for which cost and/or revenue data is individually collected (e.g. a division, department, process, product).
Percentage component bar chart	The VAT charged by a business on its sales or taxable supplies.
Pictogram	Is a simple diagram which uses pictures to represent numbers.
Pie chart	Is a circle divided up into segments, each proportion-ately representing a category of data.

Term	Description
Primary data	Data used solely for the purpose for which it was originally collected.
Private sector enterprise	A business owned and funded by individual investors, e.g. sole trader, partnership, limited company.
Productivity	A measure of the efficiency with which inputs are processed to produce output.
Proforma invoice	Is not a VAT invoice but a demand for payment, which allows the supplier to collect the VAT in from the customer before it has to be paid over to HMRC.
Public sector enterprise	An organisation owned and funded by central or local government, e.g. hospital, library, school.
Raw data	Numerical information or figures that have been collected but not processed or analysed.
Regulatory organisations	UK examples include HM Revenue & Customs, DTI, the Stock Exchange.
Report	An orderly and objective communication of factual information, e.g. by formal written document, letter, completed form, memo or spoken presentation.
Resource utilisation	A measure of the extent to which resources available were used productively.
Retail Prices Index (RPI)	A monthly index reflecting changes in price of a 'basket' of consumer goods and services.
Return on capital employed (ROCE)	A measure of how profitably the business has been using its assets: $\text{ROCE} = \dfrac{\text{Net profit before interest and tax}}{\text{Capital employed}} \times 100\%$
Return on equity (RoE)	A measure of shareholder profitability: $\text{RoE} = \dfrac{\text{Net profit after interest and tax}}{\text{Equity (share capital + reserves)}} \times 100\%$
Secondary data	Data used for one purpose but that was originally collected for another, e.g. published statistics.
Simple bar chart	Represents each category of data by a bar, whose height or length is proportionate to the size of the category.
Spreadsheet	A computerised table of rows and columns, forming cells into which numbers, text and formulae can be entered.
Tax point	The date on which a taxable supply is recorded as having taken place, and on which the output tax liability arises. Can be **basic** or **actual**.
Time series	A series of figures measured at regular time intervals, e.g. monthly sales, annual populations.

Term	Description
Traceable costs	Costs incurred as a result of an organisational unit being in existence, used in unit evaluation.
Trade associations	Bodies that represent and look after the interests of organisations in the same line of business, e.g. Association of British Travel Agents (ABTA).
Transfer price	The price charged by one organisational unit for goods/services provided to another.
Trend	The general direction in which the graph of a time series is moving in the long term.
Two-way table	Summarises data by two characteristics (e.g. invoices by age and value).
Value Added Tax (VAT)	Tax paid by consumers on goods and services, collected by businesses on behalf of HM Revenue and Customs (HMRC).
VAT Guide	A booklet issued by the HMRC with guidance on the rules and procedures of VAT.
VAT invoice	An invoice for the supply of goods or services that contains specific VAT and other details, that is used as a basis for collecting VAT from customers and reclaiming VAT suffered on purchases.
VAT return	A statement of input and output tax and net amount payable/receivable for a given period, submitted by a business to HMRC.
VAT return	A statement of input and output tax and net amount payable/receivable, submitted by a business to HMRC at the end of each tax period (normally three months).
Weighted index number (aggregate)	Several items are combined, on a weighted average basis, into one index number.
What if? analysis	The use of spreadsheets in assessing the impact of different input values on revenues, profits, etc.

INDEX